So Noted!

The Genesis Commentary by Dr. Henry Morris

First printing: August 2017
Fifth printing: April 2022

Master Books, P.O. Box 726, Green Forest, AR 72638
Master Books® is a division of the New Leaf Publishing Group, Inc.

ISBN: 978-1-68344-076-5
ISBN: 978-1-61458-446-9 (digital)

Scripture taken from the King James Version.

Please consider requesting that a copy of this volume be purchased by your local library system.

Printed in the United States of America

Please visit our website for other great titles:
www.masterbooks.com

Master
Books®
A Division of New Leaf Publishing Group
www.masterbooks.com

Acknowledgments

A respected ministry leader, educator and scientist, Dr. Henry M. Morris was actively involved in the study and defense of the Christian faith for almost 60 years. After teaching engineering in secular universities for 28 years, he founded the Institute for Creation Research in 1970. His books include *The Genesis Flood* (with Dr. John Whitcomb), *Many Infallible Proofs, The Biblical Basis for Modern Science, The Genesis Record, The Remarkable Record of Job, The Revelation Record, Scientific Creationism, Biblical Creationism, The Long War Against God*, and *God and the Nations*. He also served as editor of the popular devotional Bible study quarterly, *Days of Praise*.

Contents

Contents

Publisher's Note

So Noted is a complete excerpt of the Book of Genesis from *The Henry Morris Study Bible*. Understanding the Book of Genesis is foundational and vital for a deeper understanding of God's Word, including historical events like creation and Noah's Flood and their aftermath.

So Noted includes all 600 of the study notes for Genesis from *The Henry Morris Study Bible*. Henry Morris' thorough notes provide readers with access to his decades of rigorous biblical study, as well as his scientific knowledge, to bring clarity to modern confusion and controversy over the intersection of science and faith. His comprehensive notes ensure readers have a firm understanding of the theological, cultural, and scientific background of the Book of Genesis. They also include cross-references to notes on other verses, which are available in the full *Henry Morris Study Bible*.

In addition, you will also find R and T superscripted within verses. The R means there is a scriptural cross-reference available, while T means a translation for a specific word or phrase is noted; the additional information is usually provided at the end of the verse. This feature provides readers with even more help in studying and understanding the connections and language in God's Word.

So Noted also includes 11 appendices from *The Henry Morris Study Bible*. These resources add further clarity to many of Dr. Morris' notes on Genesis.

So Noted includes a complete King James Version translation of the Book of Genesis, as well as the extensive extra study helps. This book is an invaluable resource for defending the scientific accuracy of Genesis, resolving alleged biblical contradictions, and explaining difficult and controversial passages.

We hope you enjoy this unique selection from Dr. Morris' commentary on the Bible. We pray it enriches your faith and answers many of your questions as you begin this biblical journey of discovery.

The Henry Morris Study Bible

With notes defending the accuracy and integrity of the Scriptures, assuming complete and verbal inspiration, inerrancy in all matters of fact and faith, and literal interpretation as intended by the writers.

The Henry Morris Study Bible by the late Henry M. Morris, Ph.D., LL.D., Litt. D., President Emeritus, Institute for Creation Research:
- Uses standard King James Version as basic text
- Defends scientific accuracy of recent special creation
- Resolves supposed contradictions in history and doctrine
- Explains difficult and controversial passages

Introduction to

The Henry Morris Study Bible

The written Word of God, with its glorious message of creation, redemption, and eternal life with God, has always been under attack by the secular world and the unseen hosts of darkness who control it. Yet, out of the ungodly world, year after year, God chooses some to follow Him, and He has provided a wonderful plan of salvation and everlasting joy for all who respond to His call, believe His Word, and receive His incarnate Son as Savior and Lord.

The Need for *The Henry Morris Study Bible*

To these redeemed sinners He has given the privilege of proclaiming His saving gospel to others yet unsaved. This means they must not only "preach the gospel to every creature" (Mk 16:15) but also defend the gospel against those who seek to destroy it. Like the apostle Paul, we who know the Lord must be "set for the defence of the gospel" (Ph 1:17). Like the apostle Peter, we must "be ready always to give an answer to every man that asketh you a reason of the hope that is in you with meekness and fear" (1 Pe 3:15). Neither ignorance nor arrogance is appropriate armor for the Christian soldier.

It is with such admonitions in mind that I have undertaken the challenging task of preparing the annotations for *The Henry Morris Study Bible.* As an engineering scientist who has spent many years among the skeptical intellectuals of the academic world, I have felt very keenly the need for this kind of Bible study tool "in the defence and confirmation of the gospel" (Ph 1:7), and have therefore spent many, many hours in the study of Christian evidences and the scientific integrity of Scripture.

More importantly, every day for over 60 years has been partially devoted to the study of the Bible itself. The result has been a deep and settled conviction, stronger every year, that the Bible is indeed the very Word of the living God. Its histories are authentic, its science is accurate and far in advance of its times, its practical wisdom for daily living is unexcelled, and its insights into the human heart are profoundly perfect for every need. Furthermore, its own internal structures, as well as the claims of its authors, provide endless evidences of its divine inspiration to all who study it with open mind and heart. "Thou hast magnified thy word above all thy name," the psalmist testified (Ps 138:2).

The Bible does have the answer; its gospel can be defended; and it is hoped that *The Henry Morris Study Bible* will prove of significant help in this great cause to those who use it. Its annotations explain the Bible's difficult passages, resolve its alleged contradictions, point out the evidences of its divine origin, confirm its historical accuracy, note its remarkable anticipations of modern science, demonstrate its fulfilled prophecies and in general remove any doubts about its inerrancy, its authority and its ability to meet every human need.

The Henry Morris Study Bible Supports Literal Biblical Creationism

Probably the most distinctive feature of *The Henry Morris Study Bible* is an uncompromising commitment to literal biblical creationism. That is, it accepts at face value the majestic revelation of special creation in the Bible's very first chapter, acknowledging and defending the literal, six-day creation of all things. This truth of recent creation, combined

with the truth of the global cataclysmic flood in the days of Noah, is the real key to the true scientific understanding of earth history. The doctrine of special creation then pervades all the rest of the Bible and is the real foundation of all other truth, especially including all the great doctrines of the Christian faith. The evolutionary concept of history, on the other hand, is Satan's greatest weapon in his long war against God, serving him as the root of every false philosophy and evil practice known to man. The annotations in *The Henry Morris Study Bible* stress these great truths wherever they surface in Scripture.

Most importantly, the person and work of the Lord Jesus Christ are emphasized throughout. Christ is both eternal God—the second Person of the three-person Godhead—and perfect man, man as God intended man to be. His uniquely miraculous conception, His virgin birth, His sinless life, His powerful teachings, His mighty miracles, and then His substitutionary death and glorious resurrection are all stressed in the notes of *The Henry Morris Study Bible*.

The Henry Morris Study Bible
Follows a Literal Approach to the Bible

The Bible does contain many teachings that Christians have disagreed about, of course, and some annotated Bibles try to take neutral positions on such controversial doctrines. I have thought it best, however, to express my own convictions on these matters, even at the risk of losing some readers who hold other views.

Thus a literal approach has been taken, not only in Genesis but throughout the whole Bible. It would seem that, if the Bible is really God's Word, intended as His authoritative revelation to all men, we ought to assume He means exactly what He says. If figures of speech or symbols or metaphors are used, they are for the purpose of helping us understand, not confusing us, so they will be explained in the biblical context itself, not requiring the professional help of specially educated priests or prophets.

Based on this literal and contextual approach, the notes become what one might call Baptistic in ecclesiology, pre-millennial in eschatology, non-charismatic in pneumatology, and moderately Calvinistic in soteriology. These are man-made terms, of course, and no attempt has been made to develop formal theological doctrines in the notes. I have tried to be irenic, rather than argumentative, in dealing with such controversial matters, so it is hoped that anyone who disagrees with any particular annotation will still find the other notes helpful and profitable.

Finally, it is hoped that *The Henry Morris Study Bible* will not only help many Christians to be able better to defend and contend for the faith, but will also be used to lead many to saving faith in the Lord Jesus Christ. Most of all, it is fervently hoped—following much prayer and many years of study—that it will honor and please our great God of creation and redemption, Jesus Christ our Lord.

Dr. Henry M. Morris
(b.1918 – d.2006)

The First Book of Moses, called

GENESIS

Introduction to Genesis

In a very real sense, the Book of Genesis is the most important book in the world, for it is the foundation upon which all the other 65 books of God's written Word have been based. When Jesus Christ, after His resurrection, gave a key Bible study to His disciples on the way to Emmaus, He began with Genesis!

"Beginning at Moses and all the prophets, He expounded unto them in all the scriptures the things concerning himself" (Lk 24:27). We would do well to follow His example. If we want to understand the New Testament, we first need to understand Genesis; the New Testament contains at least 200 direct quotations or clear allusions to events described in Genesis—more than from any other book in the Old Testament.

All the great doctrines of Christianity—sin, atonement, grace, redemption, faith, justification, salvation, and many others—are first encountered in Genesis. The greatest doctrine of all—the special creation of all things by the eternal, self-existent God—is revealed in the very first chapter of Genesis, the foundation of all foundations.

It is hardly surprising, therefore, that the greatest attacks on the Bible have been directed against the integrity and authority of Genesis. Since the only alternative to creation is evolution, these attacks are all ultimately based on evolutionism, the assumption that this complex universe can somehow be explained apart from the infinite creative power of God.

The creation account in Genesis is supported by numerous other references throughout the Bible, and this is true for all the later events recorded in Genesis as well. To some degree, archaeological discoveries, as well as other ancient writings and traditions, also support these events, but the only infallibly correct record of creation and primeval history is the Book of Genesis. Its importance cannot be overestimated.

Authorship

Until about 200 years ago, practically all authorities accepted the fact that Moses wrote Genesis and all the rest of the Pentateuch as well. The first writer to question this seems to have been a French physician, Jean Astruc, about the time of the French revolution. Astruc argued that two writers wrote the two creation accounts in Genesis 1 and 2, on the basis of the different names for God used in the two chapters. Later writers during the 19th century, notably the German higher critic Julius Wellhausen, developed this idea into the elaborate documentary hypothesis of the origin of the Pentateuch.

According to this notion, the Pentateuch was written much later than the time of Moses, by at least four different writers or groups of writers, commonly identified now by J, E, D and P (standing for the Jehovist, Elohist, Deuteronomist, and Priestly documents, respectively). Although some form of this theory is still being taught in most liberal seminaries and college departments of religion, it has been thoroughly discredited by conservative scholars. This is discussed further in the Introductions to Exodus and other books of the

Pentateuch. In any case, there is no valid reason to question the Mosaic authorship of the Pentateuch, except for Genesis itself.

For Genesis, however, there is real substance to the documentary idea, though certainly not in the Astruc/Wellhausen form. In fact, it seems very likely that Moses was the compiler and editor of a number of earlier documents, written by Adam and other ancient patriarchs, rather than being the actual writer himself. After all, the events of Genesis took place long before Moses was born, whereas he was a direct participant in the events recorded in the other four books of the Pentateuch.

It is reasonable that Adam and his descendants all knew how to write and, therefore, kept records of their own times (note the mention of "the book of the generations of Adam" in 5:1). These records (probably kept on stone or clay tablets) were possibly handed down from father to son in the line of the God-fearing patriarchs until they were finally acquired by Moses when he led the children of Israel out of Egypt. During the wilderness wanderings, Moses compiled them into the Book of Genesis, adding his own explanatory editorial comments where needed. Genesis is still properly considered as one of the books of Moses, since its present form is due to him, but it really records the eyewitness records of these primeval histories, as written originally by Adam, Noah, Shem, Isaac, Jacob and other ancient patriarchs.

The divisions of Genesis can be recognized by the recurring phrase: "These are the generations of...." The archaeologist P. J. Wiseman has shown that these statements probably represent the "signatures," so to speak, of the respective writers as they concluded their accounts of the events during their lifetimes.

The Hebrew word for "generations" (*toledoth*) was translated in the Septuagint Greek by the Greek word *genesis* (used in the New Testament only in Ma 1:1, there translated "generation"). Thus these divisional notations have indirectly provided the very name for the Book of Genesis, which means "beginnings."

It is interesting to note, as an indirect confirmation of this concept of Genesis authorship, that while Genesis is cited at least 200 times in the New Testament, Moses himself is never noted as the *author* of any of these citations. On the other hand, he is listed at least 40 times in reference to citations from the other four books of the Pentateuch. There are also frequent references to Moses in the later books of the Old Testament, but never in relation to the Book of Genesis.

In sum, we can be absolutely confident that the events described in Genesis are not merely ancient legends or religious allegories, but the actual eyewitness accounts of the places, events, and people of those early days of earth history, written by men who were there, then transmitted down to Moses, who finally compiled and edited them into a permanent record of those ancient times.

CHAPTER 1
The Creation of the World

IN the ᴿbeginning ᴿGod created the heaven and the earth.   [Jo 1:1-3] • Ac 17:24

2 And the earth was ᴿwithout form, and void; and darkness *was* upon the face of the deep. ᴿAnd the Spirit of God moved upon the face of the waters.   Je 4:23 • Is 40:13,14

1:1 God. This opening verse of the Bible is unique, the foundation of foundations, probably the first words ever written down, either revealed to Adam, or even written directly by God Himself. One who really believes Genesis 1:1 will have no difficulty believing the rest of Scripture. God (*Elohim*) is eternal, existing before the universe, and is omnipotent, having created the universe. Therefore, nothing is impossible with God, and He alone gives meaning to everything. No attempt is made in this verse to *prove* God; it was recorded in the beginning when no one *doubted* God.

1:1 *created*. No other cosmogony, whether in ancient paganism or modern naturalism, even mentions the absolute origin of the universe. All begin with the space/time/matter universe, already existing in a primeval state of chaos, then attempt to speculate how it might have "evolved" into its present form. Modern evolutionism begins with elementary particles of matter evolving out of nothing in a "big bang" and then developing through natural forces into complex systems. Pagan pantheism also begins with elementary matter in various forms evolving into complex systems by the forces of nature personified as different gods and goddesses. But, very significantly, the concept of the special creation of the universe of space and time itself is found nowhere in all religion or philosophy, ancient or modern, except here in Genesis 1:1.

Appropriately, therefore, this verse records the creation of space ("the heaven"), of time ("in the beginning"), and of matter ("the earth"), the tri-universe, the space/time/matter universe which constitutes our physical environment. The Creator of this tri-universe is the triune God, *Elohim*, the uni-plural Old Testament name for the divine "Godhead," a name which is plural in form (with its Hebrew "*im*" ending) but commonly singular in meaning.

The existence of a transcendent Creator and the necessity of a primeval special creation of the universe is confirmed by the most basic principles of nature discovered by scientists:

(1)   The law of causality, that no effect can be greater than its cause, is basic in all scientific investigation and human experience. A universe comprising an array of intelligible and complex effects, including living systems and conscious personalities, is itself proof of an intelligent, complex, living, conscious Person as its Cause;

(2)   The laws of thermodynamics are the most universal and best-proved generalizations of science, applicable to every process and system of any kind, the First Law stating that no matter or energy is now being created or destroyed, and the Second Law stating that all existing matter and energy is proceeding irreversibly toward ultimate equilibrium and cessation of all processes. Since this eventual death of the universe has not yet occurred and since it will occur in time, if these processes continue, the Second Law proves that time (and, therefore, the space/matter/time universe) had a beginning. The universe must have been created, but the First Law precludes the possibility of its self-creation. The only resolution of the dilemma posed by the First and Second Laws is that "in the beginning God created the heavens and the earth." The so-called big bang theory of the origin of the cosmos, postulating a primeval explosion of the space/mass/time continuum at the start, beginning with a state of nothingness and then rapidly expanding into the present complex universe, contradicts both these basic laws and contradicts Scripture.

1:2 *the earth*. In an attempt to accommodate the supposed evolutionary geological ages in Genesis, certain theologians postulated a long gap in time here between Genesis 1:1 and Genesis 1:2, in which it was hoped that these ages could be pigeon-holed and forgotten as far as biblical exegesis was concerned. This gap theory, however, requires a worldwide cataclysm at the end of the geological ages, in order to account for the globally flooded and darkened earth described in Genesis 1:2. The cataclysm, in turn, is hypothetically connected with the fall of Lucifer in heaven (Is 14:9-14) and his expulsion to the earth (Eze 28:12-15), though such a cataclysm is nowhere mentioned in Scripture. However, in addition to its obvious contradictions with other important and clear Bible passages (1:31; Ex 20:11), the gap theory is self-defeating geologically. The geological age system (which is the necessary framework for modern evolutionism) is based entirely on the principle of uniformitarianism, a premise which denies any such worldwide cataclysm, and requires that we interpret earth history by the applying of present geological processes into the remote past. The concept of geological ages is based entirely on a uniformitarian explanation of the fossil beds and sedimentary rocks of the earth's crust, which would all have been destroyed by such a pre-Adamic cataclysm. Thus, any attempt to ignore or explain away the supposed great age of the earth by the gap theory makes an unnecessary compromise with evolutionism, and displays a lack of understanding of the geological structures and processes to which evolutionists appeal in defending their long ages.

3 ᴿAnd God said, ᴿLet there be ᴿlight: and there was light. Ps 33:6,9 • 2 Co 4:6 • [He 11:3]

4 And God saw the light, that *it was* good: and God divided the light from the darkness.

5 And God called the light Day, and the darkness he called Night. And the evening and the morning were the first day.

6 And God said, ᴿLet there be a firma-

The real answer to the geological ages is not an imaginary pre-Adamic cataclysm, but the very real cataclysm of the Noah's flood (see comments on ch. 6–9), which provides a much better explanation of the fossil beds and sedimentary rocks, eliminating all evidence of geological ages and confirming the biblical doctrine of recent creation.

1:2 *was without form, and void.* The verb "was" in Genesis 1:2 is the regular Hebrew verb of being (*hayetha*) and does not denote a change of state unless the context so requires. It only rarely is translated "became," as the gap theory postulates here. Neither does the phrase *tohu waw bohu* need to mean "ruined and desolated," as the gap theory requires. The King James translation "without form and void" is the proper meaning.

1:2 *was upon the face of the deep.* The universe, as first called into existence by *Elohim* was in elemental existence, still "unformed" and unenergized, not yet ready for habitation, "void" (see notes on Ps 33:6-9; Pr 8:22-31; Is 45:18; 2 Pe 3:5). It would not be perfect (i.e., finished) until the end of creation week, when God would pronounce it "very good" and "finished" (1:31–2:3). The "earth" material was suspended in a matrix of water (the "deep") completely static and therefore in "darkness."

1:2 *And the Spirit...moved.* However, this condition prevailed only momentarily. Then, the "Spirit" (Hebrew *ruach*) of "God" (*Elohim*) proceeded to "move upon the face of the waters" (literally, "vibrate in the presence of the waters"). Waves of gravitational energy and waves of electromagnetic energy began to pulse forth from the great "Breath" (another meaning of *ruach*) of God, the *Prime Mover* of the universe. The unformed "earth" material (Hebrew *eretz*), as well as the "waters" permeating it (Hebrew *shamayim*) quickly coalesced into spherical form under the new force of gravity, and the first material body (Planet Earth) had been formed at a point in space.

1:3 *God said.* As the "Spirit" of God "moved" (1:2), so now the Word of God speaks in Genesis 1:3. The result is light, the energizing of the vast cosmos through the marvelous electromagnetic force system which maintains all structures and processes in matter. These varied energies include not only visible light, but also all the shortwave radiations (ultraviolet, x-rays, etc.) and the long-wave radiations (infrared, radio waves, etc.), as well as heat, sound, electricity, magnetism, molecular interactions, etc. "Light," the most basic form of energy, is mentioned specifically, but its existence necessarily implies the activation of all forms of electromagnetic energies. Light was not created, since God Himself dwells in light. On the other hand, He created darkness (Is 45:7).

The existence of visible light prior to the establishment of the sun, moon and stars (1:16) emphasizes the fact that light (energy) is more fundamental than light givers. God could just as easily (perhaps more easily) have created waves of light energy as He could construct material bodies which generate light energy. The first is direct (since God *is* light!), the second indirect. For the creation of such light generators, see note on Genesis 1:14.

1:4 *darkness.* It is obvious that these rays of light energy included the visible light spectrum by its separation from the newly created "darkness." Most of this visible light emanated from one direction in space and, further, the newly-sphericized earth began now to rotate on its axis, as is shown by the establishment of a cyclical succession of "Day" and "Night," which has continued ever since.

1:5 *Day.* The use of "day" (Hebrew *yom*) in Genesis 1:5 is its first occurrence in Scripture, and here it is specifically defined by God as "the light" in the cyclical succession of light and darkness which has, ever since, constituted a solar day. Since the same word is used in defining all later "*yoms*" as used for this "first" *yom*, it is undeniable that God in-

ment in the midst of the waters, and let it divide the waters from the waters. Je 10:12

7 And God made the firmament, Rand divided the waters which *were* under the firmament from the waters which *were* Rabove the firmament: and it was so. Pr 8:27-29 • Ps 148:4

8 And God called the Tfirmament Heaven. And the evening and the morning were the second day. *expanse*

9 And God said, RLet the waters under

---

tends us to know that the days of creation week were of the same duration as any natural solar day. The word *yom* in the Old Testament almost always is used in this natural way, and is never used to mean any other definite time period than a literal day. This becomes especially clear when it is combined with a number (e.g., "first day") or with definite bounds (e.g., "evening and morning"), neither of which usages in the Old Testament allow non-literal meanings. It is occasionally, though rarely, used symbolically or in the sense of indefinite time (e.g., "the day of the Lord"), but such usage (as in English or other languages) is always evident from the context itself. Thus the so-called day-age theory, by which the days of creation are assumed to correspond to the ages of geology, is precluded by this definitive use of the word in its first occurrence, God Himself defining it!

1:5 *evening and the morning*. The use of "evening and morning" in that order is significant. As each day's work was accomplished during the "light," God's activity ceased during the "darkness." Consequently, there was nothing to report between evening and morning. The beginning of the next day's activity began with the next period of light, after the "morning," or better, "dawning." The literal sense of the formula after each day's work is: "Then there was dusk, then dawn, ending the first day."

1:6 *firmament*. The "firmament" is not a great vaulted dome in the sky, as some have interpreted it, but is simply the atmospheric expanse established between the waters above and below. The Hebrew word, *raqiya*, means "expanse" or perhaps better, "stretched-out thinness." Since God specifically identified it with "Heaven," it also can be understood simply as "space." Thus, on the second day, God separated the primeval deep into two deeps, with a great space between. The waters below the space retained the elemental earth materials which would be utilized on the following day to form the land and its plant cover. The waters above the firmament had apparently been transformed into the vapor state in order to be separated from the heavier materials and elevated above the atmosphere, where it could serve as a thermal blanket for the earth's future inhabitants.

Such a vapor canopy would undoubtedly have provided a highly efficient "greenhouse effect," assuring a perennial springlike climate for the entire earth. Water vapor both shields the earth against harmful radiations from space and also retains and spreads incoming solar heat. A vapor canopy would thus provide an ideal environment for abundant animal and plant life and for longevity and comfort in human life. Water vapor is invisible, and thus would be translucent, allowing the stars to be seen through it. This would not be the case with a liquid water or ice canopy.

1:7 *above the firmament*. The "waters which were above the firmament" are clearly not the clouds or the vapor which now float in the atmosphere. The Hebrew word *al* definitely requires the meaning "above." Furthermore, the absence of rain (2:5) and the rainbow (9:13) is not only explained but required by a vapor canopy, not by an atmosphere like that of the present. These waters extending far out into space eventually condensed and fell back to the earth at the time of the great deluge, providing the source of the worldwide rainstorm that contributed to the flood. Although the exact extent and structure of this canopy is still being researched by computer simulations, there are no major scientific problems with the concept.

1:9 *dry land*. The work of the third day began with the laying of the foundations of the earth (see notes on Job 38:4; Ps 33:7; Pr 8:29) by the power of God's spoken Word. The waters "under the firmament" apparently still contained all the material elements of the earth

the heaven be gathered together unto one place, and ᴿlet the dry *land* appear: and it was so.   Job 26:10 • Ps 24:1,2; 33:7; 95:5

10 And God called the dry *land* Earth; and the gathering together of the waters called he Seas: and God saw that *it was* good.

11 And God said, Let the earth ᴿbring forth grass, the herb yielding seed, *and the* ᴿfruit tree yielding fruit after his kind, whose seed *is* in itself, upon the earth: and it was so.   He 6:7 • 2 Sa 16:1

12 And the earth brought forth grass, *and* herb yielding seed after his kind, and the tree yielding fruit, whose seed *was* in itself, after his kind: and God saw that *it was* good.

13 And the evening and the morning were the third day.

---

in solution or suspension until the energizing Word initiated a vast complex string of chemical and physical reactions, to precipitate, combine and sort all the rock materials and metals comprising the solid earth. The "earth" (Hebrew *eretz*) thus formed was the same "earth" which had initially been "without form" (the same word *eretz* is used in 1:1-2,10), but it was now "dry land," no longer mixed in the initial watery matrix.

1:10 *Seas.* The solid materials separated out of the water, and then moved down and around under the forces of gravity, internal heat, and other electromagnetic energies (not to mention the outflowing energy of the divine Word) great basins opened up to receive and store the waters. Some of these waters were trapped and stored in the "great deep" (7:11), subterranean chambers beneath the earth's crust. Others accumulated in surface basins. However, all were evidently interconnected through a network of subterranean channels, so that they were both singular and plural—gathered together into "one place," yet called "Seas."

Thus were established the primeval continents and primeval oceans. We do not now know the original geography, however, since all was cataclysmically changed at the time of the great flood. We can infer that the topography was gently rolling and the waterways were relatively shallow and narrow, since all was "very good" and was made for man's enjoyment and utilization (1:26-28,31).

1:11 *bring forth grass.* The ability of the earth to begin immediately producing abundant plant life everywhere, on the very same day as the forming of the land surfaces, shows that the upper portion of the crust was a rich soil, fertile in chemical nutrients and retaining adequate moisture to sustain the lush vegetation. This fact illustrates an important principle. True creation necessarily involves the theory of a "creation of apparent age," or better, "creation of functioning maturity." That is, the soil did not gradually form over hundreds of years by rock weathering and other modern uniformitarian processes. It was readied instantaneously by divine command. The plants did not develop from seeds; rather the herb was formed "yielding seed." Similarly, the fruit trees were "yielding fruit," not requiring several years of preliminary growth as do modern fruit trees.

1:11 *seed.* The "seed" which God designed guaranteed reproduction of each plant "after his kind." This phrase, repeated nine more times in Genesis 1 after this first occurrence, obviously precludes transmutation of one kind into another. The "seed" was programmed for stable reproduction of each kind, through a remarkable system known today as the "genetic code," the complex information program in the DNA molecule. This system allows wide "horizontal" variation within the kind, but no "vertical" evolution from one kind into a more complex kind. It is significant that, despite widespread belief in evolution, no scientist has yet documented a single instance of true vertical evolution occurring today. The modern equivalent of "kind" is probably broader than the "species" in many cases, since the latter term is an arbitrary manmade category. That is, the many varieties of dogs are all part of the created "dog kind," just as all tribes and nations of men constitute one "mankind" (Ac 17:25-26).

1:12 *grass.* It should also be noted that plant life, in all its forms, was created before animal life, thus contradicting the order postulated by evolutionists. There are over 20 such contradictions between the order of creation in Genesis and that in evolutionary paleontology.

14 And God said, Let there be ᴿlights in the firmament of the heaven to divide the day from the night; and let them be for signs, and for ᴿseasons, and for days, and years: Ps 74:16; 136:5-9 • Ps 104:19

15 And let them be for lights in the firmament of the heaven to give light upon the earth: and it was so.

16 And God made two great ᵀlights; the ᴿgreater light to rule the day, and the ᴿlesser light to rule the night: *he made* ᴿthe stars also.   Ps 136:8 • Ps 8:3 • Job 38:7 • *luminaries*

17 And God set them in the firmament of the heaven to give light upon the earth,

18 And to ᴿrule over the day and over the night, and to divide the light from the darkness: and God saw that *it was* good.   Je 31:35

19 And the evening and the morning were the fourth day.

20 And God said, Let the waters bring forth abundantly the moving creature that hath life, and fowl *that* may fly above the earth in the open firmament of heaven.

21 And God created great ᵀwhales, and

1:14 *lights.* On the first day, God had said: "Let there be light" (Hebrew *or*). Now He says: "Let there be lights" (*ma-or*). Light energy was activated first, but now great masses of material (part of the "earth" elements created on the first day) were gathered together in one of the firmaments, or spaces, of the cosmos—the space beyond the waters above the space adjacent to the earth. These great bodies were set burning in complex chemical and nuclear reactions, to serve henceforth as "light-givers" for the earth.

1:14 *signs.* The Hebrew word for "signs" is the same word (*oth*) as used for Cain's "mark" (4:15) and for Noah's "token" (meaning the rainbow—9:12). Evidently the stars were arranged by God to "signify" something to those on the earth, not just scattered evenly or randomly around in space. God even named the stars and their constellations (Job 38:31-33; Is 40:26). For their possible significance, see notes on Amos 5:8; Job 9:9; 26:13; 38:32.

1:14 *seasons.* The establishment of "seasons" (and these were not simply religious seasons, but actual climatological seasons) indicates that the earth was formed with an axial inclination from the beginning, for this is the basic cause of its seasons.

1:16 *the stars also.* These stars were scattered in tremendous numbers throughout the infinite recesses of the heavens (note Is 55:9). The light energy emanating from them would henceforth travel across space to "give light upon the earth," providing patterns and movements which would also enable man to keep records of time and history. In order to serve these purposes, however, light energy trails would need to be established already in place in space between each star and earth. Thus, men would have been able to see stars billions of light-years away at the very moment of their formation, in accordance with the principle of mature creation, or creation of apparent age.

1:17 *light upon the earth.* The establishment of the sun and moon in their light-giving functions for the earth halfway through creation week is obviously inconsistent with the day-age theory. This is compounded by the fact that plant life on the earth was made one day before the sun, a situation which would be absurdly impossible if this "day" was an "age." Furthermore, these "lights" were to be used to measure days and years. This is the plural (*yamin*) of the Hebrew "day" (*yom*). They were also to "rule over the day and over the night," and all this was done on the fourth day. This repeated use of the same word in the passage requires the meaning in each case to be the same. The fourth "day" was thus obviously a solar day like all the rest.

1:20 *open firmament.* Both the "lights" (1:15) and the "fowl" are said to be in the "firmament of heaven." However, the fowl were to be in the "open" (Hebrew *pene*) firmament of heaven, or better, "the *face* of the firmament of heaven." Thus, birds fly only in the lower reaches of the vast spaces of the heavens. Or, it may be that there are two different "firmaments of heaven."

1:21 *great whales.* Fish and other marine organisms were created simultaneously with birds and other flying creatures, in obvious contradiction to the sequence imagined by evolutionists. The "moving creature" (Hebrew *sherets*) of Genesis 1:20 is elsewhere always

every living creature that moveth, which the waters brought forth abundantly, after their kind, and every winged fowl after his kind: and God saw that *it was* good.   *sea creatures*

22 And God blessed them, saying, Be fruitful, and multiply, and fill the waters in the seas, and let fowl multiply in the earth.

23 And the evening and the morning were the fifth day.

24 And God said, Let the earth bring forth the living creature after his kind, cattle, and creeping thing, and beast of the earth after his kind: and it was so.

25 And God made the beast of the earth after his kind, and cattle after their kind, and every thing that creepeth upon the earth after his kind: and God saw that *it was* good.

26 And God said, Let us make man in

---

translated "creeping thing," and here evidently refers to marine invertebrates and marine reptiles, as well as the fishes. The word translated "great whales" (Hebrew *tannin*) is elsewhere the regular word for "dragons," and most probably refers to the great marine reptiles often called dinosaurs.

1:21 *living creature.* It is significant that the word "create" (Hebrew *bara*) is applied to the introduction of animal life, but not to plant life. Plants are highly complex replicating chemical systems, as are animals, with reproductive programs based in the remarkable DNA molecule in both cases. However, animals possess another entity—that of consciousness—which plants do not possess, and this required a second act of true creation (the first was in 1:1, the creation of the basic space/mass/time universe). Such "consciousness" is the essential meaning of the Hebrew word *nephesh*, commonly translated "soul," but in Genesis 1:20 (its first occurrence) translated "life," and then in Genesis 1:21 "living creature." In Genesis 2:7, referring to man, it is rendered "living soul." Thus, both men and animals possess the specially-created *nephesh* or consciousness.

1:24 *earth bring forth.* The land animals were brought forth (no need for a further act of creation, since the *nephesh* principle had already been created) in the early part of the sixth day. There was a natural threefold categorization (no correlation with the arbitrary classification system used by modern biologists) consisting of cattle (domestic animals), beasts of the earth (large non-domestic animals) and creepers (small animals that crawl or creep close to the ground). The reversal of the sequence in Genesis 1:24-25 indicates that all were formed simultaneously. The bodies of these animals, like that of man (2:7), were all formed from the basic elements of the earth.

1:24 *it was so.* Note the logical order of God's formation of things. On the first day, He made the earth's atmosphere and hydrosphere, on the second day its lithosphere and biosphere. On the central day of the week, the heavenly astrosphere was formed. Then, on the fifth day living creatures were formed for earth's atmosphere and hydrosphere, and on the sixth day for its lithosphere and biosphere. On the first day God had created and energized His elemental universe; on the last day, God blessed and sanctified His completed universe.

1:25 *after his kind.* The phrase "after his kind" occurs repeatedly, stressing the reproductive integrity of each land animal kind, of the same sort as that of each plant kind (1:11-12) and each air animal and water animal (1:21). All of these reproductive systems are programmed in terms of the biochemical genetic code, utilizing the basic elements of the earth. Both plants and animals are formed from the created *eretz* ("earth"), only animals from the created *nephesh* ("soul" or consciousness).

1:26 *in our image.* God is, as it were, taking counsel here with Himself, not with angels, since man was to be made in the image of God, not of angels. "Our image," therefore, implies human likeness to the triune Godhead. Plants possess a body, and animals a body and consciousness. Man was not only to have a body (of the created "earth") and a consciousness (of the created "soul"), but man was also to possess a third created entity, the image of God, an eternal spirit capable of communion and fellowship with his Creator.

our image, after our likeness: and let them have dominion over the fish of the sea, and over the fowl of the air, and over the cattle, and over all the earth, and over every creeping thing that creepeth upon the earth.

27 So God created man ^Rin his *own* image, in the image of God created he him; male and female created he them.   Ge 5:2

28 And God blessed them, and God said unto them, ^RBe fruitful, and multiply, and replenish the earth, and subdue it: and have dominion over the fish of the sea, and over the fowl of the air, and over every living thing that moveth upon the earth.   Ge 9:1,7

29 And God said, Behold, I have given you every herb ^Tbearing seed, which *is* upon

---

1:26 *likeness.* Man was not only created in God's spiritual image; he was also made in God's physical image. His body was specifically planned to be most suited for the divine fellowship (erect posture, upward-gazing countenance, facial expressions varying with emotional feelings, brain and tongue designed for articulate speech—none of which are shared by the animals). Furthermore, his body was designed to be like the body which God had planned from eternity that He Himself would one day assume (1 Pe 1:20).

1:26 *dominion.* The "dominion" man was to exercise was to be over both "the earth" and also all the other living creatures on the earth. Such dominion obviously was under God as a stewardship, not as autonomous sovereign. Man was to care for the earth and its creatures, developing and utilizing the earth's resources, not to despoil and deplete them for selfish pleasure.

1:27 *male and female.* Note that "man" is here (and often in Scripture) used in a generic sense to include both man and woman. Both male and female were created (the details of their physical formation being given in ch. 2) in God's image. Thus both possess equally an eternal spirit capable of personal fellowship with their Creator. Shared equally by men and women are all those spiritual attributes not shared by animals—moral conscience, abstract thought, appreciation of beauty, emotional feelings, and, especially, the capacity for worshiping and loving God.

1:28 *replenish.* God's first command to man was that of producing abundant progeny sufficient to fill the earth (not "replenish," a misleading translation of the Hebrew word *male*). Perhaps the animals had been created in large numbers of each kind, but the human population began with only two people. The function of subduing the earth and having dominion over it would necessarily require a long time—first, for the growth of a large enough population to fill the earth, and second, for the acquiring of enough knowledge and skill to enable man to bring it under full control and development.

1:28 *have dominion.* This primeval commandment to conquer and rule the earth has been called the dominion mandate, though a better term might be the first commission to mankind. It has never been revoked, but was specifically renewed and extended after the flood (see notes on 9:1-7). The military terminology in no way implies hostility and resistance from the earth, for it was all "very good" (1:31). It suggests, rather, intensive study of the earth and its creatures (that is, "science") and then application of that knowledge (that is, technology and commerce) for the optimum benefit of mankind and the animals, and for the glory of God.

Note that no instruction was given to exercise dominion over other men, but only over the earth and the animals. Had man not rebelled against God's Word, all would have remained in perfect fellowship with God and, therefore, with one another. There was no initial need for the so-called social sciences and technologies, but only the natural sciences and their implementation. This situation was radically changed at the fall, and God's commandment accordingly expanded officially after the flood.

1:29 *given you every herb.* It is plain that both men and animals were originally intended to be vegetarian. There was adequate nourishment and energy value available in the fruits and herbs to enable both to accomplish the work God had given them to do. The supply

the face of all the earth, and every tree, in the which *is* the fruit of a tree yielding seed; ᴿto you it shall be for ᵀmeat. Ge 9:3 • *yielding* • *food*

30 And to ᴿevery beast of the earth, and to every ᴿfowl of the air, and to every thing that creepeth upon the earth, wherein *there is* life, *I have given* every green herb for meat: and it was so. Ps 145:15 • Job 38:41

31 And ᴿGod saw every thing that he had made, and, behold, *it was* very good. And the evening and the morning were the sixth day. [Ps 104:24]

CHAPTER 2

Thus the heavens and the earth were finished, and ᴿall the host of them. Ps 33:6

2 ᴿAnd on the seventh day God ended his work which he had made; and he rested on

---

could not be exhausted, since these plants were designed to reproduce themselves through the seeds they produced.

1:29 *all the earth*. The fact that their food would be available everywhere, "upon the face of all the earth," shows that in the originally created world there were no deserts or other uninhabitable regions, no frozen tundras or ice caps, no rugged high mountain ranges. With lush vegetation everywhere, the animals no doubt soon had populated all the earth.

1:29 *be for meat*. The question as to how or when some of the animals became carnivorous is not definitely answerable at this late date, since the Bible does not say. In the future kingdom age, there will again be no killing or struggle between animals or between animals and men (Is 11:6-9; Ho 2:18). Even today, both animals and men can (and do, on occasion) live on a strictly vegetarian diet. The development of fangs and claws, as well as other such structures and practices, may be explained as either (1) recessive created features which became dominant by selection processes as the environment worsened following the fall and flood; (2) features created originally by the Creator in foreknowledge of the coming curse; or (3) mutational changes following the curse, converting originally benign structures into predatory and defensive structures.

1:31 *very good*. This one verse precludes any interpretation of Genesis which seeks to accommodate the geological ages in its system. The "geological ages" are identified by the fossils found in the sedimentary rocks of the earth's crust, which supposedly depict a billion-year history of the evolution of life on the earth. In this case simple fossils are found in ancient rocks and more complex fossils in younger rocks. But fossils really depict a world in which death reigns! Fossils are the remains of dead organisms, from amoebae to man, and thus represent a world full of suffering and death, *not* a world pronounced by God as "very good."

Six times before in this chapter, God had adjudged His work to be "good." Now, after completing everything (even the "host of heaven"—see 2:1), He declared it all to be "*exceedingly* good" (literal meaning of the Hebrew word rendered "very"). The evolutionary ages of geology represent a billion years of wasteful inefficiency and profound cruelty if they were, indeed, a part of God's work. They would completely discredit God as a God of order, intelligence, power, grace and love. Death represents "the wages of sin" (Ro 6:23), not of divine love.

Thus, the "gap theory" (placing the geological ages *before* creation week) and the "day-age" or "progressive creation" theory (incorporating the geological ages *during* creation week) in effect imply that the Creator is either a bumbler or a monster. In reality, the geological ages are nothing but evolutionary delusions; the fossils are much more realistically explained in terms of the flood.

Even Satan himself (with all the "host of heaven" who later followed him in rebelling against God) was still perfect in all his ways (Eze 28:15) at the end of the creation week. His fall from heaven to the earth could only have been after God's universal "very good" proclamation.

2:1 *finished*. The strong emphasis in these verses on the completion of all of God's creat-

the seventh day from all his work which he had made. Ex 20:9-11; 31:17

3 And God ^Rblessed the seventh day, and sanctified it: because that in it he had rested from all his work which God created and made. [Is 58:13]

The Creation of Mankind

4 ^RThese^T *are* the generations of the heavens and of the earth when they were created, in the day that the LORD God made the earth and the heavens, Ge 1:1 • This is the history

---

ing and making activity is a clear refutation of both ancient evolutionary pantheism and modern evolutionary materialism, which seek to explain the origin and development of all things in terms of natural processes and laws innate to the universe. Creation is complete, not continuing (except in miracles, of course; if evolution takes place at all, it would require continuing miraculous intervention in the present laws of nature).

2:2 *ended his work.* This statement of completed creation anticipates the modern scientific laws of thermodynamics. The First Law states essentially the same truth: the universe is not now being created but is being conserved, with neither matter nor energy being created or destroyed. On the Second Law, (the universal law of increasing disorder) see notes on Genesis 3:17 and Genesis 1:1.

2:3 *sanctified it.* God's "rest" on the seventh day is not continuing; the verb is in the past tense—"rested," not "is resting." His blessing and hallowing of the seventh day could not apply to this present age of sin and death, but only to the "very good" world He had just completed.

Nevertheless, this "hallowing" of every seventh day was for man's benefit (Mk 2:27), and was obviously intended as a permanent human institution, not controlled by the heavenly bodies which mark days, months, seasons and years, but by the physical and spiritual need of all men for a weekly day of rest and worship, in thankfulness for God's great gift of creation and (later) for His even greater gift of salvation. The Sabbath (literally "rest") day was incorporated in the Mosaic covenant with Israel in a special way, but its use preceded Israel and will continue eternally (Is 66:23). However, the emphasis is on a "seventh" day, not necessarily Saturday. Since Christ's resurrection, in fact, most Christians have identified their weekly cycle as centering on the first day of the week. The age-long, worldwide observance of the "week" is not contingent on the movements of the sun and moon (like the day, the month and the year) but rather is mute testimony to its primeval establishment as a memorial of God's literal seven-day creation week.

2:4 *generations.* "Generations" (Hebrew *toledoth*) is the word from which the Book of Genesis gets its name. In the Septuagint it is rendered by the Greek *genesis*, which in Matthew 1:1 is translated "generation." This is the first occurrence of the formula which marks the key subdivisions of the book: "These are the generations of...." The others are at Genesis 5:1; 6:9; 10:1; 11:10,27; 25:19; 36:1,9; 37:2.

In all except this first one, the name of a specific patriarch is attached. Parallels with the terminology of the ancient Babylonian tablets indicate that these names are actually the signatures of the original writers of the particular tablets. That is, each of these primeval patriarchs kept the narrative records of his own generations, inscribing them on stone or clay tablets, then appending his name at the end, when he was ready to turn over the tablets and the task of writing the *toledoth* to the next in line. They eventually came down into Moses' possession, who wrote the last section of Genesis (37:3ff), obtaining the information from "the sons of Jacob" (Ex 1:1), as well as organizing and editing all the rest under divine inspiration, so that the entire collection finally became, in effect, the first of the five books of Moses. Since the first tablet (1:1–2:4a) tells of events prior to the existence of any witness to record them, God Himself either wrote this section directly or specifically revealed it to Adam. It describes the generations of no person, therefore, but rather those of the cosmos itself.

2:4 *in the day.* As per the ancient Babylonian practice, the next tablet, beginning at 2:4b, keys in to the previous one by a phrase which both associates with the preceding histories

5 And every plant of the field before it was in the earth, and every herb of the field before it grew: for the LORD God had not caused it to rain upon the earth, and *there was* not a man [R]to till the ground. Ge 3:23

6 But there went up a mist from the earth, and watered the whole face of the ground.

7 And the LORD God formed man *of* the [R]dust of the ground, and breathed into his nostrils the breath of life; and [R]man became a living soul. Ge 3:19,23 • 1 Co 15:45

8 And the LORD God planted [R]a garden [R]eastward in Eden; and there he put the man whom he had formed. Is 51:3 • Ge 3:23,24

9 And out of the ground made the LORD God to grow [R]every tree that is pleasant to the sight, and good for food; the tree of life also in the midst of the garden, and the tree of knowledge of good and evil. Eze 31:8

---

and initiates the new narrative. The "day" of this verse does not necessarily refer to the entire creation week, as day-age theory advocates claim. It more likely refers to the first day of that week, when God created the earth and the heavens, as just stated in Genesis 2:4a, then proceeded also to "make" them through the rest of the six days.

2:5 *before it grew.* This statement clearly teaches the fact of a mature creation, or creation of apparent age. The first plants did not grow from seeds, but were created full grown.

2:5 *rain upon the earth.* The primeval water cycle was from underground rather than from the atmosphere (see note on 1:7), the absence of rain being a consequence of the water vapor above the firmament and the uniform temperature which it maintained over the earth. Rain today is dependent on the global circulation of the atmosphere, transporting water evaporated from the ocean inland to condense and precipitate on the lands. This circulation is driven by worldwide temperature differences in the atmosphere and would be impossible with the global warmth sustained by the canopy.

2:6 *mist.* The "mist" was not a river, as some writers think. The Hebrew word simply means water vapor (compare Job 36:27); it refers merely to the local daily cycle of evaporation and condensation brought about by the day/night temperature cycle.

2:7 *dust of the ground.* Man's body was formed out of the "elements of the earth," the same materials (carbon, hydrogen, oxygen, etc.) from which both plants and the bodies of the animals had been formed (1:12,24). This unity of physical composition is a fact of modern science thus long anticipated by Scripture.

2:7 *breath of life.* Though animals also possess the "breath" (Hebrew *neshama*—7:22) and the "soul" (Hebrew *nephesh*—1:24), man's breath (same word as "spirit") and soul were imparted to him by God *directly*, rather than indirectly, as imparted to the animals.

2:7 *living soul.* Evolution is again refuted at this point. If man's body had been derived from an animal's body by any kind of evolutionary process, he would already have possessed the *nephesh*, rather than "becoming a living soul" when God gave him the breath of life.

2:8 *Eden.* Eden was evidently a region somewhere east of where Adam first received consciousness, so that he could watch as God "planted" a beautiful garden there for his home. Though this was to be his base, he was actually instructed to "subdue" and "rule" the whole earth (1:26-28). This verse is a summary, with Genesis 2:9-14 going back to give more details concerning Adam's home.

2:9 *tree of life.* The "tree of life" was an actual tree, with real fruit (note 3:22; Re 22:2) whose properties would have enabled even mortal men to live indefinitely. Though modern scientists may have difficulty in determining the nature of such a remarkable food, they also have been unable so far even to determine the basic physiological cause of aging and death. Thus it is impossible to say scientifically that no chemical substance could exist which might stabilize all metabolic processes and thereby prevent aging.

2:9 *tree of knowledge.* The same cautions apply to any discussions of the fruit of the tree of knowledge of good and evil, which likewise was genuinely physical. It is conceivable that

10 And a river went out of Eden to water the garden; and from thence it was parted, and became into four ᵀheads. *riverheads*

11 The name of the first *is* Pi'-son: that *is* it which compasseth ᴿthe whole land of Hav'-i-lah, where *there is* gold; Ge 25:18

12 And the gold of that land *is* good: ᴿthere *is* bdellium and the onyx stone. Nu 11:7

13 And the name of the second river *is* Gi'-hon: the same *is* it that compasseth the whole land of ᵀE-thi-o'-pi-a. *Cush*

14 And the name of the third river *is* ᴿHid'-de-kel:ᵀ that *is* it which goeth toward the east of ᵀAssyria. And the fourth river *is* Eu-phra'-tes. Da 10:4 • *The Tigris* • He *Ashshur*

15 And the LORD God took ᵀthe man, and put him into the garden of Eden to ᵀdress it and to keep it. *Adam* • *tend or cultivate*

16 And the LORD God commanded the man, saying, Of every tree of the garden thou mayest freely eat:

17 But of the tree of the knowledge of

---

the fruit contained substances capable of catalyzing physiological decay processes in the body, perhaps affecting even the genetic system. Whether or not this was the case, a "knowledge" of evil would necessarily follow its eating, since evil is fundamentally merely rejection of God's Word. Man had abundant knowledge of good already, since everything God had made was "very good" (1:31), but disobedience would itself constitute an experimental knowledge of evil.

2:10 *out of Eden.* The geography described in these verses obviously corresponds to nothing in the present world, although some of the names sound familiar. The Noahic flood was so cataclysmic in its effects (note 2 Pe 3:6) that the primeval geography was obliterated, with the post-flood continents and oceans completely different.

The similarity of certain names (e.g., Ethiopia, Euphrates) is best explained in terms of the ascription by Noah or his sons of these names to post-flood features which reminded them of pre-flood geographic features, just as the explorers of America often gave European names to American sites.

2:10 *four heads.* The rivers described in this section could not have derived their waters from rainfall (2:5), and so must have been fed by artesian springs, or controlled fountains from the great deep. This implies a network of subterranean pressurized reservoirs and channels fed from the primeval seas and energized by the earth's internal heat (see notes on 1:9-10).

2:12 *is good.* The present tense in which this description is written indicates it to be an eyewitness account, and thus most likely a record originally from Adam himself. However, the past tense in Genesis 2:10 ("went") may suggest that, at the time when Adam actually wrote it, the garden of Eden was no longer there.

2:12 *bdellium.* The "bdellium" was evidently a precious gum, likened to the bread from heaven sent to the Israelites in the wilderness (Nu 11:7).

2:15 *keep it.* The ideal world, both before the entrance of sin and after the removal of sin (see Re 22:3), is not one of idleness and frolic, but one of serious activity and service. Adam was placed in an ideal environment and circumstances, so he had no excuse for rejecting God's love and authority.

2:17 *not eat of it.* For true fellowship with God (having been created in His image), man must be free to reject that fellowship. The restriction imposed here by God is the simplest, most straightforward test that could be devised for determining man's volitional response to God's love. There was only one minor restraint placed on Adam's freedom and, with an abundance of delicious fruit of all types available, there was no justification for his desiring the one forbidden fruit. Nevertheless, he did have a choice, and so was a free moral agent, capable of accepting or rejecting God's will.

2:17 *die.* "Thou shalt surely die" could be rendered, "Dying, thou shalt die!" In the very day that he would experimentally come to "know evil," through disobeying God's Word, he would die spiritually, being separated from God's direct fellowship. Adam would also begin to die physically, with the initiation of decay processes in his body which would ultimately cause his physical death.

good and evil, Rthou shalt not eat of it: for in the day that thou eatest thereof Rthou shalt surely Rdie.   Ge 3:1,3,11,17 • Ge 3:3,19 • Ro 5:12

18 And the LORD God said, *It is* not good that the man should be alone; RI will make him an help meet for him.   1 Co 11:8,9

19 And out of the ground the LORD God formed every beast of the field, and every fowl of the air; and Rbrought *them* unto Adam to see what he would call them: and whatsoever Adam called every living creature, that *was* the name thereof.   Ps 8:6

20 And Adam gave names to all cattle, and to the fowl of the air, and to every beast of the field; but for Adam there was not found an help meet for him.

21 And the LORD God caused a Rdeep sleep to fall upon Adam, and he slept: and he took one of his ribs, and closed up the flesh instead thereof;   1 Sa 26:12

22 And the rib, which the LORD God had taken from man, made he a woman, Rand Rbrought her unto the man.   1 Ti 2:13 • He 13:4

23 And Adam said, This *is* now Rbone of my bones, and flesh of my flesh: she shall be called TWoman, because she was Rtaken out of TMan. Ge 29:14 • 1 Co 11:8,9 • He *Ishshah* • He *Ish*

24 RTherefore shall a man leave his father

2:18 *meet for him.* The events described here all took place on the sixth day of the creation week, after which God pronounced all things "very good." All the animals had been created "male and female" (6:19) and instructed to "multiply in the earth" (1:22), but man still needed a "helper like him" (literal meaning).

2:19 *God formed.* A better, and quite legitimate, translation is "had formed." Thus there is no contradiction with the order of creation in Genesis 1 (animals before man). The first chapter of Genesis gives a summary of the events on all six days of creation; the second chapter provides more details of certain events of the sixth day.

2:19 *the name thereof.* The animals named by Adam included only birds, domesticable animals, and the smaller wild animals that would live near him. It would be possible for him to name about 3,000 of the basic kinds of these animals in about five hours (one every six seconds), and this would be adequate both to acquaint Adam with those animals and also to show clearly that there were none who were sufficiently like him to provide companionship for him. This is still further proof that man did not evolve from any of the animals, even those that were most directly associated with him.

2:20 *not found.* As far as fossil evidence is concerned, many fossils of true men have been found (Neanderthal, Cro-Magnon, etc.) as well as fossils of true apes. The so-called "hominids" (*Australopithecus, Homo erectus*, etc.) are fragmentary and controversial, even among evolutionists, and can all be interpreted either as extinct apes or degenerated men.

2:21 *deep sleep.* The "deep sleep" was not simply an anesthetized state to prevent pain, since there was as yet no pain in the world. It was most likely ordained as a primeval picture of the future death of the second Adam, whose sacrificial death would result in the formation of His bride (Ep 5:30-32; 2 Co 11:2).

2:21 *ribs.* The "rib" was actually the "side" of Adam (the Hebrew *tsela* occurs 35 times in the Old Testament, and is nowhere else translated "rib"). The side contained both "bone" and "flesh" (2:23), but it may be that both are implied in the blood that would necessarily flow from the opened side. The "life of the flesh is in the blood" (9:4; Le 17:11) and a primeval blood "transfusion" would more perfectly fit the event as a type of the opened side of Christ on the cross (Jo 19:34-36). Even if the operation did actually extract a rib from Adam, this would not suggest that men should have one less rib than women, since "acquired characteristics" are not hereditary.

2:22 *made he a woman.* This remarkable record of the formation of the first woman could hardly have been invented by human imagination. Neither can it be interpreted in the context of theistic evolution, even if one could interpret the formation of Adam's body from the dust in evolutionary terms. Its historicity is confirmed in the New Testament (1 Ti 2:13; 1 Co 11:8). All other men have been born of woman, but the first woman was made from man.

and his mother, and shall cleave unto his wife: and they shall be one flesh.   Ma 19:5

25 And they were both naked, the man and his wife, and were not ^Rashamed.   Is 47:3

CHAPTER 3

The Temptation of Mankind

Now ^Rthe serpent was ^Rmore subtil than any beast of the field which the LORD

2:24 *one flesh*. The literal historicity of this event and its primary importance in human life are confirmed by both the apostle Paul (Ep 5:30-31) and the Lord Jesus Christ (Ma 19:3-9; Mk 10:2-12). Although men and women through the ages have corrupted this divine institution in many ways (adultery, divorce, polygamy, homosexuality, etc.), "from the beginning it was not so" (Ma 19:8). The institution of the home is the first and most basic human institution, and it was intended to be monogamous and permanent until death (Ro 7:2-3). It is significant that cultures of all times and sorts have acknowledged the superiority of monogamy, even though they have not always practiced it. Such an awareness could not be a product of evolution, since it does not characterize most animals, and thus can only be explained in terms of this primeval creation and revelation. Furthermore, the fact that it took place at the very "beginning of the creation," rather than billions of years after the beginning, was confirmed by the Lord Jesus Christ Himself (Mk 10:6).

2:25 *not ashamed*. The lack of shame at nakedness was not because of a hardened conscience, as is true today, but because the physiological differences of Adam and Eve had been divinely created in accord with God's purpose and they had been brought together by God with the express commandment to "be fruitful and multiply" (1:28). At this time they were still without sin and thus without consciousness of moral guilt. Later, however, their sin brought an awareness that the springs of human life had been poisoned, both in themselves and in their offspring. This discovery made them painfully aware of their reproductive organs and they were then "ashamed."

3:1 *serpent*. The "serpent" was not merely a talking snake, but was Satan himself (Re 12:9; 20:2) possessing and using the serpent's body to deceive Eve. Satan had been originally "created" (see notes on Eze 28:14-15) as the highest of all angels, the anointed cherub covering the very throne of God in heaven. He, along with all the angels, had been created to be "ministering spirits, sent forth to minister for them who shall be heirs of salvation" (He 1:14). Not content with a role inferior in two important respects to man (angels were not created in God's image, nor could they reproduce after their kind, there being no female angels), Satan led a third of the angels (Re 12:4,9) to rebel against God, seeking to become God himself. Evidently, he did not really believe that God was the omnipotent Creator, but rather that all had evolved from the primeval chaos (probably the explanation for the widespread ancient pagan belief that the world began in a state of watery chaos). God, therefore, "cast [him] to the ground" (Eze 28:17), thus allowing Satan to tempt the very ones he had been created to serve.

3:1 *subtil*. The physical serpent was clever, and possibly originally able to stand upright, eye-to-eye with man (the Hebrew word is *nachash*, possibly meaning originally a shining, upright creature).

3:1 *he said*. There is a possibility that some of the animals may have originally been able to communicate on an elementary level with their human masters, an ability later removed by the curse. More likely, God merely allowed Satan to use the serpent's throat (as He later allowed Balaam's ass to speak—Nu 22:28) and Eve was, in her innocence, not yet aware of the strangeness of it.

3:1 *hath God said*. The root of all sin is doubting God's Word. Satan used this approach successfully even with one who had never sinned before and who had no sin-nature inclining her to sin. Satan merely implanted a slight doubt concerning God's truth and His sovereign goodness. The approach, so successful in this case, has provided the pattern for his temptations ever since.

God had made. And he said unto the woman, Yea, hath God said, Ye shall not eat of every tree of the garden?   1 Ch 21:1 • 2 Co 11:3

2 And the woman said unto the serpent, We may eat of the ᴿfruit of the trees of the garden: Ge 2:16,17

3 But of the fruit of the tree which *is* in the midst of the garden, God hath said, Ye shall not eat of it, neither shall ye ᴿtouch it, lest ye die.   Ex 19:12,13

4 ᴿAnd the serpent said unto the woman, Ye shall not surely die: [2 Co 11:3]

5 For God doth know that in the day ye eat thereof, then your eyes shall be opened, and ye shall be as ᵀgods, knowing good and evil.   *God*

The Fall of Mankind

6 And when the woman ᴿsaw that the tree *was* good for food, and that it *was* pleasant to the eyes, and a tree to be desired to make *one* wise, she took of the fruit thereof, and did eat, and gave also unto her husband with her; and he did eat.   1 Jo 2:16

7 And the eyes of them both were opened, ᴿand they knew that they *were*

3:3 *touch it.* Eve, in her developing resentment against God, fell into Satan's trap, both taking away from God's Word and adding to it. God had said that they could "freely eat of every tree" (2:16); Eve quoted Him merely as saying that they could eat of the trees. God had said that they should not eat of the fruit of one tree; Eve added the statement that they should not even touch it. These are the very sins God warned about after His written Word was finally completed (Re 22:18-19). Doubting God's Word, augmenting, then diluting, and finally rejecting God's Word—this was Satan's temptation and Eve's sin, and this is the common sequence of apostasy even today.

3:4 *the serpent.* It is interesting that two clay seals found in the archaeological digs at Nineveh may reflect the story of the fall of Adam and Eve. One seems to show the man and woman being tempted by the serpent, the other their expulsion from the garden.

3:5 *be as gods.* Satan's sin led him to desire to be as God, and this was the desire he placed in Eve's mind (see notes on Is 14:13-14). In fact, when one questions or changes the Word of God, he is, for all practical purposes, making himself to be "god."

3:5 *knowing good and evil.* Satan's deceptions are always most effective when they have some truth in them. Through eating the forbidden fruit, Adam and Eve would indeed come to "know good and evil," but not "as gods!"

3:6 *make one wise.* The threefold temptation, appealing to body ("good for food"), soul ("pleasant to the eyes") and spirit ("make one wise"), was the same by which Satan appealed to Christ in the wilderness (Lk 4:1-12), and against which Christians are warned in 1 John 2:16 ("the lust of the flesh, and the lust of the eyes, and the pride of life").

3:6 *he did eat.* It was at this point that "by one man sin entered into the world, and death by sin" (Ro 5:12). There could have been no death in the world before man brought sin into the world. Thus, the fossils in the earth's crust cannot be a record of the evolution of life leading up to man but must be a record of death after man. In the evolutionary scenario, struggle and death in the animal kingdom eventually, after a billion years, brought man into the world. The truth is, however, that man brought death into his whole dominion by his sin.

3:7 *naked.* The sudden recognition of their nakedness indicates the realization of Adam and Eve that their descendants, as well as themselves, would suffer the effects of this original sin. The ability and instruction to be fruitful, given by God as a unique blessing, now would also convey the curse of sin and death. Adam was the federal head of the human race, and it was "through the offence of one many be dead" (Ro 5:15).

3:7 *fig leaves.* The hasty fabrication of fig leaf aprons might conceal their procreative organs from each other, but could hardly hide their sin from God. Neither will the "filthy rags" of self-made "righteousnesses" (Is 64:6) cover sinful hearts today. The "garments of salvation" and the "robe of righteousness" (Is 61:10) can be provided only by God, just as God provided coats of skins for Adam and Eve (3:21).

naked; and they sewed fig leaves together, and made themselves aprons. Ge 2:25

The Judgment on Mankind

8 And they heard ᴿthe voice of the LORD God walking in the garden in the cool of the day: and Adam and his wife hid themselves from the presence of the LORD God amongst the trees of the garden. Job 38:1

9 And the LORD God called unto Adam, and said unto him, Where *art* thou?

10 And he said, I heard thy voice in the garden, ᴿand I was afraid, because I *was* naked; and I hid myself. Ge 2:25

11 And he said, Who told thee that thou *wast* naked? Hast thou eaten of the tree, whereof I commanded thee that thou shouldest not eat?

12 And the man said, ᴿThe woman whom thou gavest *to be* with me, she gave me of the tree, and I did eat. [Pr 28:13]

13 And the LORD God said unto the woman, What *is* this *that* thou hast done? And the woman said, ᴿThe serpent ᵀbeguiled me, and I did eat. 2 Co 11:3 • *deceived*

14 And the LORD God said unto the serpent, Because thou hast done this, thou *art* cursed above all cattle, and above every beast of the field; upon thy belly shalt thou go, and ᴿdust shalt thou eat all the days of thy life: De 28:15-20

15 And I will put enmity between thee and the woman, and between thy seed and her seed; ᴿitᵀ shall bruise thy head, and thou shalt bruise his heel. Ro 16:20 • Lit. *he*

16 Unto the woman he said, I will greatly

3:8 *walking in the garden*. This is not a crude figure of speech, but an actual appearance of God. The "Word of God," Christ in His preincarnate state, regularly appeared in the garden for fellowship and communication with His people. How long this period of fellowship had endured is not stated, but it was long enough for the satanic rebellion in heaven and expulsion to earth. Since it was not long enough for Eve to conceive children, however, and since she and Adam had been instructed by God to do so, it was probably not more than a few days or weeks.

3:10 *hid myself*. The shame associated with nudity is no artificial inhibition of civilization, but has its source in this primeval awareness of sin. It is only lost when consciences are so hardened as to lose sensitivity to sin. Clothing is even worn in heaven (Re 1:13; 19:14).

3:11 *Hast thou eaten*. God's questions were not to obtain information, but to encourage Adam and Eve to confess their sin. Instead of repentance, however, they responded by feeble attempts at self-justification, each blaming someone else. In this, they behaved like most of their descendants.

3:14 *cursed above all cattle*. God's curse fell first on the serpent, representing man's great enemy, the devil, as a perpetual reminder to man of his fall. All other animals were also placed under the curse, as part of man's dominion, but the serpent was cursed above all others, becoming a universal object of dread and loathing. Whatever may have been its original posture, it would henceforth glide on its belly, eating its prey directly off the ground, and covered with the dust of the earth.

3:15 *enmity between thee*. This verse is famous as the Protevangel ("first gospel"). The curse was directed immediately towards the serpent, but its real thrust was against the evil spirit possessing its body, "that old serpent, called the Devil" (Re 12:9). Satan may have assumed that he had now won the allegiance of the woman and all her descendants, but God told him that there would be enmity between him and the woman.

3:15 *her seed*. The "seed of the woman" can only be an allusion to a future descendant of Eve who would have no human father. Biologically, a woman produces no seed, and except in this case biblical usage always speaks only of the seed of men. This promised Seed would, therefore, have to be miraculously implanted in the womb. In this way, He would not inherit the sin nature which would disqualify every son of Adam from becoming a Savior from sin. This prophecy thus clearly anticipates the future virgin birth of Christ.

3:15 *bruise thy head*. Satan will inflict a painful wound on the woman's Seed, but Christ in turn will inflict a mortal wound on the serpent, crushing his head. This prophecy was

multiply thy sorrow and thy conception; ᴿin sorrow thou shalt bring forth children; ᴿand thy desire *shall be* to thy husband, and he shall ᴿrule over thee.   Jo 16:21 • Ge 4:7 • 1 Co 11:3

17 And unto Adam he said, ᴿBecause thou hast hearkened unto the voice of thy

wife, and hast eaten of the tree, ᴿof which I commanded thee, saying, Thou shalt not eat of it: ᴿcursed *is* the ground for thy sake; ᴿin ᵀsorrow shalt thou eat *of* it all the days of thy life;   1 Sa 15:23 • Ge 2:17 • Ro 8:20-22 • Ec 2:23 • *toil*

18 Thorns also and thistles shall it bring

---

fulfilled in the first instance at the cross, but will culminate when the triumphant Christ casts Satan into the lake of fire (Re 20:10).

3:15 *bruise his heel*. This primeval prophecy made such a profound impression on Adam's descendants that it was incorporated, with varying degrees of distortion and embellishment, in all the legends, mythologies and astrologies of the ancients, filled as they are with tales of mighty heroes engaged in life-and-death struggles with dragons and other monsters. Mankind, from the earliest ages, has recorded its hope that someday a Savior would come who would destroy the devil and reconcile man to God.

3:16 *multiply thy sorrow*. Had Eve not sinned, the experience of childbirth would have been easy and pleasant, like every other experience in the perfect world God had made. The curse, however, fell in a peculiar way on Eve and her daughters, and the pain and sorrow of birth would be greatly multiplied.

Nevertheless, the bearing of children, especially by a woman who loves God and seeks to obey Him, is a time of blessing and rejoicing even though accompanied by a time of suffering (Jo 16:21). In the experience of giving birth, every woman experiences by proxy, as it were, the privilege granted Mary when she became the mother of the promised Seed. Furthermore, she even becomes a type of Christ, who "shall see His seed....He shall see of the travail of His soul, and shall be satisfied" (Is 53:10-11). The suffering is forgotten in the rejoicing, and this in itself goes far toward easing the physical pain (note 1 Ti 2:15).

3:16 *rule over thee*. She who had acted independently of her husband in her desire for the forbidden fruit must henceforth exercise her desires through her husband, and he would be ruler in the family. This prophecy has been fulfilled throughout history, in every time and nation.

To the woman who knows God, however, especially in the full light of Christianity, her role of submission to God and to her husband becomes her means of greatest fulfillment and happiness. The "rule" of a true Christian husband is not one of harshness and subjugation, but one of loving companionship and caring responsibility (Ep 5:22-33; Col 3:18-21; 1 Pe 3:1-7).

3:17 *unto Adam*. The full force of the curse fell on Adam, as the responsible head of the human race, and on all his dominion. Instead of believing God's Word, Adam had "hearkened to the voice of his wife," and she had been beguiled by the voice of the serpent. It is always a fatal mistake to allow the words of any creature to take precedence over the Word of God.

3:17 *cursed is the ground*. The "ground" is the same word as "earth." The very elements of matter, out of which all things had been made, were included in the curse, so that the "whole creation" (Ro 8:22) was brought under bondage to a universal principle of "corruption" (literally "decay"—Ro 8:21). That is, all things had been built up by God from the basic elements of matter ("the dust of the earth"), but now they would all begin to decay back to the dust again. The curse evidently applies to the entire physical cosmos, as well as to the planet Earth, though it is possible that the decay principle operating in the stars and the other planets may relate also to the prior sin of the angelic "host of heaven."

3:17 *for thy sake*. The curse was not only a punishment for man's disobedience but also a provision for man's good, forcing him to recognize the seriousness of his sin, to realize the

forth to thee; and ᴿthou shalt eat the herb of the field;   Ps 104:14
19 ᴿIn the sweat of thy face shalt thou eat bread, till thou return unto the ground; for out of it wast thou taken: for dust thou *art*, and unto dust shalt thou return.   2 Th 3:10

---

folly of trusting anyone but his Creator, and his inability to save himself from destruction. This would encourage him to a state of true repentance toward God and to trust in God to save him. The Second Law of Thermodynamics, which is the modern scientific statement of this decay principle (see notes on 1:1), points toward an ultimate death of the universe, and at the same time points back to a primeval creation, and therefore compels men to look toward the Creator as its only possible Savior.

3:18 *thistles*. It seems unlikely that God actually created thorns and thistles at this time. More probably, He allowed the beneficent processes and structures He had made previously, all of which were "very good" initially, to deteriorate in varying degrees, some even becoming harmful to man and to each other. There exists now a host of systems in nature (disease, bacteria, viruses, parasites, fangs and claws, weeds and poisons, etc.) which reflect a state of conflict and struggle for existence in the plant and animal kingdoms, as well as in human life, all of which seems, at first, to be inconsistent with the concept of an ideal creation. In the physical world there are storms and earthquakes, extremes of heat and cold, weathering and disintegration, and many other unpleasant phenomena. There is still need for research to understand the mechanisms by which this change of state from the perfect creation was brought about. In plants and animals, beneficent structures may either have mutated to malevolent structures or else have been replaced through natural selection by recessive characteristics coded into the genetic system by God at the time of creation in anticipation of the future environmental changes that might become necessary if Adam used his freedom wrongfully.

These systems and processes now maintain a balance of nature and so are indirectly beneficial in maintaining life on a cursed earth, even though individual organisms all eventually die. Had the fall and curse not taken place, populations would probably have eventually been stabilized at optimum values by divine constraints on the reproductive process. With God's personal presence withdrawn for a time, however, it is better to maintain order by these indirect constraints associated with the curse, adding still further to the testimony that the world is now in pain, awaiting its coming Redeemer.

3:19 *sweat of thy face*. The curse on Adam had four main aspects: (1) *sorrow*, because of the futility of endless struggle against a hostile environment; (2) *pain*, signified by the thorns; (3) *sweat*, or *tears*, the "strong crying" occasioned by the labor necessary to maintain life and hope; and (4) eventual physical *death* in spite of all his efforts, returning back to the dust.

But Christ, as the second Adam, has borne the curse for us (Ga 3:13), as the "man of sorrows" (Is 53:3), wearing the *thorns* and suffering the greatest *pain* (Mk 15:17), acquired by *strong crying* (He 5:7) to *sweat* as it were drops of blood before being finally brought into the *dust of death* (Ps 22:15). And because He so suffered for us, once again someday God will dwell with men, and "there shall be no more *death*, neither *sorrow*, nor *crying*, neither shall there be any more *pain*" (Re 21:4). Indeed there shall be "no more curse" (Re 22:3).

3:19 *dust thou art*. The curse thus applies to man and woman, to the animals and to the physical elements, God's whole creation. It is so universal as to have been discovered and recognized empirically as a general scientific law, the law of increasing entropy ("in-turning"). This famous Second Law of Thermodynamics is sometimes also called the law of morpholysis ("loosing of structure"). It expresses the universal tendency for systems to decay and become disordered, for energy to be converted into forms unavailable for further work, for information to become confused, for the new to become worn, for the young to become old, for the living to die, even for whole species to become extinct. One

20 And Adam called his wife's name ᴿEve;ᵀ because she was the mother of all living. 2 Co 11:3 • *Life* or *Living*

21 Unto Adam also and to his wife did the Lᴏʀᴅ God make ᵀcoats of skins, and clothed them. *tunics*

22 And the Lᴏʀᴅ God said, Behold, the man is become as one of us, to know good and evil: and now, lest he put forth his hand, and take also of the tree of life, and eat, and live for ever:

23 Therefore the Lᴏʀᴅ God sent him forth from the garden of Eden, ᴿto till the ground from whence he was taken. Ge 4:2; 9:20

24 So ᴿhe drove out the man; and he placed ᴿat the east of the garden of Eden

---

of the most amazing anomalies of human thought is the concept of evolution, which has never been observed in action scientifically and is exactly the opposite of the universally proved scientific principle of increasing entropy. This theory is nevertheless believed to be the most fundamental principle of nature by almost the entire intellectual establishment!

3:20 Eve. Eve means "life," and her name indicates Adam's faith in God's promise that the "woman" would bear a Seed. Even though he realized that he was going to die, Adam still believed that God would provide life. He had disobeyed God's Word by partaking of his wife's forbidden fruit; now he believed God's Word concerning his wife's fruitfulness. Since true faith is always accompanied by repentance, it is evident that Adam had turned away from Satan and back to God. No doubt Eve had done the same, desiring now to follow her husband instead of leading him.

3:20 all living. There were no children at this time, so this statement is apparently an editorial insertion by Moses, testifying that all mankind had descended from Adam and Eve. There were no "pre-Adamite" men (compare 1 Co 15:45, speaking of "the first man Adam"), nor were there any pre-fall children, since "in Adam all die" (1 Co 15:22).

3:21 coats of skins. This action is very instructive in several ways: (1) God considers clothing so vital in this present world that He Himself provided it for our first parents; (2) the aprons fashioned by Adam and Eve were inadequate, testifying in effect that man-made efforts to prepare for God's presence will be rejected; (3) the clothing provided by God required shedding the blood of two animals, probably two sheep, who were thus the first creatures actually to suffer death after Adam's sin, illustrating the basic biblical principle of substitutionary atonement (or "covering"), requiring the shedding of innocent blood as a condition of forgiveness for the sinner.

3:22 as one of us. Once again there is a divine council of the Godhead, this time to decree man's expulsion from the garden. Man's ultimate restoration requires his full instruction in the effects of sin and separation from God.

3:22 tree of life. The delicious fruit of the tree of life had been freely available to Adam and Eve, but it was not *necessary* for their survival. It was only eating the fruit of the tree of knowledge of good and evil that would result in death (2:17). The same will apply when the tree of life is planted again in the new earth. Its fruit and leaves will be freely available for food (Re 22:2), but it will not be necessary for survival, since there will be no more death there (Re 21:4). However, it did contain such wonderful health-giving ingredients that it would have enabled people to survive to tremendous ages even after sin and death entered the world, and this would have undermined God's intended purpose for death (see note on 3:17). The words "for ever" in this verse are from the Hebrew *olam*, which can also legitimately be translated a "long time," depending on context (Is 42:14). It is also used for the "lasting hills" (De 33:15).

3:22 live for ever. The fruit of the tree of life will be freely available to all in the new earth (Re 2:7; 22:1-2).

3:23 sent him forth. Evidently Adam and Eve were reluctant to leave their beautiful garden home and God's personal fellowship, but it was for their own good, and God finally "drove out" those whom He loved (3:24).

RCher'-u-bims, and a flaming sword which turned every way, to keep the way of the tree of Rlife.   Eze 31:3,11 • Ge 2:8 • Ps 104:4 • Ge 2:9

CHAPTER 4

Cain Slays His Brother Abel

And Adam knew Eve his wife; and she conceived, and bare TCain, and said, I have gotten a man from the LORD.   Lit. *Acquire*

2 And she again bare his brother TAbel. And Abel was a keeper of sheep, but Cain was a tiller of the ground.   Lit. *Breath* or *Nothing*

3 And in process of time it came to pass, that Cain brought of the fruit Rof the ground an offering unto the LORD.   Nu 18:12

4 And Abel, he also brought of Rthe firstlings of his flock and of Rthe fat thereof. And the LORD had Rrespect unto Abel and to his offering: Nu 18:17 • Le 3:16 • He 11:4

5 But unto Cain and to his offering he had not respect. And Cain was very Twroth, and his countenance fell.   *angry*

6 And the LORD said unto Cain, Why art thou wroth? and why is thy countenance fallen?

3:24 *Cherubims.* The cherubim are apparently the highest beings in the hierarchy of angels, always associated with the immediate presence of God (Ps 18:10; 80:1; 99:1; Eze 1:4-28; 10:1-22; Re 4:6-8). Satan himself had once been the "anointed cherub" on God's holy mountain (Eze 28:14). The appointment of the cherubim to keep (or "guard") the way to the tree of life, with swordlike tongues of flame flashing around them, suggests that God's personal presence continued to be associated with the garden and the tree. The representations of the cherubim in the holy of holies in the tabernacle (Ex 25:17-22; He 9:3-5), suggest that God may have continued to meet at stipulated intervals with His people at the entrance to the garden (see notes on 4:3-5).

4:1 *Cain.* The name "Cain" means "acquisition," expressing Eve's thankfulness that the Lord was keeping His promise to her, and her faith that her son would grow to manhood. Possibly Eve jumped to the unwarranted conclusion that Cain was the promised Deliverer. Actually, however, he was "of that wicked one" (1 Jo 3:12), and thus was the first in the long line of the serpent's seed.

4:2 *Abel.* "Abel" means "vapor" or "vanity." By the time Abel was born, Eve was fully aware of the effect of God's curse on the creation, which was made "subject to vanity" (Ro 8:20).

4:2 *tiller of the ground.* Both Cain and Abel had honorable occupations, Cain producing food for the family and Abel sheep for clothing and sacrifice. As time would pass and populations would multiply, such specializations could provide the basis for trade and help subdue the earth.

4:3 *process of time.* Literally, "at the end of the days," undoubtedly a reference to the "seventh day," which God had hallowed as a day of rest and blessing (2:3). On such a day, men would follow God's example in ceasing from their regular labors in order to have fellowship with God, possibly meeting with Him at the entrance to Eden (3:24).

4:3 *an offering.* Such fellowship, however, required that worshipers approach God with an offering that would make them suitable for His presence. Adam and Eve no doubt had instructed their sons that this required a substitutionary sacrifice of innocent blood (3:21). Cain, however, chose to bring another type of offering on this occasion.

4:4 *Abel.* Abel was a man of faith, the first listed in the chapter of faith (He 11). Since he brought "by faith...a more excellent sacrifice" (He 11:4), it is evident that God had given instruction concerning the sacrifice, which Abel believed and obeyed. The Lord Jesus described him as "righteous" (Ma 23:35) and even as one of God's prophets (Lk 11:50-51).

4:5 *his countenance fell.* Cain's anger reflects pride in his own works which, because of that very fact, God regarded as "evil" (1 Jo 3:12).

4:6 *Why art thou wroth.* God's questions reminded Cain that he knew the type of sacrifice required and had no reason to be surprised when God would not accept another.

7 If thou doest well, shalt thou not be accepted? and if thou doest not well, sin lieth at the door. And unto thee *shall be* his desire, and thou shalt rule over him.

8 And Cain talked with Abel his brother: and it came to pass, when they were in the field, that Cain rose up against Abel his brother, and Rslew him.   [1 Jo 3:12-15]

9 And the LORD said unto Cain, Where *is* Abel thy brother? And he said, RI know not: *Am* I Rmy brother's keeper?   Jo 8:44 • 1 Co 8:11-13

10 And he said, What hast thou done? the voice of thy brother's blood Rcrieth unto me from the ground.   He 12:24

11 And now *art* thou cursed from the earth, which hath opened her mouth to receive thy brother's blood from thy hand;

12 When thou tillest the ground, it shall not henceforth yield unto thee her strength; a fugitive and a vagabond shalt thou be in the earth.

13 And Cain said unto the LORD, My Tpunishment *is* greater than I can bear. *iniquity*

14 Behold, thou hast driven me out this day from the face of the earth; and Rfrom thy face shall I be Rhid; and I shall be a fugitive and a vagabond in the earth; and it

---

4:7 rule over him. Note the similar terminology to that of Genesis 3:16b. Just as Eve's desire would be toward Adam and he would lead her, so would an unrepentant Cain become so committed to rebellion that "sin" (personified as a crouching animal) would rule Cain unless he made sin his obedient servant.

4:8 talked with Abel. Abel was a prophet and no doubt urged Cain to repent and believe God's Word, but this only angered Cain further. The serpent was quickly striking at the Seed of the woman, corrupting her first son and slaying her second, trying to prevent the fulfillment of the Lord's promise.

4:9 I know not. Cain thus added blatant lying to his sins of self-righteous pride and murder. However, in one sense, he was speaking the truth. He knew where Abel's blood was spilled but not where Abel himself was. Abel was now the first human inhabitant of Sheol (or Hades), that place in the heart of the earth where departed spirits would reside while awaiting the coming of the Savior (Lk 16:22-26; Ep 4:8-10; 1 Pe 3:18-20).

4:10 thy brother's blood. This first mention of "blood" in Scripture prefigures the innocent blood of Christ, which "speaketh better things than that of Abel" (He 12:24). The voice of Abel's blood cried for vengeance (compare Re 5:9-10), but the blood of Christ speaks of cleansing and forgiveness (1 Jo 1:7; Ep 1:7).

4:11 cursed from the earth. The earth had been cursed because of Adam's sin; now the earth itself had been defiled by Cain's sin. God's curse was *on* the earth; Cain's curse was *from* the earth. His boastful pride in the fruits he had been able to grow from the cursed earth had been the occasion of his sin, but now he would no longer be able to till the ground even for his own food. Those who trust in their own good works eventually find it impossible to produce them any more.

4:12 vagabond. As yet there was no law given to order man's behavior. Therefore Cain's crime could not be punished by governmental means, but only by its natural consequences.

4:13 punishment. The word "punishment" is usually translated "iniquity," and its use by Cain indicates that, for the first time, Cain acknowledged his sin and guilt to the Lord. This may partially explain the degree of mercy shown by God in sparing his life after Abel's murder.

4:14 every one. Adam had daughters as well as sons (5:4), and brother/sister marriages were necessary at least in the first generation, before the accumulation of genetic mutations could make such close marriages genetically dangerous. Since the people prior to the flood lived for hundreds of years and since they could propagate children for hundreds of years (note 5:15,32), the population multiplied rapidly. This concern of Cain's, therefore, was quite realistic. Since Cain could not produce his own food, he would have to purchase it from others, but other people would naturally tend to fear him and try to avoid him or even to do away with him.

shall come to pass, *that* every one that findeth me shall slay me. Ps 51:11 • Is 1:15

15 And the LORD said unto him, Therefore whosoever slayeth Cain, vengeance shall be taken on him ᴿsevenfold. And the LORD set a ᴿmark upon Cain, lest any finding him should kill him. Ge 4:24 • Eze 9:4,6

The Wicked Lineage of Cain

16 And Cain ᴿwent out from the presence of the LORD, and dwelt in the land of Nod, on the east of Eden. 2 Ki 13:23; 24:20

17 And Cain knew his wife; and she conceived, and bare E′-noch: and he builded a city, ᴿand called the name of the city, after the name of his son, E′-noch. Ps 49:11

18 And unto E′-noch was born I′-rad: and I′-rad begat Me-hu′-ja-el: and Me-hu′-ja-el begat Me-thu′-sa-el: and Me-thu′-sa-el begat La′-mech.

19 And La′-mech took unto him ᴿtwo wives: the name of the one *was* A′-dah, and the name of the other Zil′-lah. Ge 2:24; 16:3

20 And A′-dah bare Ja′-bal: he was the father of such as dwell in tents, and *of such as have* ᵀcattle. livestock

---

4:15 *mark.* The "mark" is not described. The Hebrew word *oth* is better rendered "sign." Whether this sign was a physical marking on Cain's body or a miraculous display of some sort, it was widely known for many generations (see 4:24) and did serve to inhibit any who might be inclined to slay Cain otherwise.

4:16 *from the presence.* Cain thus becomes the type of those "that obey not the gospel of our Lord Jesus Christ: Who shall be punished with everlasting destruction from the presence of the Lord" (2 Th 1:8-9).

4:16 *Nod.* "Nod" means "wandering," and so may be a figurative expression depicting Cain's vagabond lifestyle. Since he built a city, however, it probably was also the name of the specific region in which he led this wandering existence.

4:17 *knew his wife.* His wife was probably one of Adam's daughters (see 5:4), although it could have been a later descendant, since it would easily have been possible for the population to grow to several hundred thousand by the time of Cain's death.

4:17 *Enoch.* Cain named his son "Enoch," meaning "dedication" or "commencement," probably signifying the beginning of a new manner of life.

4:17 *city.* Urbanization is usually considered by evolutionary archaeologists to be one of the first indicators of the emergence of true civilization from a hunting-and-gathering culture (so-called stone age culture). It is significant that true civilized cultures, by this definition, have existed since the very first generation following Adam, with no suggestion whatever of a long evolutionary advance from an imaginary stone age. Evidently Cain, unable to survive either as a farmer or by trade, had to develop his own self-sufficient economy, through the patriarchal clan which he established around his son Enoch and the city which Cain built for him.

4:18 *Lamech.* The possible meanings of these names are: Irad, meaning "Townsman," Mehujael, meaning "God gives life;" Methusael, meaning "Man of God;" Lamech, meaning "Conqueror." The similarity of some of the names to those in Seth's line, as well as their religious "*-el*" endings, probably indicates that the two families kept in touch with each other and that Cain's line continued to believe in God as long as Adam remained alive to exercise some degree of patriarchal leadership.

4:19 *two wives.* Lamech is the first recorded rebel against the divine command of monogamous marriage. It is probable that Adam died during Lamech's time (by comparison with the chronological data in Seth's line) and the Cainites then became more openly rebellious against God.

4:19 *Zillah.* "Adah" apparently means "ornament" and "Zillah" means "shade." Lamech's motivation in taking two wives may have been partially physical lust and partially the desire to establish a large clan in the increasingly violent pre-flood society.

4:20 *bare Jabal.* Lamech's children were given names associated with their talents: "Jabal" seems to mean "wanderer," "Jubal" means "sound" and "Naamah" means "pleasant."

21 And his brother's name *was* Ju'-bal: he was the father of all such as handle the harp and ᵀorgan. *flute*

22 And Zil'-lah, she also bare Tu'-bal–cain, an ᵀinstructer of every artificer in brass and iron: and the sister of Tu'-bal–cain *was* Na'-a-mah. *Lit. craftsman in bronze*

23 And La'-mech said unto his wives, A'-dah and Zil'-lah, Hear my voice; ye wives of La'-mech, hearken unto my speech: for I have ᵀslain a man to my wounding, and a young man to my hurt. *killed a man for wounding me*

24 ᴿIf Cain shall be avenged sevenfold, truly La'-mech seventy and sevenfold. Ge 4:15

The Godly Lineage of Seth 1 Ch 1:1-4; Lk 3:36-38

25 And Adam knew his wife again; and she bare a son, and called his name Seth: For God, *said she*, hath appointed me another seed instead of Abel, whom Cain slew.

26 And to Seth, ᴿto him also there was born a son; and he called his name ᵀE'-nos: then began men ᴿto call upon the name of the LORD. Ge 5:6 • Zep 3:9 • He Enosh; Gr. Enos

CHAPTER 5

This *is* the book of the generations of Adam. In the day that God created man, in the likeness of God made he him;

2 Male and female created he them; and blessed them, and called their name Adam, in the day when they were created.

3 And Adam lived an hundred and thirty years, and begat *a son* in his own likeness, after his image; and called his name Seth:

"Tubal-cain" is of uncertain meaning but is associated etymologically with the Roman God Vulcan. The inventions of these talented progeny no doubt contributed greatly to the wealth and power of Lamech's clan, and to the increasing materialism of the Cainite civilization in general.

4:22 brass and iron. Evolutionary archaeologists have attempted to organize human history in terms of various supposed "ages"—Stone Age, Bronze Age, Iron Age, etc. The Noahic record, however, indicates that early men were very competent in brass and iron metallurgy, as well as agriculture, animal husbandry, and urbanization. It is significant that many kinds of bronze and iron implements are known to have been used in the earliest civilizations of Sumeria and Egypt. The same is true of musical instruments, and it is evident that the science and art of both metallurgy and music, as well as agriculture and animal husbandry, had been handed down from ancient times to these earliest post-flood civilizations. Modern archaeology is confirming the high degree of technology associated with the earliest human settlers all over the world.

4:23 speech. This fragment of Lamech's song is history's first recorded poem, and exhibits the humanistic attitude often typical of both ancient and modern literature.

4:24 sevenfold. A Jewish tradition (no more than that) suggests that one of the men slain by Lamech was his ancestor, Cain himself. In any case, Lamech's boast is nothing less than blasphemy against God in promising protection for Cain.

4:24 seventy and sevenfold. Contrast Lamech's vindictiveness with the forgiving attitude enjoyed by Christ, who urged Peter to forgive his brother "seventy times seven" times (Ma 18:22).

4:25 Seth. "Seth" means "appointed" or "substitute." Contrast Eve's attitude of thankfulness and trust with Lamech's attitude (in 4:24) of vengeance and pride.

4:26 Enos. "Enos" means "mortal frailty." It is interesting that Eve gave the name to *her* son, while Seth gave the name to *his* son. This probably suggests that both husband and wife normally consulted with one another in deciding on appropriate names for their children.

4:26 call upon the name. To "call upon the name of the LORD" normally implies a definite action of prayer and worship. It was evidently at this time that godly men and women first initiated formal public services of sacrifice, worship and prayer, replacing the earlier practice of meeting personally with God, as Cain and Abel had done. The practice of individual prayer is also intimated, implying that God's personal presence was no longer regularly available. In any case, an act of faith is implied. In later times, "calling upon the name of the LORD" was accompanied by the building of an altar and the offering of a sacrifice (12:8;

4 ᴿAnd the days of Adam after he had begotten Seth were eight hundred years: and he begat sons and daughters: Lk 3:36-38

5 And all the days that Adam lived were nine hundred and thirty years: and he died.

6 And Seth lived an hundred and five years, and begat ᴿE'-nos:ᵀ Ge 4:26 • He Enosh

7 And Seth lived after he begat E'-nos eight hundred and seven years, and begat sons and daughters:

26:25). Since Christ's sacrifice on Calvary, however, men need only call in faith on the name of the Lord Jesus Christ. "For whosoever shall call upon the name of the Lord shall be saved" (Ro 10:13).

4:26 *the Lord.* The name of the self-existing, redeeming Lord, *Jehovah*. There is no contradiction with Exodus 6:3, especially if the statement there is punctuated with a question mark: "But by my name JEHOVAH was I not known to them?" The obvious answer to this rhetorical question is yes.

5:1 *book.* The use of the word "book" in this connection strongly implies that reading and writing were abilities commonly shared by the earliest generations of mankind. These records, finally edited and assembled by Moses, must originally have come from eyewitnesses, and there is no reason (other than evolutionary presuppositions) why their transmission could not have been by written records instead of orally-repeated tales.

5:1 *generations.* This is the second of the *toledoth* statements in Genesis (the first at 2:4a). Since only Adam could have personal knowledge of all the events in Genesis 2, 3 and 4, it is reasonable to conclude that this section was originally written by him. Genesis 5:1a is thus Adam's signature at its conclusion.

5:1 *made he him.* If Genesis 5:1a is the concluding statement of Adam's record, then Genesis 5:1b is the opening statement of Noah's record, which concludes with Noah's signature at Genesis 6:9a. As is true with the corresponding opening statements following the other *toledoth* endings in Genesis, as well as similar phenomena in Babylonian tablets, each statement ties in to the previous division by keying in to relevant statements. The opening statement in Genesis 5:1-2 obviously refers back to Genesis 1:26-28. Note that God "created" man in His spiritual image, and "made" man in His physical "likeness" (anticipating His future incarnation in human flesh).

5:2 *their name Adam.* "Adam" and "man" are both translations of the same Hebrew word. Its generic use in this context would perhaps better warrant the translation "...and called their name Man."

5:3 *hundred and thirty years.* It is possible that other children were born to Adam, particularly daughters, during this 130-year period, with only Seth being mentioned by name, in view of an implied revelation to Eve that he was the appointed son leading eventually to Christ.

5:3 *begat a son.* Adam was "created" in God's likeness (5:1), whereas Adam "begat" Seth in his own likeness. Jesus Christ is the *only* "begotten" Son of God (Jo 3:16).

5:4 *sons and daughters.* Probably many children were born to Adam during his long life; the ancient quibble about "Cain's wife" is easily resolved in terms of brother/sister marriages in the first generation. Close marriages are genetically dangerous today because of the accumulation of harmful mutations in the human genetic system over many generations, and incest has been prohibited since Moses' time (Le 20:11-20). In the first few generations, including those after the flood, marriages of near relatives were necessary in order for mankind to obey God's command to "multiply" (1:28; 9:1), and accumulated mutations were few.

5:6 *begat Enos.* These records provide three items of necessary information nowhere else available: (1) the names of the pre-flood patriarchs in the line of the promised Seed who would ultimately fulfill God's promise (these names are accepted as authentic and repeated in 1 Ch 1:1-4 and Lk 3:36-38); (2) the chronological framework of primeval history, showing a total of 1,656 years from Adam to the flood (there is no internal evidence to suggest

8 And all the days of Seth were nine hundred and twelve years: and he died.

9 And E'-nos lived ninety years, and begat Ca-i'-nan:

10 And E'-nos lived after he begat Ca-i'-nan eight hundred and fifteen years, and begat sons and daughters:

11 And all the days of E'-nos were nine hundred and five years: and he died.

12 And Ca-i'-nan lived seventy years, and begat ᵀMa-ha'-la-le-el: *Maleleel, Lk 3:37*

13 And Ca-i'-nan lived after he begat Ma-ha'-la-le-el eight hundred and forty years, and begat sons and daughters:

14 And all the days of Ca-i'-nan were nine hundred and ten years: and he died.

15 And Ma-ha'-la-le-el lived sixty and five years, and begat Ja'-red:

16 And Ma-ha'-la-le-el lived after he begat Ja'-red eight hundred and thirty years, and begat sons and daughters:

17 And all the days of Ma-ha'-la-le-el were eight hundred ninety and five years: and he died.

18 And Ja'-red lived an hundred sixty and two years, and he begat ᴿE'-noch: Jude 14,15

19 And Ja'-red lived after he begat E'-noch eight hundred years, and begat sons and daughters:

20 And all the days of Ja'-red were nine hundred sixty and two years: and he died.

21 And E'-noch lived sixty and five years, and begat Me-thu'-se-lah:

22 And E'-noch walked with God after he begat Me-thu'-se-lah three hundred years, and begat sons and daughters:

23 And all the days of E'-noch were three hundred sixty and five years:

---

any gaps in these records); (3) the lifespans of those living before the flood averaged over 900 years (912 to be exact, excluding Enoch), indicating vastly superior environmental conditions then.

5:8 *nine hundred and twelve years.* These great ages have been questioned. However, a "king list" was excavated near Babel, which tells of 10 kings who had lived to great ages before the flood. Although these ages were first deciphered as thousands of years, improved translations have brought them more in line with those in the Bible record. The Egyptians, Chinese, Greeks, and Romans also recorded a tradition that the ancient men lived to great ages.

5:21 *Methuselah.* "Methuselah" may mean "when he dies, judgment." He died in the same year that God sent the flood, suggesting that his father Enoch received a prophecy concerning this coming judgment at the time Methuselah was born.

5:22 *walked with God.* Enoch presumably did not literally walk with God, as had Adam before the fall, but walked "by faith" (He 11:5) in prayer and obedience to God's Word. There seems to be an implication that this spiritual walk had a special beginning at the time of his son's birth, and the accompanying revelation. Note also Genesis 6:9.

5:22 *sons and daughters.* It is worth noting that Enoch's walk with God was not such a mystical, pietistic experience as to prevent him from having an effective family life or a strong and vocal opposition to the apostasy and wickedness of his day (Jude 14-15).

5:24 *Enoch walked.* Twice Enoch's walk with God is mentioned, and he is elsewhere (Jude 14-15) said to have been a great prophet who prophesied of God's ultimate judgment on all ungodliness at His coming, as well as its initial fulfillment at the coming deluge. There are at least three apocryphal books that have been attributed to Enoch, and they may have preserved certain elements of his prophecies. However, in their present form at least, they actually date from shortly before the time of Christ and are certainly not part of the inspired Scriptures.

5:24 *was not.* It is not said of Enoch that he "died," like the other pre-flood patriarchs, but only that suddenly he was no longer present on earth. The New Testament makes it plain that he "was translated that he should not see death" (He 11:5). Elijah had a similar experience 25 centuries later (2 Ki 2:11). Both Enoch and Elijah were prophets of judgment to come, ministering in times of deep apostasy. Enoch, as the "seventh from Adam" (Jude 14), a contemporary of ungodly Lamech (4:18-24), prophesied midway between Adam and Abraham, when God was dealing directly with mankind in general. Elijah

24 And ᴿE'-noch walked with God: and he *was* not; for God ᴿtook him. 2 Ki 2:11 • He 11:5

25 And Me-thu'-se-lah lived an hundred eighty and seven years, and begat La'-mech:

26 And Me-thu'-se-lah lived after he begat La'-mech seven hundred eighty and two years, and begat sons and daughters:

27 And all the days of Me-thu'-se-lah were nine hundred sixty and nine years: and he died.

28 And La'-mech lived an hundred eighty and two years, and begat a son:

29 And he called his name Noah, saying, This *same* shall comfort us concerning our work and toil of our hands, because of the ground which the LORD hath cursed.

30 And La'-mech lived after he begat Noah five hundred ninety and five years, and begat sons and daughters:

31 And all the days of La'-mech were

prophesied midway between Abraham and Christ, when God was dealing with Israel in particular. Both were translated in the physical flesh directly to heaven (not yet glorified, as at the coming rapture of the church, described in 1 Th 4:13-17, since Christ had not yet been glorified).

5:24 God took him. The text does not say where God took him, but presumably he, like Elijah, was taken into heaven and into the personal presence of God. Elijah is definitely scheduled to return to earth to preach again (Mal 4:5-6; Ma 17:11), and it may well be that Enoch will accompany Elijah, and they will serve as the two prophetic witnesses of Revelation 11:3-12, prophesying again of God's coming judgment, this time to the whole world, both Jew and Gentile.

5:25 Lamech. "Lamech" probably means "conqueror." It is interesting that Lamech and his grandfather Enoch both appear to have been named after their older relatives in the line of Cain, possibly as a gesture of family affection in hope of leading the Cainites back to God. It is also interesting that these are the only two pre-flood patriarchs in the Seth's line who did not outlive their fathers. Furthermore, Enoch and Lamech are the only two of these patriarchs from whom have been handed down to us fragments of their prophecies (5:29; Jude 14-15).

5:27 nine hundred sixty and nine. Methuselah's 969-year life span is the longest ever recorded, possibly testifying to God's "longsuffering...in the days of Noah" (1 Pe 3:20; 2 Pe 3:9), since the flood was to be sent to destroy the world immediately after Methuselah's death.

5:29 Noah. Noah means "rest," and his father prophesied that he would bring the rest and comfort so desired by the godly remnant in that day.

5:29 hath cursed. The memory of God's curse on the ground was still fresh in the memory of Adam's godly descendants, showing that the million or more years of human history imagined by evolutionary anthropologists are an absurd dream. Lamech was undoubtedly one of those in Peter's mind when he preached about those holy prophets who "since the world began" had been promising the "times of restitution (i.e., 'restoration') of all things" (Ac 3:21).

5:30 begat sons. All the pre-flood patriarchs are said to have begotten sons and daughters, probably many of each, so the world population grew explosively. The names listed are not those of the firstborn, but of the one in each family who would serve as spiritual leader of his people and who would be in the line of promise. In Noah's case, his brothers and sisters were probably ungodly like the rest of their generation, finally perishing in the flood.

5:32 begat Shem. Shem, Ham, and Japheth were not triplets. Japheth is later called "the elder" (10:21) and Ham the "younger son" (9:24). However, Noah was 500 years old before any of these sons—who were the ones who chose to go with him on the ark—were born. Evidently all of Noah's older "sons and daughters" had followed the ungodliness of their aunts and uncles and of the world in general, and thus eventually perished in the flood.

5:32 Japheth. The meanings of the names are probably as follows: Shem, meaning "name;" Ham, meaning "warm;" Japheth, meaning "enlarged." The common notion that

Genesis 5:32

seven hundred seventy and seven years: and he died.

32 And Noah was five hundred years old: and Noah begat ᴿShem, Ham, ᴿand Ja'-pheth.
Ge 6:10; 7:13 • Ge 10:21

CHAPTER 6

The Multiplication of the Wicked

And it came to pass, ᴿwhen men began to multiply on the face of the earth, and daughters were born unto them,
Ge 1:28

their names corresponded to three different skin colorations ("dark," "black," and "fair") has no substance. Note, however, the significant fact that all the personal names listed for men and women who lived before the confusion of languages at Babel seem to have a distinctive meaning in the Hebrew language. This implies that the original language of mankind was Hebrew.

6:1 *multiply.* God had commanded Adam and Eve to "multiply" (1:28). With each man and woman enjoying hundreds of years of parental productivity plus almost ideal environmental conditions, the earth could well have been "filled" with people long before the flood. For example, an initial population of two people, increasing at the rate of two percent annually (estimated to be the annual growth rate at present) would generate a population of well over 10 trillion people in 1,656 years (the time span from Adam to the flood).

6:2 *sons of God.* The identity of these "sons of God" has been a matter of much discussion, but the obvious meaning is that they were angelic beings. This was the uniform interpretation of the ancient Jews, who translated the phrase as "angels of God" in their Septuagint translation of the Old Testament. The apocryphal books of Enoch elaborate this interpretation, which is also strongly implied by the New Testament passages (1 Pe 3:19-20; 2 Pe 2:4-6; Jude 6). The Hebrew phrase is *bene elohim*, which occurs elsewhere only in Job 1:6; 2:1; 38:7. In these three explicitly parallel usages, the contextual meaning can be nothing except that of angels. A similar phrase *bar elohim*, occurs in Daniel 3:25, and another, *bar elim*, occurs in Psalm 29:1 and Psalm 89:6. All of these also refer explicitly to angels. The intent of the writer of Genesis 6 (probably Noah) was clearly that of introducing a monstrous irruption of demonic forces on the earth, leading to universal corruption and eventual judgment.

6:2 *took them wives.* The "taking" of these women most likely refers to fallen angels, or demons, "possessing" their bodies. The word "wives" (Hebrew *ishshah*) is better translated "women." There is no necessary intimation of actual marriage involved. By this time in history, anarchism and amorality were so widespread that these demons were easily able to take possession of the bodies of multitudes of ungodly men; these in turn engaged in promiscuous sex with demon-possessed women, with a resulting rapid population growth, Satan perhaps hoping thereby to generate a vast army of human recruits to his rebellion and also to thwart the coming of God's promised Seed by thus corrupting all flesh.

6:3 *My spirit.* One of the ministries of God's Holy Spirit has always been to convict man's spirit of "sin, and of righteousness, and of judgment" (Jo 16:8). Man is also "flesh," however, and there is perpetual conflict between the flesh and the spirit, even in the life of a believer (Ro 8:5; Ga 5:16-17). God is long-suffering with respect to man's rebellion, but only for a time: the hour of His judgment must eventually arrive.

6:3 *hundred and twenty years.* This prophecy was apparently given, perhaps through Methuselah, just 120 years before the coming flood. The prophet Enoch had already been translated. Shem, Ham, and Japheth had not yet been born and God's specific commands to Noah (5:32; 6:10,13,21) not yet given.

6:4 *giants.* These "giants" were the monstrous progeny of the demon-possessed men and women whose illicit activities led to God's warning of imminent judgment. The Hebrew word is *nephilim* ("fallen ones"), a term possibly relating to the nature of their spiritual "parents," the fallen angels. That they were also physical giants is evident from the fact that the same word is later used in connection with the giants in Canaan at the time of Joshua

38

2 That the sons of God saw the daughters of men that they *were* fair; and they ᴿtook them wives of all which they chose.   De 7:3,4

3 And the LORD said, ᴿMy spirit shall not always ᴿstrive with man, ᴿfor that he also *is* flesh: yet his days shall be an hundred and twenty years.   [Ga 5:16,17] • 2 Th 2:7 • Ps 78:39

4 There were ᵀgiants in the earth in those ᴿdays; and also after that, when the sons of God came in unto the daughters of men, and they bare *children* to them, the same *became* mighty men which *were* of old, men of renown.   Nu 13:32,33 • He *nephilim, mighty* or *fallen ones*

The Wicked Sin Continually

5 And ᵀGOD saw that the wickedness of man *was* great in the earth, and *that* every ᴿimagination of the thoughts of his heart *was* only evil continually.   Ge 8:21 • MT *LORD*

The Wicked To Be Destroyed

6 And ᴿit repented the LORD that he had made man on the earth, and it ᴿgrieved him at his ᴿheart.   1 Sa 15:11,29 • Is 63:10 • Mk 3:5

7 And the LORD said, I will ᴿdestroy man whom I have created from the face of the

(Nu 13:33) and by the fact that the word here was translated in the Septuagint by the Greek word *gigantes*.

6:4 *also after that.* "After that" clearly refers to Numbers 13:33 and probably represents an editorial insertion in Noah's record by Moses. These giants in Canaan may also have had demonically-controlled parents; they were also known as the Anakim, the sons of Anak.

6:4 *daughters of men.* The idea that these "daughters of men" were actually descendants of Cain, and the "sons of God" descendants of Seth has been a widely held Christian naturalistic interpretation. This was not the intended meaning of the writer, however, who could certainly have written that the male descendants of Seth began to take wives from the daughters of Cain if that were his meaning. The descendants of Seth were not "sons of God" (most of them perished in the flood) and the female descendants of both Cain and Seth were certainly "daughters of men" (literally, daughters of *Adam*). Besides, Adam had many other sons in addition to Cain and Seth. Further, even though intermarriage between believers and unbelievers is wrong, it could not in itself have produced universal wickedness and violence.

6:4 *men of renown.* The pre-flood giants had, by the time of Moses, become renowned heroes of antiquity, as far as the world was concerned. They, like their parents, were probably demon-controlled, their giant stature engineered by genetic manipulations discovered and carried out by these evil spirits. They could not have been demi-gods (half man, half "god"), however, as ancient mythology claims, since such imaginary beings are beyond the pale of God's creative purposes. Fallen angels are not prospects for salvation, whereas fallen men and women are. A half-angel, half-human being would be an impossible anomaly. The only apparent solution to all the problems posed by these verses is demon possession of both parents and progeny, *not* demonic marriage or procreation.

6:5 *only evil continually.* Universal wickedness requires a universal cause adequate to produce it. Nothing less than a worldwide influx of demonic control seems adequate to explain it.

6:6 *his heart.* The first mention of the word "heart" occurs here, connecting the evil in man's heart with grief in God's heart. This figure occurs often in Scripture, the "heart" representing the deepest seat of one's emotions and decisions.

6:7 *repenteth me.* The apparent contradiction involved in the biblical record of God "repenting" when the Bible also says God does *not* repent (contrast 1 Sa 15:11 and 15:29) is resolved in terms of man's viewpoint versus God's viewpoint. To "repent" means to "change the mind." God cannot repent, since He cannot change His mind concerning evil. He *seems* to repent, when man changes *his* mind concerning evil. God's attitude toward man is con-

earth; both man, and beast, and the creeping thing, and the fowls of the air; for it repenteth me that I have made them. Ge 7:4,23

God Makes Provision for the Righteous

8 But Noah ᴿfound grace in the eyes of the LORD. Ge 19:19

9 ᵀThese *are* the generations of Noah: Noah was a just man *and* perfect in his generations, *and* Noah walked with God.

10 And Noah begat three sons, ᴿShem, Ham, and Ja'-pheth. Ge 5:32; 7:13

11 The earth also was corrupt before God, and the earth was filled with violence.

12 And God looked upon the earth, and, behold, it was corrupt; for all flesh had corrupted his way upon the earth.

13 And God said unto Noah, The end of all flesh is come before me; for the earth is filled with violence through them; and, behold, I will destroy them with the earth.

14 Make thee an ark of go'-pher wood; rooms shalt thou make in the ark, and shalt pitch it within and without with pitch.

---

ditioned by man's attitude toward Him. It is because God does *not* repent that He must *seem* to repent when man "changes his mind."

6:8 *found grace.* This is the first mention of "grace" in the Bible: the first mention in the New Testament is Luke 1:30, where Mary "found favour" (same word as "grace") with God. God's grace is found, not earned! Note the consistent biblical order here: Noah first found grace, then he was a justified, righteous man, finally becoming perfect (complete or mature) in his relation to both God and man, and ultimately walking with God in a life of total faith and fellowship.

6:9 *generations of Noah.* This seems to be Noah's signature concluding his personal record (5:29–6:9a). It is significant that his last word emphasizes only that he was being saved from a sinful world merely by the grace of God.

6:9 *perfect in his generations.* It is likewise significant that the first sentence of the *toledoth* of Noah's sons (note 10:1) stresses the godliness of their father. Noah is an outstanding example of parental example and guidance. His sons were saved on the ark because of his own righteousness (note 7:1).

6:11 *filled with violence.* In order to be "filled" with violence, the earth by this time had become filled with people.

6:12 *all flesh.* Since "all flesh," as destroyed in the flood, included animals (7:21), some have suggested that animals also had "corrupted their ways" and were contributing to the worldwide violence. This is doubtful, since animals do not make moral judgments. However, as a part of man's dominion, they shared in his curse and now in the judgment of the flood. This verse may possibly imply the development of carnivorous appetites and increasing hostility to man by the animals.

6:13 *with the earth.* God did not promise to destroy man *from* the earth, but *with* the earth. The physical earth-system itself, as man's home and dominion, must share in his judgment. The flood obviously was to be global and cataclysmic, not local or tranquil, as many modern compromising Christians have sought to interpret it.

6:14 *pitch.* The ark (an ancient Hebrew word used also for the small box in which the infant Moses floated on the Nile) was made of a hard dense wood whose species has not yet been identified; it was made waterproof, not by a bituminous pitch (a different Hebrew word) but by some as-yet-unknown "covering." The Hebrew word is *kopher*, equivalent to *kaphar*, frequently translated later as "atonement" (Le 17:11). In providing a protective covering against the waters of judgment, it thus becomes a beautiful type of Christ.

6:15 *three hundred cubits.* The dimensions of the ark were ideally designed both for stability and capacity. It has been shown hydrodynamically that the ark would have been practically impossible to capsize and would have been reasonably comfortable,

15 And this *is the fashion* which thou shalt make it *of*: The length of the ark *shall be* three hundred cubits, the breadth of it fifty cubits, and the height of it thirty cubits.

16 A window shalt thou make [T]to the ark, and in a cubit shalt thou finish it above; and the door of the ark shalt thou set in the side thereof; *with* lower, second, and third *stories* shalt thou make it.

17 [R]And, behold, I, even I, do bring a [R]flood of waters upon the earth, to destroy all flesh, wherein *is* the breath of life, from under heaven; *and* every thing that *is* in the earth shall [R]die.   2 Pe 2:5 • 2 Pe 3:6 • Lk 16:22

18 But with thee will I establish my [R]covenant; and thou shalt come into the ark, thou, and thy sons, and thy wife, and thy sons' wives with thee.   Ge 8:20—9:17; 17:7

19 And of every living thing of all flesh, [R]two of every *sort* shalt thou bring into the ark, to keep *them* alive with thee; they shall be male and female.   Ge 7:2,8,9,14-16

20 Of fowls after their kind, and of cattle after their kind, of every creeping thing of the earth after his kind, two of every *sort* shall come unto thee, to keep *them* alive.

21 And take thou unto thee of all food that is eaten, and thou shalt gather *it* to

---

even during violent waves and winds. Assuming the ancient cubit to have been only 17.5 inches (the smallest suggested by any authority), the ark could have carried as many as 125,000 sheep-sized animals. Since there are not more than about 25,000 species of land animals known (that is, mammals, birds, reptiles, amphibians), either living or extinct, and since the average size of such animals is certainly much less than that of a sheep, it is obvious that all the animals could easily have been stored in less than half the capacity of Noah's ark, each pair in appropriate "rooms" (literally "nests").

6:16 *window.* The "window" was probably an opening for light and ventilation extending around the ark, with a parapet to keep out the rain. The one large door in the side was to be closed only once (after the animals were in) and opened only once (to release them a year later).

6:16 *third stories.* The three decks may have been laid out as follows: large animals on the bottom; small animals and food storage on the middle deck; family quarters, possessions, records, etc., on the top deck. Water could have been stored in cisterns on the roof and piped throughout the ark where needed. Overhead water storage could also have provided fluid pressure for various other uses.

6:17 *a flood.* The flood (Hebrew *mabbul*) was a unique event. Various other words were used in Scripture for local floods. The *mabbul* was *the* flood.

6:17 *every thing that is in the earth.* The purpose of the flood—to destroy all flesh—could only have been accomplished by a worldwide deluge. The idea of a local flood is merely a frivolous conceit of Christians seeking to avoid imagined geological difficulties. Although many marine organisms would perish in the upheavals, everything in the earth (that is, "on the land") would die.

6:19 *two of every sort.* Two of each kind of bird, cattle, and creeping thing (the "beasts" are also included in 7:14) were to be put on the ark. Again, marine animals are omitted, as representatives of their kinds could survive outside the ark. Note that the animals were to "come unto thee." God directed to the ark, by a miraculous selection process, those animals who possessed the necessary genes for the migratory instincts which would be needed by their survivors in the post-flood world. Noah did not have to gather the animals himself, but merely to take into the ark two of each kind as God sent them to him.

6:21 *all food.* Since the pre-flood world was essentially uniform in climate, it was probably equally uniform ecologically, with representatives of all plants and animals located reasonably near Noah's home base.

Genesis 6:22

thee; and it shall be for food for thee, and for them.

22 [R]Thus did Noah; according to all that God commanded him, so did he.   Ge 7:5; 12:4,5

CHAPTER 7

God Commands Noah to Enter the Ark

And the [R]LORD said unto Noah, [R]Come thou and all thy house into the ark; for [R]thee have I seen righteous before me in this generation.   Ma 11:28 • Ma 24:38 • Ge 6:9

2 Of every [R]clean beast thou shalt take to thee by sevens, the male and his female: [R]and of beasts that *are* not clean by two, the male and his female.   Le 11 • Le 10:10

3 Of fowls also of the air by sevens, the male and the female; to keep [T]seed alive upon the face of all the earth.   *the species*

4 For [T]yet [R]seven days, and I will cause it to rain upon the earth [R]forty days and forty nights; and every living substance that I have made will I destroy from off the face of the earth.   Ge 7:10 • Ge 7:12,17 • *after seven more days*

5 [R]And Noah did according unto all that the LORD commanded him.   Ge 6:22

6 And Noah *was* [R]six hundred years old when the flood of waters was upon the earth.   Ge 5:4,32

7 And Noah went in, and his sons, and his wife, and his sons' wives with him, into the ark, because of the waters of the flood.

8 Of clean beasts, and of beasts that *are* not clean, and of fowls, and of every thing that creepeth upon the earth,

9 There went in two and two unto Noah into the ark, the male and the female, as God had commanded Noah.

10 And it came to pass after seven days, that the waters of the flood were upon the earth.

The Earth Is Flooded

11 In the six hundredth year of Noah's life, in the second month, the seventeenth day of the month, the same day were all the

---

6:22 *so did he.* This simple statement summarizes a whole century of absolute obedience to God's Word by Noah, under the most difficult and discouraging of circumstances. Not only here but three other times (7:5,9,16), it is said that Noah did all God commanded him.

7:1 *have I seen righteous.* This is the first mention of the doctrine of justification in the Bible—that is, of being "seen as righteous" by God. The same word is translated "just" in Genesis 6:9 ("Noah was a just man"). The reason why Noah could be seen as "justified" was that he had "found grace in the eyes of the LORD" (6:8). Also, see note on Genesis 15:6.

7:2 *by sevens.* The "clean" kinds of beasts and birds were those suitable for domestication and a form of fellowship with man, as well as for sacrificial offerings. Apparently three pairs of each of these were preserved in order to allow for wider variation in breeding after the flood. The seventh was offered by Noah in sacrifice when they left the ark (8:20).

7:3 *keep seed alive.* God's purpose for the ark was to "keep seed alive" in the earth, a statement meaningful only in the context of a universal flood. The ark was far too large to accommodate merely a local or regional fauna. In fact, if the flood were only local, the ark would not have been needed at all. Noah's family, as well as the birds and beasts, could far more easily have simply migrated away from the region to be flooded.

7:4 *seven days.* This seven-day period of final warning and preparation marks the first of many references to seven-day intervals during the flood year. This fact makes it obvious that the practice of measuring time in seven-day weeks had been in effect throughout the period between the creation week and the flood.

7:4 *forty days.* A worldwide rain lasting 40 days would be impossible under present meteorologic conditions. The condensation of the pre-flood vapor canopy, the "waters above the firmament" (1:6-8) is the only adequate explanation.

7:4 *every living substance.* "Every living substance" includes the plant life on the land. The lush vegetation of the pre-flood world was all to be uprooted, transported and buried in great sedimentary beds, many of which would eventually become the world's coal beds.

7:11 *seventeenth day.* The exact date of the flood's onset must have been noted for some reason. The ark landed on the mountains of Ararat exactly 150 days or five months later

42

fountains of the great deep broken up, and the windows of heaven were opened.

12 [R]And the rain was upon the earth forty days and forty nights. Ge 7:4,17

13 In the selfsame day entered Noah, and Shem, and Ham, and Ja'-pheth, the sons of Noah, and Noah's wife, and the three wives of his sons with them, into the ark;

14 [R]They, and every beast after his kind, and all the cattle after their kind, and every creeping thing that creepeth upon the earth after his kind, and every fowl after his kind, every bird of every [R]sort. Ge 6:19 • Ge 1:21

15 And they [R]went in unto Noah into the ark, two and two of all flesh, wherein *is* the breath of life. Ge 6:19,20; 7:9

16 And they that went in, went in male and female of all flesh, as God had commanded him: and the LORD shut him in.

17 [R]And the flood was forty days upon the earth; and the waters increased, and [T]bare up the ark, and it [T]was lift up above the earth. Ge 7:4,12; 8:6 • *lifted* • *rose high*

18 And the waters prevailed, and were increased greatly upon the earth; [R]and the ark went upon the face of the waters. Ps 104:26

(see 8:3-4). The implication is that the primeval year contained 12 months of 30 days each (see also Re 11:2-3).

7:11 *fountains of the great deep*. The physical cause of the flood is clearly identified as the eruption of the waters in the "great deep" and the opening of the floodgates of heaven. These are quite sufficient in themselves to cause and explain all the phenomena of the flood. The pre-flood water cycle was apparently controlled by a system of subterranean pressurized reservoirs and conduits, but these fountains were all cleaved open in one day, releasing tremendous quantities of water and magma to the earth's surface and dust and gas into the atmosphere. The resulting combination of atmospheric turbulence and dust was probably the immediate cause of the precipitation of the vapor canopy. The cataclysmic restoration of the primeval deep that resulted left the pre-flood world completely devastated and inundated.

7:15 *two of all flesh*. Two of every kind of land animal entered the ark, including those animals (e.g., dinosaurs) that have become extinct in the millennia following the flood. The animals were all young animals, since they would have to spend the year in the ark without reproducing and then emerge to repopulate the earth after the flood. The animals entering the ark were those individuals possessing genes for the remarkable physiologic abilities of migration and hibernation. These were not needed in the climates of the primeval world, but would be vital for survival in the post-flood world. After being installed in their respective "rooms" in the ark, and after a good meal, most of them probably spent most of the flood year in a state of hibernation.

7:17 *bare up the ark*. The ark was 30 cubits high and, when loaded, probably had a draft of almost 15 cubits. As soon as the water level rose to a level of 15 cubits above the platform on which it had been constructed, it would begin to float.

7:18 *prevailed*. The word "prevailed" in the original Hebrew text conveys the meaning "were overwhelmingly mighty." Not only would all land animals eventually drown, but the plant covering would be uprooted and rafted away, the soils eroded and finally even the mountains and hills washed away. In the sea depths, the eruption of the fountains of the great deep would also profoundly affect marine life. Great quantities of magma, metals and other materials were extruded from the earth's mantle. The sediments from the lands were transported down to be deposited in the encroaching sea basins. Complex hydrodynamic phenomena—tsunamis, vortices, turbidity flows, cyclic erosion and deposition, and a variety of geomorphologic activity—took place throughout the year. Earth movements of great magnitude, and tremendous volcanic explosions shook the earth again and again, until finally, "the world that then was, being overflowed with water, perished" (2 Pe 3:6).

7:18 *face of the waters*. The occupants of the ark, unaware of the convulsions in the depths below, rode safely and in comparative comfort, steered by God's unseen hand away from the zones of hydrodynamic violence.

19 And the waters prevailed exceedingly upon the earth; and all the high hills, that *were* under the whole heaven, were covered.

20 Fifteen cubits upward did the waters prevail; and the mountains were covered.

21 And all flesh died that moved upon the earth, both of fowl, and of cattle, and of beast, and of every creeping thing that creepeth upon the earth, and every man:

22 All in whose nostrils *was* the breath of life, of all that *was* in the dry *land*, died.

23 And every living substance was destroyed which was upon the face of the ground, both man, and cattle, and the creeping things, and the fowl of the heaven; and they were destroyed from the earth: and ^RNoah only remained *alive*, and they that *were* with him in the ark. 2 Pe 2:5

24 ^RAnd the waters prevailed upon the earth an hundred and fifty days. Ge 8:3,4

CHAPTER 8

The Waters Dry Up

And God ^Rremembered Noah, and every living thing, and all the ^Tcattle that *was* with him in the ark: ^Rand God made a wind to pass over the earth, and the waters ^Tasswaged; Ge 19:29 • Ex 14:21; 15:10 • *animals* • *subsided*

7:19 all the high hills. The double superlative precludes the use of "all" in a relative sense here. The obvious intent of the writer was to describe a universal inundation.

7:20 mountains. The words "high hills" and "mountains" are the same in the original Hebrew. The waters were 15 cubits (22.5 feet) above the highest mountains, patently including Mount Ararat, which is now 17,000 feet high. In the "local flood" theory, Mt. Ararat would have had the same elevation before and after the flood, but it should be obvious that a 17,000-foot flood is not a *local* flood!

7:21 moved upon the earth. "All flesh" died that moved on land. In a local flood, at least *most* of the animals (certainly all the birds!) would escape to higher ground.

7:22 breath of life. The "breath (Hebrew *neshamah*) of life" is clearly stated here to be a component of animal life as well as human life. Thus animals possess "spirit," but not the "image of God."

7:23 every living substance. The rocks of the earth's crust now contain the fossil remains of unnumbered billions of plants and animals, buried in water-transported sediments which quickly became stone. This "geologic column" has been grossly distorted by evolutionists into the record of an imagined three-billion-year history of evolution during the geological ages. Actually it represents the deposits of the cataclysmic flood, with the fossil order primarily depicting the relative elevations of the habitats—and therefore the usual order of sedimentary burial in the flood—of the organisms of the pre-flood world. Many modern geologists are again admitting the necessity of catastrophic formation and burial to explain the fossil rocks in the geologic column. The reason why very few fossilized men (also few fossilized flying birds) are found in the rocks is their high mobility and ability to escape burial in sediments. When eventually drowned, their bodies would remain on the surface until they decayed.

7:24 prevailed. The third emphasis is on the waters "prevailing" (7:18-19,24). This highest intensity of flood action continued for five months.

8:1 a wind. The uniform temperatures of the pre-flood world would have prevented the great atmospheric circulations that now prevail, so that significant wind movements were impossible. With the almost complete precipitation of the waters in the primeval canopy after 150 days, the present temperature fluctuations were soon functioning to initiate tremendous winds all over the earth. These winds, blowing on a shoreless ocean, would certainly generate gigantic surface waves and tidal surges. The latter, superimposed on all the other hydrodynamic and geophysical forces at work, evidently served as the critical factor to trigger great forces that eventually would restore at least partial equilibrium to the disturbed surface of the earth. The earth's crust was in a highly unstable condition, with the tremen-

2 ʳThe fountains also of the deep and the windows of heaven were stopped, and the rain from heaven was restrained;   Ge 7:11

3 And the waters ᵀreturned from off the earth continually: and after the end ᴿof the hundred and fifty days the waters ᵀwere abated.   Ge 7:24 • *receded* • *decreased*

4 And the ark rested in the seventh month, on the seventeenth day of the month, upon the mountains of Ar′-a-rat.

5 And the waters decreased continually until the tenth month: in the tenth *month,* on the first *day* of the month, were the tops of the mountains seen.

---

dous subterranean reservoirs now emptied of their pressurized waters and with vast depths of light sediments piling up in the sea basins.

8:1 *assuaged.* As a result of the water subsiding, the phenomena described in Psalm 104:6-9 began to take place. The earth's crust collapsed deep into the previous subterranean reservoir chambers, forming the present ocean basins, and causing further extrusions of magmas around their peripheries and through openings in their floors. The light sediments in the sea troughs were forced upward to form mountain ranges and plateaus. Thus the waters originally stored in the vapor canopy and the subterranean chambers are now stored mainly in the present ocean basins (these waters would be sufficient to cover a "smoothed" earth to a depth of almost two miles) after the vast topographic adjustments that terminated and followed the flood.

8:3 *continually.* This expression, to some degree, suggests a cyclic tidal action, but especially suggests rapid drainage. It is significant that all the world's oceans bear evidence (e.g., sea mounts, submarine canyons, etc.) of former lower levels and that all the world's continental drainage systems (rivers, lakes) bear evidence of former higher water levels and quantities of flow (e.g., old raised river terraces and lake beaches, vast alluvial valleys and "underfit" streams). These worldwide evidences clearly picture a world emerging from a recent global inundation.

8:4 *seventeenth day of the month.* This "resting" of the ark, after its labor of protecting its precious cargo against the terrible cataclysm for five long months, occurred exactly 150 days after the flood began. It may be significant that, on the anniversary of this date many years later, Jesus Christ rose from the dead! That is, the seventh month of the civil year used by the Jews (almost certainly the calendar used in the flood narrative) was later set as the first month of their religious year. The Passover was on the 14ᵗʰ day of the first month, and Christ rose three days after the Passover. Thus, He "rested" in Joseph's tomb and then rose from the dead on the 17ᵗʰ day of the seventh month of the civil calendar.

8:4 *mountains of Ararat.* "Ararat" in the Bible is the same as "Armenia." The "mountains of Ararat" could apply to the entire region; however, the present Mount Ararat, 17,000 feet high, is the only logical site for the ark to rest. The ark landed the very day the waters began to recede, and it was another 2½ months until the tops of nearby mountains could even be seen. Furthermore, there have been many reported sightings of the ark, seemingly still preserved on an almost inaccessible ledge, most of the time encased in the stationary ice cap near its summit. Though none of these reports are sufficiently documented to constitute proof, the very number and variety of them is at least intriguing evidence that the ark has been divinely preserved, awaiting God's timing for its confirmed discovery and manifestation. Mount Ararat is a volcanic mountain, formed evidently during the early months of the flood year (there were no volcanoes before the flood). There is also considerable geological evidence that it was further uplifted sometime after the flood, so that it may well have been much lower and easier to access during the years immediately following the flood. That even the summit of Ararat was at one time under water, however, is evident both from the marine fossils that have been found there and the extensive pillow lavas (lavas formed under high hydrostatic pressure) which exist there.

8:7 *raven.* The raven, a hardy flier and carrion eater, could survive indefinitely even be-

6 And it came to pass at the end of forty days, that Noah opened ᴿthe window of the ark which he had made: Ge 6:16

7 And he sent forth a raven, which went forth to and fro, until the waters were dried up from off the earth.

8 Also he sent forth a dove from him, to see if the waters were abated from off the face of the ground;

9 But the dove found no rest for the sole of her foot, and she returned unto him into the ark, for the waters *were* on the face of the whole earth: then he put forth his hand, and took her, and pulled her in unto him into the ark.

10 And he stayed yet other seven days; and again he sent forth the dove out of the ark;

11 And the dove came in to him in the evening; and, lo, in her mouth *was* an olive leaf pluckt off: so Noah knew that the waters were abated from off the earth.

12 And he stayed yet other seven days; and sent forth the dove; which returned not again unto him any more.

13 And it came to pass in the six hundredth and first year, in the first *month*, the first *day* of the month, the waters were dried up from off the earth: and Noah removed the covering of the ark, and looked, and, behold, the face of the ground was dry.

14 And in the second month, on the seven and twentieth day of the month, was the earth dried.

15 And God spake unto Noah, saying,

16 Go forth of the ark, ᴿthou, and thy wife, and thy sons, and thy sons' wives with thee.   Ge 7:13

17 Bring forth with thee every living thing that *is* with thee, of all flesh, *both* of fowl, and of cattle, and of every creeping thing that creepeth upon the earth; that they may breed abundantly in the earth, and be fruitful, and multiply upon the earth.

18 And Noah went forth, and his sons, and his wife, and his sons' wives with him:

19 Every beast, every creeping thing, and every fowl, *and* whatsoever creepeth upon the earth, after their ᵀkinds, went forth out of the ark.   Lit. *families*

---

fore there was much dry land. The dove, however, required fresh plant material and dry ground.

8:10 *other seven days.* The frequent references to "seven days" in the flood account, plus the fact that Noah left the ark 371 days (53 weeks) after entering it, indicates that they were following a calendar based on seven-day weeks. Confined in the ark, the crew could not use the moon or stars for navigation or chronology, but could, of course, count days.

8:11 *olive leaf.* The olive tree is extremely hardy and can grow and thrive on almost barren rocky slopes. The fresh olive leaf plucked by the dove proved that the land was beginning to produce a vegetal cover and so would soon be ready to support its human and animal residents again. Both seeds and cuttings from pre-flood plants were abundant in the sediments of the flood and could grow again as soon as adequate sunlight and dry land were available. Experiments have shown that seeds of a wide variety of plants will sprout even after many months of submergence in salt water. Actually the waters of the earth changed only gradually and slightly in salinity during the flood, certainly not so much as to prevent the survival and multiplication of all kinds of plants and marine animals after the flood.

8:17 *multiply upon the earth.* This is a repetition of the Edenic command to the created animal kinds (1:20,22). In order to do this, they must migrate from Ararat, each finding its proper ecological niche in the drastically changed and widely varied environments of the post-flood world. During the Ice Age following the flood, land bridges existed across the Bering Strait from Siberia to Alaska and down the Malaysian Strait into New Guinea, facilitating such migrations. Also, Noah's descendants certainly knew how to build and use boats, and some of the animals may well have been transported in this way, as well as on rafts of vegetation transported out to sea during river floods.

8:19 *out of the ark.* Here it is again asserted, as clearly as could be expressed, that *all* the present land animals in the earth have descended from those on the ark.

Noah Worships God

20 And Noah builded an ᴿaltar unto the LORD; and took of ᴿevery clean beast, and of every clean fowl, and offered ᴿburnt offerings on the altar.   Ge 12:7 • Le 11 • Ex 10:25

21 And the LORD smelled ᴿa sweet savour; and the LORD said in his heart, I will not again ᴿcurse the ground any more for man's sake; for the ᴿimagination of man's heart *is* evil from his youth; neither will I again smite any more every thing living, as I have done.   Ex 29:18,25 • Ge 3:17; 6:7,13,17

22 ᴿWhile the earth remaineth, seedtime and harvest, and cold and heat, and summer and winter, and ᴿday and night shall not cease.   Is 54:9 • Je 33:20,25

CHAPTER 9

God's Covenant with Noah

And God blessed Noah and his sons, and said unto them, Be fruitful, and multiply, and replenish the earth.

2 ᴿAnd the fear of you and the dread of you shall be upon every beast of the earth, and upon every fowl of the air, upon all that moveth *upon* the earth, and upon all the fishes of the sea; into your hand are they ᵀdelivered.   Ps 8:6 • Lit. *given*

8:20 *offered burnt offerings.* Noah thus sacrificed what amounted to one-seventh of his flocks and herds of domestic animals, a real act of thanksgiving and faith on his part. The world was far more forbidding in aspect than when they had entered the ark: rugged and desolate, cold and stormy, barren and silent. It had been purged and cleansed of its wicked and violent inhabitants, however, and God had preserved His remnant through the awful cataclysm, so this was a service of both great praise and earnest petition.

8:21 *not again curse.* The promise of God, given in response to Noah's sacrificial prayer of thanksgiving and intercession, is tremendous in scope. He would never again "curse the ground" with a worldwide curse as He had done following Adam's sin. The Edenic curse is still in effect, of course, but there would be no other. Noah had, indeed, brought "comfort" to the world concerning "the ground which the LORD had cursed" (5:29).

8:21 *every thing living.* Neither would God ever again bring a worldwide cataclysm to the earth as He had with the flood.

8:22 *remaineth.* This dual promise would be kept as long as the earth existed in its probationary state, with man still in his sinful condition, his "heart evil from his youth." Eventually, the earth would be renovated and the curse removed altogether (Re 22:3).

8:22 *shall not cease.* The principle of uniformity is here established by God for the post-flood world. Not only would the basic laws of nature still continue in effect (these had, of course, operated even during the flood) but also the regular operation of its natural processes (these had been greatly intensified during the flood). The basic processes of earth are its rotation on its axis and its orbital revolution around the sun. These control all annual and daily processes, which in turn control practically all biological and geological processes. Absolute uniformity of the day/night cycle and the seasonal cycles assures at least general uniformity of functioning of other processes. Thus the principle of uniformitarianism is valid absolutely for the *laws* of nature ever since the imposition of God's curse (except for special miracles) and is valid statistically for the *processes* of nature since the flood.

9:1 *replenish the earth.* This is the same command given to Adam and Eve; the word "replenish" (Hebrew *male*), simply means "fill."

9:2 *are they delivered.* In essence the primeval commission to mankind (the so-called "dominion mandate") is here reiterated to Noah and his descendants, though with some amendments. Man is still to be in dominion over all other creatures and over the earth itself, even though Satan's usurpation of that dominion must continually be recognized and rectified, with God's enablement. Man's relation to the animals (except perhaps for the domestic animals not mentioned here) has been changed by God's imposition on them of literally the "terror" of man. Their newly-developed carnivorous appetites and other abilities,

3 ᴿEvery moving thing that liveth shall be meat for you; even as the green herb have I given you all things.   De 12:15; 14:3,9,11

4 ᴿBut flesh with the life thereof, *which is* the blood thereof, shall ye not eat.   1 Sa 14:33,34

5 And surely your blood of your lives will I require; ᴿat the hand of every beast will I require it, and ᴿat the hand of man; at the hand of every ᴿman's brother will I require the life of man.   Ex 21:28 • Ge 4:9,10 • Ac 17:26

6 ᴿWhoso sheddeth man's blood, by man shall his blood be shed: ᴿfor in the image of God made he man.   Le 24:17 • Ge 1:26,27

7 And you, ᴿbe ye fruitful, and multiply; bring forth abundantly in the earth, and multiply therein.   Ge 9:1,19

---

combined with their more rapid multiplication, might otherwise have resulted in man's extermination.

9:3 *meat for you.* For the first time, human beings are given divine permission to eat animal flesh. Initially, they were to have been vegetarians (1:29). The reason for this change was due to the greater need for animal protein in man's diet in view of the nutrient-impoverished soils of the post-flood world and the much more rigorous climatic conditions. A second reason may have been to emphasize the great gulf between man and the animals. Evolutionary and polytheistic philosophies, then as now, had seriously blurred that distinction (note Ro 1:21-25).

9:4 *the blood thereof.* The profoundly scientific truth that "the life of the flesh is in the blood" (see also Le 17:11) is here mentioned for the first time. This, as well as the other principles of the Edenic mandate and the Noahic covenant, is still in effect and should be observed by Christians especially. The blood, both in symbol and in reality, is "the life of the flesh." Thus, it is appropriate to offer in sacrifice (until the offering of Christ, that is) but never to consume, either as food or as a religious ritual.

9:5 *will I require.* If the blood of animals is to be regarded as too sacred to be eaten, since it represents the "life" (or "soul"—Hebrew *nephesh*) of the animal and is acceptable as a substitutionary sacrifice for man's sins, how much more sacred is the blood of man himself! His blood represents *his* life and, since he alone is "in the image of God," the Creator of life, man's blood is not even to be shed, let alone eaten! If either man or beast slays a man, that man or that animal is judicially to be slain himself, the reason being the divine sacredness of human life.

9:6 *blood be shed.* This establishment of capital punishment, administered judicially by man, has never been changed or withdrawn. It is still God's law today, and forms the basic authorization of the institution of human government. It implies also the enactment and enforcement of regulations for those human activities (e.g., stealing, adultery) which if unrestrained, would lead to murder. It does not stipulate the form, but only the fact of government. It extends the primeval mandate by giving man the responsibility to control not only the animals but his own society also. The original commission in effect had authorized the natural sciences and technologies; this new extension incorporated in God's covenant with Noah in effect authorizes the social sciences and their technologies (e.g., psychology, law, sociology, anthropology, political science, government, police, criminology).

Although capital punishment is the proper prerogative of human society ("every man's brother") in so far as strict justice is concerned, mitigating circumstances (especially sincere repentance and restitution) may warrant extension of mercy in individual cases. Nevertheless, the basic right of governments to exact capital punishment as penalty for murder cannot legitimately be revoked as far as God is concerned. This is clear even in the Christian dispensation. The eating of meat (1 Ti 4:3-4), the abstinence from blood (Ac 15:19-20) and the authority of the governmental sword (Ro 13:4; Ac 25:11) were reaffirmed to the early church, making it clear that the Noahic mandate still applied.

9:9 *my covenant.* The Noahic covenant (Hebrew *berith*) is the first covenant mentioned in

8 And God spake unto Noah, and to his sons with him, saying,

9 And I, ^Rbehold, I establish ^Rmy covenant with you, and with your ^Tseed after you;   Ge 6:18 • Is 54:9 • *descendants*

10 ^RAnd with every living creature that *is* with you, of the fowl, of the cattle, and of every beast of the earth with you; from all that go out of the ark, to every beast of the earth.   Ps 145:9

11 And ^RI will establish my covenant with you; neither shall all flesh be cut off any more by the waters of a flood; neither shall there any more be a flood to destroy the earth.   Is 54:9

12 And God said, ^RThis *is* the token of the covenant which I make between me and you and every living creature that *is* with you, for perpetual generations: Ge 9:13,17; 17:11

13 I do set ^Rmy ^Tbow in the cloud, and it shall be for a ^Ttoken of a covenant between me and the earth.   Eze 1:28 • *rainbow* • *sign*

14 And it shall come to pass, when I bring a cloud over the earth, that the ^Tbow shall be seen in the cloud: *rainbow*

15 And I will remember my covenant, which *is* between me and you and every living creature of all flesh; and the waters shall no more become a flood to destroy all flesh.

16 And the ^Tbow shall be in the cloud; and I will look upon it, that I may remember ^Rthe everlasting covenant between God and every living creature of all flesh that *is* upon the earth.   Ge 17:13,19 • *rainbow*

17 And God said unto Noah, This *is* the ^Ttoken of the covenant, which I have established between me and all flesh that *is* upon the earth.   *sign*

The Sons of Noah

18 And the sons of Noah, that went forth of the ark, were Shem, and Ham, and Ja'-pheth: and Ham *is* the father of Canaan.

19 ^RThese *are* the three sons of Noah: ^Rand of them was the whole earth ^Toverspread.   Ge 5:32 • 1 Ch 1:4 • *populated*

The Sin of Ham

20 And Noah began *to be* ^Ran husbandman, and he planted a vineyard: Ge 3:19,23; 4:2

Scripture and is everlasting (9:16). It applied not only to Noah and his seed (9:9), but also to the animal kingdom (9:10) and even to the earth itself (9:13). It was unconditional, promising the age-long endurance of the post-flood cosmos, and also reconfirming and amplifying God's primeval commission to mankind, involving human stewardship over the earth and its inhabitants.

9:13 *my bow.* The rainbow, requiring small water droplets in the air, could not form in the pre-flood world, where the high vapor canopy precluded rain (2:5). After the flood, the very fact that rainfall is now possible makes a worldwide rainstorm impossible, and the rainbow "in the cloud" thereby becomes a perpetual reminder of God's grace, even in judgment.

9:16 *everlasting covenant.* This is the first of 16 references to an "everlasting covenant" made by God, and therefore to an unconditional, unbreakable promise. This first such everlasting covenant was made with "all flesh," and the second was with Abraham's seed (17:7). The last was with all who are redeemed with the blood of Christ (He 13:20).

9:18 *Japheth.* The original meanings of these names are uncertain, but the most probable meanings are: Shem means "Name" or "Renown;" Ham means "Warm" or "Hot;" Japheth means "Enlarged" or "Beautiful."

9:19 *whole earth overspread.* This plain declaration (see also 10:32) leaves no possibility that any other people survived the worldwide flood. All the world's present peoples are descendants of Noah's three sons and their wives. The gene pool from these six individuals (all originally from Adam and Eve, of course) provided far more than enough genetic variational potential to account for the wide range in national and tribal characteristics which have surfaced since the flood. The world's present population of approximately six billion people likewise could easily have been developed in, say, 4,000 years. An average annual growth rate of one-half percent (only one-fourth the present rate), or an average family size of only 2.5 children per family, could easily accomplish this.

21 And he drank of the wine, ᴿand was drunken; and he was uncovered within his tent. Pr 20:1

22 And Ham, the father of Canaan, saw the nakedness of his father, and told his two brethren without.

23 ᴿAnd Shem and Ja'-pheth took a garment, and laid *it* upon both their shoulders, and went backward, and covered the nakedness of their father; and their faces *were* ᵀbackward, and they saw not their father's nakedness. Ex 20:12 • *turned away*

24 And Noah awoke from his wine, and knew what his younger son had done unto him.

The Curse on Canaan

25 And he said, ᴿCursed *be* Canaan; a ᴿservant of servants shall he be unto his brethren. De 27:16 • Jos 9:23

9:21 *wine.* This is the first mention of wine in Scripture, but there is no reason to doubt that the people used wine and intoxicating beverages before the flood. Christ said they were characterized by much "eating and drinking" (Ma 24:38). Although the vapor canopy filtered much of the harmful radiation from space, fermentation as a decay process had probably been controlled and utilized by man since soon after the fall.

9:24 *done unto him.* Though Noah was guilty of the sin of carelessness and drunkenness, the sin of Ham was much more serious, revealing a hitherto suppressed carnal and rebellious nature, a resentment against his father and, probably, against God. Shem and Japheth, on the other hand, sought to cover and restore their father.

9:25 *Cursed be Canaan.* Noah's curse was spoken concerning Canaan instead of Ham for possibly one or more of the following reasons: (1) As Ham was his youngest son, so Canaan was Ham's youngest son, and Noah wished to emphasize that the prophecy extended through Ham to all his seed, even his youngest; (2) Noah could gladly bless his two faithful sons, but could not bear to pronounce the prophetic curse *directly* on his other son, whom he also loved dearly; (3) He knew his grandsons well enough to recognize in the sons of Ham the same rebellious attitudes that were in Ham, and he knew that they would actually experience the resultant effects of his sin even more than would Ham himself.

9:25 *servant of servants.* The phrase "servant of servants" is never used elsewhere in Scripture. If it means "slave of slaves," then the prophecy has failed, for neither the Hamitic nations in general nor the Canaanitic nations in particular have ever been such. The Hamites have included such great empires as Sumeria, Phoenicia, Egypt, Ethiopia, etc., and quite possibly the great Asian nations (China, Japan, etc.) as well. The word "servant," however, is more often used in the sense of "steward," so the prophecy more likely speaks of Ham's descendants as superlative stewards. That is, all men were stewards of God's created world, in the sense of exercising dominion over its resources; and Ham, with his physical and materialistic bent, would be especially effective in subduing the world and developing its resources. Since the ground had been cursed, however, this meant that Ham's lot would be uniquely associated with the physical world, thus itself becoming a curse. Noah's statement, it should be remembered, was a prophecy and not an imprecation, given under divine inspiration and on the basis of Noah's own insight into the developing characters of his sons and grandsons and, therefore, of their descendants. As a prophecy, this interpretation is fitting, since the Hamitic nations have, indeed, been the great explorers, cultivators, builders, navigators, tradesmen, inventors and warriors of mankind.

9:25 *unto his brethren.* It is obvious that his prophecy applies not only to Canaan but also to all of Ham's descendants, for the following reasons: (1) its scope is obviously intended to be symmetrical, worldwide and age-long, with all the progeny of the three sons of Noah included; (2) if taken as applicable only to Canaan specifically, then it must also apply specifically only to Canaan's brethren, who were Cush, Mizraim and Phut. Their descendants included the nations of Ethiopia, Egypt and Libya. Not only would such a judg-

26 And he said, Blessed *be* the Lord God of Shem; and Canaan shall be his servant.

27 God shall ᴿenlarge Ja'-pheth, and he shall dwell in the tents of Shem; and Canaan shall be his servant. 　Ge 10:2-5; 39:3

The Death of Noah

28 And Noah lived after the flood three hundred and fifty years.

29 And all the days of Noah were nine hundred and fifty years: and he died.

CHAPTER 10

The Generations of Japheth 1 Ch 1:5-7

Now ᵀthese *are* the generations of the sons of Noah, Shem, Ham, and Ja'-pheth: ᴿand unto them were sons born after the flood. 　Ge 9:1,7,19 • *this is the genealogy*

---

ment be unfair (it was Ham who sinned, not Canaan), but it was never fulfilled, since the Canaanites were never servants of the Libyans or Ethiopians, and only briefly of the Egyptians; (3) as a matter of fact, the descendants of Canaan, who included the Phoenicians and Hittites, were prominent nations through most of their history, not slave nations.

9:26 Shem. Noah associated Shem especially with the worship of Jehovah, recognizing the dominantly spiritual motivations of Shem and thus implying that God's promised Deliverer would ultimately come from Shem. The Semitic nations have included the Hebrews, Arabs, Assyrians, Persians, Syrians and other strongly religious-minded peoples.

9:27 enlarge Japheth. The enlargement of Japheth was not to be primarily geographical (Hamitic and Semitic nations have been enlarged geographically as much as the Japhethites) but intellectual. The Japhetic peoples (Greeks, Romans, Aryans, Europeans) have largely supplied the philosophers and scientists of mankind. The tripartite nature of man (body, mind, spirit) is shared by every man and every nation. However, each man (and each nation) reflects one of these as a predominant characteristic. Noah recognized that Ham, Japheth, and Shem were dominated, respectively, by physical, intellectual, and spiritual considerations, and so could see prophetically that these attributes would likewise be emphasized in the nations descending from them. Thus, every nation would contribute its own part to the corporate life of mankind as a whole.

9:27 tents of Shem. Japheth was peculiarly God's steward in the intellectual analysis and utilization of earth's resources, and Shem was peculiarly His steward with respect to the propagation of God's will and plan for mankind, especially the transmission of His saving Word. Both services would require an adequate physical base from which to operate, and thus would require the stewardship of Ham in the physical world. Thus, Ham was steward to Shem and Japheth in their stewardship—in this sense also, he would be a servant of servants.

10:1 the generations. This is the fourth *toledoth* of the Book of Genesis (previously noted at 2:4; 5:1; 6:9), presumably marking the signatures of Shem, Ham and Japheth after completing their narrative of the flood and the immediate post-flood years. Shem then took over the task (11:10) and his family records, now known as the Table of Nations, constitute (according to premier archaeologist William P. Albright) an "astonishingly accurate document."

10:1 Japheth. It is possible that the name Japheth was later corrupted by the Romans to Jupiter (or Iu-pater—the "father" of the gods).

10:1 after the flood. This marks the end of the first—and only authentic—account of the great flood, written down by the only eyewitnesses who could record it accurately, the men who experienced it and survived to tell about it. As their descendants scattered over the earth, especially after their dispersion from Babel (11:9), they carried the story with them. However, with the changes in language and the passage of time, the story assumed different forms in the different cultures, though always still recognizable as coming from the same source. One of the earliest of the more than 300 of these "flood legends" from all over the world is the one found in Babylon itself, the famous Gilgamesh Epic.

2 ᴿThe sons of Ja'-pheth; Go'-mer, and Ma'-gog, and Ma'-dai, and Ja'-van, and Tu'-bal, and Me'-shech, and Ti'-ras.   1 Ch 1:5-7

3 And the sons of Go'-mer; Ash'-ke-naz, and Ri'-phath, and To-gar'-mah.

4 And the sons of Ja'-van; E-li'-shah, and Tar'-shish, Kit'-tim, and Dod'-a-nim.

5 By these were the isles of the Gentiles divided in their lands; every one after his tongue, after their families, in their nations.

The Generations of Ham 1 Ch 1:8-12

6 ᴿAnd the sons of Ham; Cush, and Miz'-ra-im, and Phut, and Canaan.   1 Ch 1:8-16

10:2 *Gomer.* The "sons of Japheth," allowing for the gradual modifications in form of their names over the millennia, can be recognized as the progenitors of the Indo-European peoples. Japheth himself is called "Iapetos," in the legends of the Greeks, and Iyapeti is the reputed ancestor of the Aryans. Gomer is identified by Herodotus with Cimmeria, a name now surviving as the Crimea. His descendants moved westward, with the name possibly further preserved in Germany and Cambria (Wales).

10:2 *Magog.* Magog can mean "the place of Gog," possibly now Georgia in the former USSR.

10:2 *Madai.* Madai is the ancestor of the Medes.

10:2 *Javan.* Javan is identified with "Ionia," and is often translated as "Greece" in the Old Testament.

10:2 *Tubal.* Tubal is a name probably preserved in the modern Tobolsk and the ancient Tibareni. He is associated with Magog and Meshech in Ezekiel 38:2 and other passages, all probably ancestral to modern Russia.

10:2 *Meshech.* Meshech is preserved in the names Muskovi and Moscow.

10:2 *Tiras.* Tiras gave rise to the Thracians, and possibly to the Etruscans.

10:3 *Ashkenaz.* Ashkenaz has long been associated with the German Jews, known still as the Ashkenazi. The name is also possibly preserved in the names Scandia and Saxon, as well as a region of Armenia once known as Sakasene.

10:3 *Riphath.* Josephus associates Riphath with the Paphlagonians. There is a possibility that the name Carpathia, and even Europe, come from Riphath.

10:3 *Togarmah.* Togarmah is probably the ancestor of the Armenians. The Jewish Targums say that Germany was derived from Togarmah. The name may also have a connection with Turkey and Turkestan.

10:4 *Elishah.* Elishah is preserved today as Hellas (Hellenists, Hellespont), another name for Greece. The Iliad mentions them as the "Eilesians."

10:4 *Tarshish.* Tarshish is a name frequently mentioned in the Old Testament as a seafaring people. Apparently the name somehow became later associated with the Phoenicians and their cities of Carthage (North Africa) and Tartessos (Spain), even though these were Canaanites. Perhaps the first settlers of these cities were Japhethites, later conquered and expanded by Phoenicians.

10:4 *Kittim.* Kittim is another name for Cyprus. The name "Ma-Kittim" (land of Kittim) is possibly preserved as Macedonia.

10:4 *Dodanim.* Dodanim is the same as Rodanim (1 Ch 1:7 in some manuscripts). The name is probably found today in the names Dardanelles and Rhodes.

10:5 *after his tongue.* The islands and coastlands to which these first Europeans migrated were "divided...everyone after his tongue." This notation indicates that the author of Genesis 10 (probably Shem) wrote it after the dispersion at Babel.

10:6 Cush. Cush, the same as "Kish," is usually translated in the Old Testament as "Ethiopia," a land identified in the Tell El Amarna tablets as "Kashi." Some of the Cushites evidently stayed in Arabia while others sailed across the Red Sea into Ethiopia.

10:6 *Mizraim.* Mizraim is the customary name for Egypt in the Bible, which is also called "the land of Ham" (Ps 105:23). It is barely possible that Mizraim is the same as Menes, Egypt's first king.

7 And the sons of Cush; Se'-ba, and Hav'-i-lah, and Sab'-tah, and Ra'-a-mah, and Sab'-te-chah: and the sons of Ra'-a-mah; She'-ba, and De'-dan.

8 And Cush begat ᴿNimrod: he began to be a mighty one in the earth. Mi 5:6

9 He was a mighty ᴿhunter before the LORD: wherefore it is said, Even as Nimrod the mighty hunter before the LORD. Je 16:16

10 ᴿAnd the beginning of his kingdom was ᴿBabel, and E'-rech, and Ac'-cad, and Cal'-neh, in the land of Shi'-nar. Mi 5:6 • Ge 11:9

11 Out of that land ᵀwent ᴿforth Assh'-ur, and builded Nin'-e-veh, and the city Re-ho'-both, and Ca'-lah, Mi 5:6 • *he went to Assyrias*

12 And Re'-sen between Nin'-e-veh and Ca'-lah: the same *is* ᵀa great city. *the principal city*

13 And Miz'-ra-im begat Lu'-dim, and An'-a-mim, and Le'-ha-bim, and Naph'-tu-him,

14 And Path-ru'-sim, and Cas'-lu-him, (ᴿout of whom came ᵀPhi-lis'-tim,) and Caph'-to-rim. 1 Ch 1:12 • *the Philistines*

10:6 Phut. According to Josephus, Phut is the same as Libya in the Bible.

10:6 Canaan. Canaan, Ham's youngest son, is obviously the progenitor of the Canaanites.

10:7 Sabtechah. The five first-named sons of Cush apparently all settled in Arabia, although Seba later migrated into the Sudan, giving his name to the Sabeans (Is 45:14).

10:7 Dedan. Sheba and Dedan were evidently well known Arabians in the days of Abraham, since two of his grandsons through Keturah were named after them (25:3).

10:8 Cush begat Nimrod. As the "son of Cush" (that is, "bar-Cush") Nimrod probably was later deified and worshiped as Baccus by the Romans. As the founder of Babylon, he also later became the chief god of the Babylonians "Merod-ach" or "Marduk." His name is preserved in various ways, in many geographical sites or names of deities, having been the most influential leader of mankind when the nations were dispersed at Babel. One of the chief cities of the Assyrians was called Nimrud. He has also been identified as the tyrant Gilgamesh, in the famous Gilgamesh Epic found in the ruins of Nineveh.

10:8 Nimrod. Nimrod, the youngest and most illustrious son of Cush, was given a name meaning "Let us rebel!" and apparently trained by his father for this purpose.

10:9 mighty hunter. This phrase connotes a man mighty in wickedness. It is possible that his hero's reputation was gained in hunting and slaying the giant animals that proliferated after the flood and were considered dangerous to the small human population of the first century. He built a great kingdom, with the capital at Babel in the plain Shinar (no doubt equivalent to Sumer) in the Tigris-Euphrates valley.

10:10 Accad. Erech is also "Uruk," 100 miles southeast of Babylon, the legendary home of Gilgamesh. Accad gave its name to the Akkadian Empire, perhaps the same as the Sumerian Empire. Calneh is unidentified.

10:11 Asshur. Asshur, a son of Shem, had evidently founded a settlement, but Nimrod "went forth into Asshur" (better rendering of "out of that land went forth Assur"), extending his empire and establishing also what would later become the Assyrian Empire.

10:11 Nineveh. Nineveh, the capital city of the Assyrians, was named after "Ninus," evidently another name for Nimrod. Although both Babylonia and Assyria were later conquered by Semites, the Hamite Nimrod was their founder and first king. Nineveh was 200 hundred miles north of Babylon, on the Tigris River.

10:11 Rehoboth. Rehoboth and Resen have not yet been identified.

10:12 a great city. About 20 miles south of Nineveh, Calah has been excavated. It is still called "Nimirud." These three satellite cities, with Nineveh, made up a metropolitan complex and is thus called a "great city."

10:14 Caphtorim. The sons of Mizraim are mostly yet unidentified in secular records; perhaps most of them migrated south and west from their father's home in Egypt, deeper into Africa. However, the Pathrusim dwelt in Pathros, or upper Egypt. The Caphtorim are identified in the Bible with the Philistim, or Philistines, and by secular writers with Crete. These people evidently migrated from Egypt to Crete and then, later, in successive waves to Philistia on the eastern shore of the Mediterranean.

The Generations of Canaan 1 Ch 1:13-16

15 And Canaan begat ᵀSi'-don his first-born, and ᴿHeth,   Ge 23:3 • *Zidon,* 1 Ch 1:13

16 ᴿAnd the Jeb'-u-site, and the Am'-or-ite, and the Gir'-ga-site,   Ge 14:7; 15:19-21

17 And the Hi'-vite, and the Ark'-ite, and the Si'-nite,

18 And the Ar'-vad-ite, and the Zem'-a-rite, and the Ha'-math-ite: and afterward were the families of the Ca'-naan-ites spread abroad.

19 ᴿAnd the border of the Ca'-naan-ites was from Si'-don, as thou comest to Ge'-rar, unto Ga'-za; as thou goest, unto Sodom, and Go-mor'-rah, and Ad'-mah, and Ze-bo'-im, even unto La'-sha.   Nu 34:2-12

20 These *are* the sons of Ham, after their families, after their tongues, in their countries, *and* in their nations.

The Generations of Shem 1 Ch 1:17-23

21 Unto Shem also, the father of all the children of E'-ber, the brother of Ja'-pheth the elder, even to him were *children* born.

22 The ᴿchildrenᵀ of Shem; E'-lam, and Assh'-ur, and ᴿAr-phax'-ad, and Lud, and A'-ram.   1 Ch 1:17-28 • Lk 3:36 • Lit. *sons*

23 And the ᵀchildren of A'-ram; Uz, and Hul, and Ge'-ther, and Mash.   Lit. *sons*

24 And Ar-phax'-ad begat ᴿSa'-lah; and Sa'-lah begat E'-ber.   Ge 11:12

10:15 *Sidon.* The city of Sidon, chief city of the Phoenicians, still exists today.

10:15 *Heth.* Heth is the ancestor of the Hittites, prominent in both the Bible and secular history, ruling a great empire in Asia Minor for over 800 hundred years. When the Hittite Empire finally crumbled, many of its people migrated east. The Hittites are identified in Egyptian inscriptions as the "Kheta." In the cuneiform inscriptions in Babylonia, this name is identified as "Khittae," which may have been modified eventually to "Cathay," a synonym for China. Archaeologists have noted similarities between the Mongols and Hittites.

10:17 *Sinite.* The other nine sons of Canaan were the Canaanite tribes that inhabited the land when the Israelites entered it. The Amorites are identified in the tablets as the Amurru. The Sinites may be connected in ethnology with the wilderness of Sin and Mount Sinai in the south, and with the Assyrian god "Sin," and even with Sinim (Is 49:12) and the people of secular history called "Sinae," or Chinese.

10:18 *spread abroad.* This statement becomes especially significant if, as intimated above, the descendants of Canaan include the Mongol peoples, who eventually spread not only throughout most of Asia but also across the Bering Strait into North and South America, becoming the American Indians.

10:20 *in their nations.* The division of the original population into "nations" was both "after their tongues" and "after their families," suggesting that each family living at Babel was given a distinctive tongue at the dispersion.

10:21 *Eber.* The term "Hebrew" comes from Eber, but the descendants of Eber also include the "Habiru." Discoveries at Ebla, in northern Syria, seem to indicate the founder and king of Ebla to be "Ebrim."

10:21 *Japheth.* Japheth was evidently the oldest son of Noah, Ham the youngest (9:24).

10:22 *Elam.* Elam is the ancestor of the Elamites, who later merged with the Medes (descendants of Madai) to form the Medo-Persian Empire.

10:22 *Asshur.* Asshur gives his name to the Assyrians, although his settlement on the Tigris was later taken over by Nimrod (10:11).

10:22 *Lud.* According to Josephus, Lud was the ancestor of the Lydians.

10:22 *Aram.* Aram is the father of the Aramaeans, or Syrians. The Aramaic language was almost a world language in the ancient world, and even some parts of the Old Testament were first written in Aramaic.

10:23 *Uz.* Uz gave his name to Job's homeland (Job 1:1) but little is known of the other three sons of Aram. Evidently the children of Aram had more contact with Shem than his other grandsons (except through Arphaxad) since none of the others are listed.

25 [R]And unto E'-ber were born two sons: the name of one *was* [T]Pe'-leg; for in his days was the earth divided; and his brother's name *was* Jok'-tan.   1 Ch 1:19 • Lit. *Division*

26 And Jok'-tan begat Al-mo'-dad, and She'-leph, and Ha'-zar–ma'-veth, and Je'-rah,

27 And Ha-do'-ram, and U'-zal, and Dik'-lah,

28 And [T]O'-bal, and A-bim'-a-el, and She'-ba,   *Ebal,* 1 Ch 1:22

29 And O'-phir, and Hav'-i-lah, and Jo'-bab: all these *were* the sons of Jok'-tan.

30 And their dwelling was from Me'-sha, as thou goest unto Se'-phar a mount of the east.

31 These *are* the sons of Shem, after their families, [T]after their tongues, in their lands, after their nations.   *according to their languages*

32 [R]These *are* the families of the sons of Noah, after their generations, in their nations: and by these were the nations divided in the earth after the flood.   Ge 10:1

CHAPTER 11
Building of the Tower

A nd the whole earth was of one [T]language, and of one speech.   Lit. *lip*

10:25 *Peleg*. Peleg means "division," and he was apparently given the name by Eber because of the great event that took place just before his birth. He may also have given his name to the Pelasgians.

10:25 *the earth divided*. The "division" that took place was, most likely, the traumatic upheaval at Babel. A division in Genesis 10:5,32 is mentioned, where the division is "after his tongue." Nimrod was in the same generation as Eber, and this is the only place in the Table of Nations where the meaning of a son's name is given, indicating the importance of the event it commemorated. However, it is true that two different words are used (*Pelag* in 10:25, *parad* in 10:5,32). Although the two words are essentially synonymous, this might indicate a different type of division. Many Bible teachers have suggested, therefore, that Genesis 10:25 might refer to a splitting of the single post-flood continent into the present continents of the world. They associated the modern scientific model of sea-floor spreading and continental drifting with this verse. It should be remembered, however, that the continental drift hypothesis has by no means been proved; and the verse seems to refer more directly to the division into families, countries, and languages. Furthermore, even if the continents have separated from a single primeval continent, such a split more likely would have occurred in connection with the continental uplifts terminating the global deluge (Ps 104:6-9).

10:29 *sons of Joktan*. Thirteen sons of Joktan are listed, most of whom are believed to have settled in Arabia. The fact that *none* of Peleg's sons are listed may indicate that Shem was living near Joktan's family.

10:31 *after their nations*. This concludes the "nations" listed in Genesis 10. There are 14 from Japheth, 30 from Ham, and 26 from Shem. Thus a total of 70 such primeval nations was included by Shem in his Table of Nations. All are descendants of Adam, through Noah. There is no hint anywhere in Scripture of any "hominids" or other "pre-Adamites" in man's ancestry. The so-called "ape-men" can all be shown to be either remains of extinct apes or of true men, probably all living after the flood.

10:32 *generations*. The word "generations" (Hebrew *toledoth*) indicates that actual genealogical records were available to Shem as he compiled the information in the Table.

10:32 *nations divided*. The 70 nations from Noah's three sons are the progenitors of all other nations (note also 9:19). These three streams of nations should not be interpreted as three races, however. The concept of race is not found in the Bible and is purely an evolutionist concept with no basis in either Scripture or true science. In evolutionary terminology, a race is a sub-species in the process of evolving into a new species, but the Bible speaks only of kinds. Where mankind is concerned, there are nations, tribes, tongues, peoples, and families, but these are not races.

11:1 *one speech*. Literally, "of one lip and one set of words"—that is, one phonology and one vocabulary, the same language as spoken before the flood. This may well have been the

2 And it came to pass, as they journeyed from the east, that they found a plain in the land of Shi'-nar; and they dwelt there.

3 And they said one to another, [T]Go to, let us make brick, and burn them throughly. And they had brick for stone, and [T]slime had they for morter.　　　*Come • asphalt*

The Rebellion at the Tower

4 And they said, Go to, let us build us a city and a tower, [R]whose top *may reach* unto heaven; and let us make us a [R]name, lest we [R]be scattered abroad [T]upon the face of the whole earth.　　　De 1:28; 9:1 • Ge 6:4 • De 4:27 • *over*

Judgment on all the Generations

5 [R]And the LORD came down to see the city and the tower, which the children of men builded.　　　Ge 18:21

6 And the LORD said, Behold, [R]the people *is* one, and they have all [R]one language; and this they begin to do: and now nothing will be restrained from them, which they [T]have [R]imagined to do.　　　Ge 9:19 • Ge 11:1 • Ps 2:1 • *propose*

Hebrew language, or some similar Semitic language since the primitive records were transmitted through Noah and Shem and since it is very unlikely that either Noah or Shem were participants in the rebellion and judgment at Babel.

11:2 *from the east.* The phrase may mean "eastward." It is also possible that, as the people migrated from Ararat, they first went farther to the east, and then turned back westward until they came to the plain of Shinar (Sumer). This fertile valley so reminded them of Eden that they named its two rivers (Tigris and Euphrates) after two of the Edenic rivers.

11:2 *land of Shinar.* The reference to Shinar ties back in to Genesis 10:10, reminding us that the leader of the population by this time was Nimrod, "the mighty hunter before the LORD" (10:9).

11:2 *dwelt there.* Their decision to "dwell" here in one location was in defiance of God's command to "replenish the earth" (9:1,7). God's design was to have a multiplicity of local governmental units (9:5-6; Ac 17:26-27), but Nimrod purposed to establish a one-government dictatorship under himself. When Shem's son Asshur settled in a separate location, Nimrod quickly took it over (10:11).

11:3 *Go to.* Literally, "give"—indicating that a council had reached a decision concerning various possible courses of action and was now pronouncing its decision.

11:3 *for morter.* The first decision was to develop a brick-making industry, with kiln-baked clay bricks and asphalt from the nearby pits as mortar. This would enable them to plan and develop strong, permanent buildings.

11:4 *a tower.* A second council, no doubt soon after the first, reached the firm decision to stay permanently in the Babel metroplex, erecting a strong capital city with a great central tower symbolizing its unity and centralizing its culture. This tower became the prototype of all the great ziggurats (stepped towers) and pyramids of the world.

11:4 *unto heaven.* The words "may reach" are not in the original. The tower was undoubtedly promoted as a great religious monument, dedicated "unto heaven." Its top would be used for worship and sacrifice, and the rank and file probably felt at first that its beauty and grandeur would honor God. Almost certainly the walls and ceiling of the shrine at the top were emblazoned with the painted representations of "man, and...birds, and fourfooted beasts, and creeping things" (Ro 1:23), which depicted the universal signs of the zodiac. This remarkable system was probably originally formulated by the pre-flood patriarchs to depict the primeval prophecies of the coming Seed of the woman and God's ultimate victory over Satan in a permanent record in the stars themselves (see note on 1:14). Under Nimrod's subtle corruption of God's truth, however, this "gospel in the stars" was soon distorted into astrology, and evolutionary pantheism, then into spiritism and polytheism, as people gradually ceased worshiping the true God of heaven and turned to "the host of heaven," the fallen angels.

11:4 *scattered abroad.* The intent of the leaders of this rebellion was flagrant rejection of God's command.

7 Go to, [R]let us go down, and there confound their language, that they may not understand one another's speech.   Ge 1:26

8 So [R]the LORD scattered them abroad from thence upon the face of all the earth: and they left off to build the city.   [Lk 1:51]

9 Therefore is the name of it called Babel; [R]because the LORD did there confound the

---

11:5 came down. God was well aware of all that was transpiring, but was long-suffering, allowing ample time for repentance. The expression "came down" is figurative, indicating that the rebellion had now gone too far and required divine intervention.

11:6 one language. In God's judgment, the main problem was the unity of the people; the one most effective way of thwarting unity would be to prevent communication.

11:6 nothing will be restrained. Nimrod, with direct access to demonic intelligence and satanic power, would be invincible without divine intervention. No doubt there was a faithful remnant (e.g., Noah, Shem), but these were helpless without God's action.

11:7 Go to. A council in heaven (perhaps mocking Nimrod's councils—note Ps 2:1-4) decrees the confusion of tongues. This act is clearly supernatural, involving the divine creative power which Satan could neither duplicate nor reverse.

11:7 confound their language. In some inexplicable manner, God altered the brain/nerve/speech apparati of the Babylonian rebels to give each family unit (possibly the 70 families of ch. 10) its own distinctive language. With all this, however, they all remained truly human, unchanged in basic thought processes or moral character. Further, their distinctive languages were still sufficiently alike that they could, with time and much effort, learn to speak each other's languages. For some time to come, however, they could no longer communicate and, therefore, they could no longer cooperate. They were thus forced to obey God's earlier command to scatter abroad and to fill the earth with different nations and governmental units.

11:8 scattered them abroad. The tower had been completed and was actively in use, but the city was still unfinished. Probably all families except that of Nimrod himself departed from Babel, leaving him and his immediate family the burden of developing his own tribe at Babel as best they could. These probably became the Sumerians. The others scattered into various regions as already described in Genesis 10, some eventually developing great civilizations. This account, originally written by Shem (11:10), is reflected in somewhat distorted form in the legends of other nations, including a tablet excavated at Ur. There is no better scientific theory to date for the origin of the various families of languages. All such theories seem to point to an origin in the Middle East.

11:8 they left off. In addition to the Babel tablet found at Ur (see note above), an inscription purportedly made by Nebuchadnezzar (16 centuries after Nimrod) on the base of the remains of a tower in Borsippa (a Greek word possibly meaning "tongue-tower"), some seven miles southwest of Babylon, claims that he (Nebuchadnezzar) was rebuilding the base of the ancient tower of Babel.

11:9 Babel. The Hebrew word *babel* means "mixed" or "confusion." It was associated by the writer with the "babble" of sounds which was the last memory held by all who scattered from the city. The word "babble" is an example of onomatopoeia, a word that imitates an actual sound, and thus is essentially the same in all languages. The name Babel, therefore, does not really mean "gate of God," as its later apologists claimed, but "confusion."

11:9 all the earth. As the people scattered, each family gradually became a tribal unit, and each had to develop its own distinctive culture as best it could. Each for a time would have to live by hunting and gathering, residing in caves or temporary shelters. The stronger families would occupy the best nearby sites (e.g., the Nile valley), while others would be forced farther away. Although they were all familiar with the arts of agriculture, animal husbandry, ceramics, metallurgy, construction, navigation, etc., each family would require time, population growth, and discovery of sources of metals and building

language of all the earth: and from thence did the LORD scatter them abroad upon the face of all the earth.   1 Co 14:23

The Generations of Abram
1 Ch 1:24-27; Lk 3:34-36

10 These *are* the generations of Shem: Shem *was* an hundred years old, and begat Ar-phax'-ad two years after the flood:

11 And Shem lived after he begat Ar-phax'-ad five hundred years, and begat sons and daughters.

12 And Ar-phax'-ad lived five and thirty years, ᴿand begat Sa'-lah: Lk 3:35

13 And Ar-phax'-ad lived after he begat Sa'-lah four hundred and three years, and begat sons and daughters.

14 And Sa'-lah lived thirty years, and begat E'-ber:

15 And Sa'-lah lived after he begat E'-ber

---

materials. They all had known how to write, but now, with a completely new speech, each tribe would need to invent an entirely new written language, and this would require still more time and ingenuity. Within a few generations, however, all these attributes of "civilization" had surfaced all over the world, even on distant continents. As populations grew, some tribes eventually reached into every part of the world. In some instances they traveled by land bridges (e.g., Bering Strait, Malaysian Strait) which existed for perhaps a millennium during the Ice Age which followed the flood. In other cases, they established colonies through sea exploration (e.g., the Phoenicians). All carried essentially the same Babylonian culture and religion with them, unfortunately, so that Babylon is called in the New Testament "THE MOTHER OF HARLOTS AND ABOMINATIONS (that is, "idola-tries") OF THE EARTH" (Re 17:5). At the same time, they also carried a faint remem-brance of the true God and His promises, especially remembering the divine judgment of the great flood in their traditions. Each retained knowledge of God, and could see enough evidence of Him in both the creation and their own natures (Jo 1:9; Ro 1:20; 2:13-15) so they were inexcusable in their almost universal descent into the religious morass of evolutionary pantheism, astrology, spiritism, polytheism and, finally, atheistic materialism.

11:10 generations of Shem. This marks the termination of Shem's tablet. Apparently Terah (11:27) acquired the ancient records at this point, and continued them.

11:10 hundred years old. Evidently Japheth was born 100 hundred years before the flood (5:32; 7:6). Shem was evidently a few years younger than Japheth (called "the elder" in 10:21). Ham was still younger. He was called Noah's "younger son" in Genesis 9:24.

11:10 after the flood. Apparently none of Noah's sons had children before the flood, pos-sibly because of the universal violence and their concentration on building the ark.

11:13 four hundred and three years. It is obvious, by comparison of the genealogies and chronologies in Genesis 5 and 11, that the longevity of mankind began a steady decline af-ter the flood. Undoubtedly the vast climatological and physiographical changes caused by the flood were the main natural causes of this. The protective vapor canopy was gone (see notes on 1:6; 7:4), the rich soils were gone, mutations were increasing in the inbreeding populations, and the general environment was much more rigorous. No doubt it was also providentially ordered that, in the post-flood world, life spans should settle at around 70 (Ps 90:10).

11:14 Salah. Luke 3:36 inserts the name "Cainan" between those of Arphaxad and Salah. This name is also found in some of the Septuagint manuscripts (though not the earliest), but it is not found in either Genesis 10:24 or 1 Chronicles 1:18, in any of the Masoretic manuscripts. The weight of evidence favors the Hebrew text with Cainan's name having accidentally been later inserted by careless scribal copying from Genesis 5:10 and/or Luke 3:37. The inclusion of essentially the same genealogy, with no sugges-tion of any omitted generations, in Genesis 10:21-25 and 11:10-26, 1 Chronicles 1:17-28, and Luke 3:34-38, including chronological data in the second, at least places the burden

four hundred and three years, and begat sons and daughters.

16 ᴿAnd E'-ber lived four and thirty years, and begat ᴿPe'-leg: 1 Ch 1:19 • Lk 3:35

17 And E'-ber lived after he begat Pe'-leg four hundred and thirty years, and begat sons and daughters.

18 And Pe'-leg lived thirty years, and begat Re'-u:

19 And Pe'-leg lived after he begat Re'-u two hundred and nine years, and begat sons and daughters.

20 And Re'-u lived two and thirty years, and begat ᴿSe'-rug: Lk 3:35

21 And Re'-u lived after he begat Se'-rug two hundred and seven years, and begat sons and daughters.

22 And Se'-rug lived thirty years, and begat Na'-hor:

23 And Se'-rug lived after he begat Na'-hor two hundred years, and begat sons and daughters.

24 And Na'-hor lived nine and twenty years, and begat ᴿTe'-rah: Jos 24:2

25 And Na'-hor lived after he begat Te'-rah an hundred and nineteen years, and begat sons and daughters.

26 And Te'-rah lived seventy years, and ᴿbegat Abram, Na'-hor, and Ha'-ran. 1 Ch 1:26

The History of Abram

27 Now these *are* the generations of Te'-rah: Te'-rah begat ᴿAbram, Na'-hor, and Ha'-ran; and Ha'-ran begat Lot. Ge 11:31; 17:5

---

of proof on any who (for archaeological reasons) would maintain that there are significant gaps involved.

11:16 *begat Peleg.* If there are no genealogical gaps in Genesis 11:10-17, then the numbers add to 101 years from the flood to the birth of Peleg right after the dispersion. In view of the longevity of the times, plus the high advantages implicit in large families, as well as God's command to multiply rapidly, a quite reasonable population growth model will indicate at least 1,000 mature adults on the earth at the time of the dispersion, and possibly many times this amount.

11:19 *two hundred and nine years.* There is a sudden drop in longevity here, from 464 years for Eber to 239 years for Peleg. This is the most likely spot, therefore, for a genealogical gap in the record. However, this sharp decline may also be explained by the traumatic changes in living conditions caused by the confusion of tongues and the resultant migrations and struggles. The close inbreeding since the flood, aggravated further by the dispersion, would also contribute to an increased mutational load carried by the population, and this would tend to further reduce the life span. In any case, even if genealogical gaps do exist (in either ch. 5 or ch. 11, for that matter) they could only involve a few generations at most; in no case could they be stretched sufficiently to accommodate the evolutionist's imagined million-year history of man.

11:26 *begat Abram.* Abram presumably was the oldest of Terah's three sons. However, when the same type of notation had been used for Noah's three sons (5:32), the first-named son was not the oldest, so Abram could possibly have been younger than one or both of his brothers.

11:27 *generations of Terah.* This statement seems to conclude Terah's tablet, which thus consisted solely of the genealogical records from Shem to himself (11:10-27). If there are no gaps in the genealogies, Shem lived until after Terah's death, so Terah could easily have gotten the earlier tablets from Shem. Likewise, he could easily have transmitted them later to Abraham, or even to Isaac, since he lived until Isaac was 35 years old (see 11:26,32; 21:5), assuming Abram was his oldest son.

11:27 *Terah begat Abram.* Isaac is apparently the author of the next *toledoth*, and he seems to have keyed his record back into Terah's simply by repeating the conclusion of the latter.

11:27 *Haran.* The names of both Nahor (named after his grandfather) and Haran are associated with cities in Mesopotamia (24:10; 28:10). Haran died when relatively young, evidently while visiting his father back in Ur (11:26,28,32). His son, Lot, soon became attached to his Uncle Abram.

28 And Ha'-ran died before his father Te'-rah in the land of his nativity, in Ur of the Chal'-dees.

29 And Abram and Na'-hor took them wives: the name of Abram's wife *was* Sa'-rai; and the name of Na'-hor's wife, Mil'-cah, the daughter of Ha'-ran, the father of Mil'-cah, and the father of Is'-cah.

30 But RSa'-rai was barren; she *had* no child.   Ge 16:1,2

31 And Te'-rah Rtook Abram his son, and Lot the son of Ha'-ran his son's son, and Sa'-rai his daughter in law, his son Abram's wife; and they went forth with them from RUr of the Chal'-dees, to go into Rthe land of Canaan; and they came unto Ha'-ran, and dwelt there.   Ge 12:1 • Ac 7:4 • Ge 10:19

32 And the days of Te'-rah were two hundred and five years: and Te'-rah died in Ha'-ran.

11:28 *Ur of the Chaldees.* Ur was an old and prosperous city in the days of Abram. Archaeological excavation has revealed a great library which has yielded thousands of clay tablets. Contrary to outmoded theories of cultural evolution, practically everyone knew how to read and write long before Abram's day.

11:29 *took them wives.* Nahor married his niece, and Sarai was Abram's half-sister (20:12), a daughter of Terah by another of his wives. Close marriages were not yet genetically dangerous and so were not prohibited until the Mosaic law was established. Perhaps they were even desirable in those families who still worshiped the true God, in order to maintain a pure faith.

11:31 *the land of Canaan.* Evidently Terah, as well as Abram, had received God's call to go to Canaan, but Terah went north to Haran instead, perhaps intending to go on to Canaan later, after settling his deceased son's affairs in Haran. Abram also had received God's call while still in Mesopotamia (Ac 7:2-3), and so he and his wife set out with Terah. However, Terah never left Haran, eventually even joining in its idolatrous practices (Jos 24:2,14-15).

11:32 *died in Haran.* According to Genesis 12:4, Abram left Haran for Canaan when he was 75 years old, which would have been 130 years before Terah's death, if indeed Abram had been born when Terah was 70 years old, or soon after (11:26). Yet Stephen, in Acts 7:4, says that Abram did not leave Haran until his father was dead. Probably Stephen was suggesting that Terah, though still alive physically, had "died" as far as God's will and calling to him were concerned, using the terminology that Christ had used in advising a young man in a similar situation (Ma 8:21-22). Otherwise, Abram would have to have been born when Terah was at least 130 years old—a very unlikely circumstance in view of the special miracle required for Abram himself to have a son when he was only 100. In any case, by the time of Abram's departure, even if Terah were only 145 years of age at the time, there would have been at least 267 years since the dispersion. This was more than adequate time for the great civilizations of the ancient world (Egypt, Babylonia, etc.) and for a large population to have developed (as much as 300 million would be a reasonable number by this time, though it was probably much less). Along with the tremendous growth of civilization and population, there was a corresponding rise in both materialism and idolatrous evolutionism, so God finally called Abram again, instructing him to delay no longer in leaving his kindred to establish a new, God-fearing nation through which God would accomplish His purposes (12:1-4).

12:1 *out of thy country.* The call of Abram marks a critical turning point in history. Heretofore God's covenant with mankind (9:8-17) applied to all men alike. With the confusion of tongues at Babel, distinct nations necessarily began to develop. Though the Noahic covenant is everlasting, it was now necessary for this to be supplemented (not replaced) by a special relation with a particular nation through which the promised Seed of the woman (3:15) would eventually enter the human race to redeem lost mankind.

CHAPTER 12

God's Covenant with Abram

Now the RLORD had said unto Abram, Get thee Rout of thy country, and from thy kindred, and from thy father's house, unto a land that I will shew thee: Ac 7:2,3 • Ge 13:9

2 RAnd I will make of thee a great nation, and I will bless thee, and make thy name great; and thou shalt be a blessing: De 26:5

3 RAnd I will bless them that bless thee, and curse him that curseth thee: and in Rthee shall all families of the earth be Rblessed. Nu 24:9 • Ac 3:25 • Is 41:27

4 So Abram departed, as the LORD had spoken unto him; and Lot went with him: and Abram *was* seventy and five years old when he departed out of Ha'-ran.

5 And Abram took Sa'-rai his wife, and Lot his brother's son, and all their Tsubstance that they had gathered, and Rthe Tsouls that they had gotten Rin Ha'-ran; and they Rwent forth to go into the land of Canaan; and into the land of Canaan they came. Ge 14:14 • Ge 11:31 • Ge 13:18 • *possessions* • *people*

6 And Abram Rpassed through the land unto the place of Si'-chem, Runto the plain of Mo'-reh. RAnd the Ca'-naan-ite *was* then in the land. He 11:9 • De 11:30 • Ge 10:18,19

7 RAnd the LORD appeared unto Abram, and said, Unto thy seed will I give this land: and there builded he an altar unto the LORD, who appeared unto him. Ge 17:1; 18:1

8 And he removed from thence unto a mountain on the east of Beth'-el, and pitched his tent, *having* Beth'-el on the west, and Ha'-i on the east: and there he builded an altar unto the LORD, and Rcalled upon the name of the LORD. Ge 4:26; 13:4; 21:33

9 And Abram journeyed, Rgoing on still toward the Tsouth. Ge 13:1,3; 20:1; 24:62 • He *Negev*

10 And there was Ra famine in the land: and Abram Rwent down into Egypt to sojourn there; for the famine *was* Rgrievous in the land. Ge 26:1 • Ps 105:13 • Ge 43:1

11 And it came to pass, when he was come near to enter into Egypt, that he said unto Sa'-rai his wife, Behold now, I know that thou *art* a fair woman to look upon:

12 Therefore it shall come to pass, when the Egyptians shall see thee, that they shall say, This *is* his wife: and they Rwill kill me, but they will save thee alive. Ge 20:11; 26:7

13 Say, I pray thee, thou *art* my sister: that it may be well with me for thy sake; and my soul shall live because of thee.

14 And it came to pass, that, when Abram was come into Egypt, the Egyptians beheld the woman that she *was* very fair.

15 The princes also of Pharaoh saw her, and commended her before Pharaoh: and the woman was taken into Pharaoh's house.

16 And he Rentreated Abram well for her sake: and he Rhad sheep, and oxen, and he asses, and menservants, and maidservants, and she asses, and camels. Ge 20:14 • Ge 13:2

17 And the LORD Rplagued Pharaoh and his house with great plagues because of Sa'-rai Abram's wife. 1 Ch 16:21

18 And Pharaoh called Abram, and said,

12:7 appeared. This is the first mention of an actual "appearance" of God to men (that is, a theophany, a pre-incarnate appearance of Christ). Note that God's promise to give Abram the land of Canaan was unconditional. Abram had already met the *only* condition; that of leaving his homeland to go to Canaan as God commanded him.

12:12 they will kill me. A papyrus document from ancient Egypt does indeed tell of a pharaoh who had a beautiful woman brought to his court after murdering her husband, which would indicate that Abram's concern was realistic.

12:13 my sister. Sarai was Abram's half-sister (20:12), so this was not an outright lie. Abram's faith was still weak. He should have stayed in Canaan in spite of the famine. Having gone into Egypt, he should have been open and consistent in his testimony, and so should Sarai. Instead, they compromised, following human reason instead of God's Word. God protected them in spite of it, but they lost their testimony with the Egyptians, whom they might otherwise have led back to God.

12:16 she asses, and camels. Contrary to the opinions of many cultural evolutionists, modern research has confirmed that all these animals had been domesticated and used well before the time of Abraham.

^RWhat *is* this *that* thou hast done unto me? why didst thou not tell me that she *was* thy wife? Ge 20:9,10; 26:10

19 Why saidst thou, She *is* my sister? so I might have taken her to me to wife: now therefore behold thy wife, take *her*, and go thy way.

20 ^RAnd Pharaoh commanded *his* men concerning him: and they sent him away, and his wife, and all that he had. [Pr 21:1]

CHAPTER 13

The Separation of Abram from Lot

And Abram went up out of Egypt, he, and his wife, and all that he had, and ^RLot with him, into the south. Ge 12:4; 14:12,16

2 ^RAnd Abram *was* very rich in cattle, in silver, and in gold. Ge 24:35; 26:14

3 And he went on his journeys ^Rfrom the south even to Beth'–el, unto the place where his tent had been at the beginning, between Beth'–el and ^THa'–i; Ge 12:8,9 • Or Ai

4 Unto the place of the altar, which he had made there at the first: and there Abram called on the name of the LORD.

5 And Lot also, which went with Abram, had flocks, and herds, and tents.

6 And ^Rthe land was not able to ^Tbear them, that they might dwell together: for their substance was great, so that they could not dwell together. Ge 36:7 • support

7 And there was a strife between the herdmen of Abram's cattle and the herdmen of Lot's cattle: and the Ca'–naan-ite and the Per'–iz-zite dwelled then in the land.

8 And Abram said unto Lot, ^RLet there be no strife, I pray thee, between me and thee, and between my herdmen and thy herdmen; for we *be* brethren. 1 Co 6:7

9 ^R*Is* not the whole land before thee? separate thyself, I pray thee, from me: if *thou wilt take* the left hand, then I will go to the right; or if *thou depart* to the right hand, then I will go to the left. Ge 20:15; 34:10

10 And Lot lifted up his eyes, and beheld all ^Rthe plain of Jordan, that it *was* well watered every where, before the LORD destroyed Sodom and Go-mor'-rah, *even* as the garden of the LORD, like the land of Egypt, as thou comest unto Zo'-ar. Ge 19:17-29

11 Then Lot chose ^Thim all the plain of Jordan; and Lot journeyed east: and they separated themselves the one from the other. *for himself*

12 Abram dwelled in the land of Canaan, and Lot dwelled in the cities of the plain, and pitched *his* tent toward Sodom.

13 But the men of Sodom *were* wicked and sinners before the LORD exceedingly.

God's Promise to Abram

14 And the LORD said unto Abram, after that Lot ^Rwas separated from him, Lift up now thine eyes, and look from the place where thou art ^Rnorthward, and southward, and eastward, and westward: Ge 13:11 • Ge 28:14

15 For all the land which thou seest, to thee will I give it, and to thy seed for ever.

16 And ^RI will make thy ^Tseed as the dust of the earth: so that if a man can number the dust of the earth, *then* shall thy seed also be numbered. Ge 22:17 • descendants

17 Arise, walk through the land in the length of it and in the breadth of it; for I will give it unto thee.

18 ^RThen Abram removed *his* tent, and came and ^Rdwelt in the plain of Mam'-re, which *is* in He'-bron, and built there an altar unto the LORD. Ge 26:17 • Ge 14:13

CHAPTER 14

Abram Rescues Lot

And it came to pass in the days of Am'-ra-phel king ^Rof Shi'-nar, A'-ri-och king of El'-la-sar, Ched-or-la'-o-mer king of E'-lam, and Ti'-dal king of nations; Ge 10:10; 11:2

2 *That these* made war with Be'-ra king of Sodom, and with Bir'-sha king of Go-mor'-

---

13:10 *well watered.* In the early centuries after the flood, a great ice sheet probably covered the northern latitudes, and this in turn led to abundant rainfall in the southern latitudes, a "pluvial age" corresponding to the "glacial age" farther north. There is much evidence of this all over the world, with remains of extensive settlements and agriculture in regions which (like the region where Sodom and Gomorrah once thrived, near the southern end of the Dead Sea) are now oppressively hot, dry and desolate.

13:16 *numbered.* It would be as impossible now to count Abraham's descendants as to count the dust of the earth. He was the progenitor of all the Israelites, of course, but also of

rah, Shi'-nab king of ᴿAd'-mah, and Shem-e'-ber king of Ze-boi'-im, and the king of Be'-la, which is ᴿZo'-ar.　De 29:23 • Ge 13:10; 19:22

3 All these were joined together in the vale of Sid'-dim, which is the salt sea.

4 Twelve years ᴿthey served Ched-or-la'-o-mer, and in the thirteenth year they rebelled.　Ge 9:26

5 And in the fourteenth year came Ched-or-la'-o-mer, and the kings that *were* with him, and ᵀsmote ᴿthe Reph'-a-ims in Ash'-te-roth Kar-na'-im, and ᴿthe Zu'-zims in

Ham, ᴿand the E'-mims in Sha'-veh Kir-i-a-tha'-im,　Ge 15:20 • De 2:20 • De 2:10 • *attacked*

6 And the Ho'-rites in their mount Se'-ir, unto El–pa'-ran, which *is* by the wilderness.

7 And they returned, and came to En–mish'-pat, which *is* Ka'-desh, and smote all the country of the Am'-a-lek-ites, and also the Am'-or-ites, that dwelt ᴿin Haz'-e-zon–ta'-mar.　2 Ch 20:2

8 And there went out the king of Sodom, and the king of Go-mor'-rah, and the king of Ad'-mah, and the king of Ze-boi'-im, and the king of Be'-la (the same *is* Zo'-ar;) and

all the Arab nations, as well as the peoples of many now-extinct nations—Edomites, Midianites, etc.

14:1 *king of Shinar.* Shinar probably refers to Sumeria and Elam to early Persia. Ellasar was the leading tribe in southern Babylonia and "nations" (Hebrew *Goiim*) was probably a tribe of northeastern Babylonia. Chedorlaomer seems to have been the chief leader of this confederacy (14:4).

14:2 *king of Sodom.* These five "cities of the plain," listed in this verse—Sodom, Gomorrah, Admah, Zeboim and Zoar—were formerly thought by critics to be fictional. However, the Ebla tablets found in northern Syria beginning in 1964 contain numerous names of cities mentioned in Genesis, including these five, listed the same as in this verse. They antedate the time of Abraham, who probably passed through Ebla on his migration from Haran to Canaan.

14:3 *Siddim.* "Siddim" meant "cultivated fields," and the vale of Siddim at this time was extremely fertile, supporting the five cities of the plain. The reference to "the salt sea" was probably a later editorial insertion by Moses. At the time of Abram, what is now the Dead Sea was still a freshwater remnant of the great flood, and the whole region was "well watered every where" (13:10). The exact location of Sodom and her four sister cities is uncertain, although most authorities believe that their remains are now submerged beneath the waters of the shallow southern arm of the Dead Sea. There is also the possibility that the actual cities were located on higher elevations overlooking five ephemeral streams ("wadis") emptying into the lake, with the inhabitants working the fields below during the daytime, then living in the cooler heights above at night.

14:5 *Rephaims.* Some of these Canaanite tribes seem actually to have been demon-possessed, in the same manner as the demon-energized population before the flood (see notes on 6:1-4). The Rephaim ("strong ones") and the Zamzummim ("powerful ones," probably the same as the Zuzim) along with the Emim, all seem to have been of "the sons of Anak" or the Anakim, and all seem to have been giants (note De 2:10,20; Jos 15:13). In Numbers 13:33, these Anakim are actually said to have been "giants" (Hebrew *nephilim*, the same word as used in 6:4). Furthermore, the term *rephaim* is also used to refer to some of the spirits of the wicked dead in Hades (Job 26:5; Pr 2:18; 9:18; 21:16; Is 14:9; 26:14). All of this suggests another irruption of demonic spirits after the flood, possibly at the rebellion at Babel, with giant progeny again being produced through demon-possessed parents. Their descendants inhabited Canaan.

14:6 *Horites.* The Horites are known to archaeologists as the Hurrians, a leading tribe of the ancient Middle East.

14:7 *Amalekites.* The Amalekites probably were descended from Amalek, a grandson of Esau, and later inhabited a region west of the Dead Sea. This note was evidently inserted by Moses in his editing of Genesis.

14:7 *Amorites.* The Amorites were probably the dominant tribe in Canaan at this time.

they joined battle with them in the vale of Sid'-dim;

9 With Ched-or-la'-o-mer the king of E'-lam, and with Ti'-dal king of ᵀnations, and Am'-ra-phel king of Shi'-nar, and A'-ri-och king of El'-la-sar; four kings ᵀwith five.   He Goyim • against

10 And the vale of Sid'-dim *was full of* ᴿslimepits; and the kings of Sodom and Go-mor'-rah fled, and fell there; and they that remained fled to the mountain.   Ge 11:3

11 And they took ᴿall the goods of Sodom and Go-mor'-rah, and all their ᵀvict-uals, and went their way.   Ge 14:16,21 • *provisions*

12 And they took Lot, Abram's ᴿbrother's son, ᴿwho dwelt in Sodom, and his goods, and departed.   Ge 11:27; 12:5 • Ge 13:12

13 And there came one that had escaped, and told Abram the Hebrew; for he dwelt in the plain of Mam'-re the Am'-or-ite, brother of Esh'-col, and brother of A'-ner: and these *were* confederate with Abram.

14 And ᴿwhen Abram heard that ᴿhis brother was taken captive, he armed his trained *servants,* born in his own house, three hundred and eighteen, and pursued *them* unto Dan.   Ge 19:29 • Ge 13:8; 14:12

15 And he divided himself against them, he and his servants, by night, and smote them, and pursued them unto Ho'-bah, which *is* on the left hand of Damascus.

16 And he ᴿbrought back all the goods, and also brought again his brother Lot, and his goods, and the women also, and the people.   Ge 31:18

Abram Refuses the Reward

17 And the king of Sodom ᴿwent out to meet him ᴿafter his return from the slaugh-ter of Ched-or-la'-o-mer, and of the kings that *were* with him, at the valley of Sha'-veh, which *is* the king's dale.   1 Sa 18:6 • 2 Sa 18:18

18 And ᴿMel-chiz'-e-dek king of Sa'-lem brought forth bread and wine: and he *was* the priest of the most high God.   He 7:1-10

19 And he blessed him, and said, ᴿBlessed *be* Abram of the most high God, ᴿpossessor of heaven and earth: Ru 3:10 • Ge 14:22

20 And ᴿblessed be the most high God, which hath delivered thine enemies into thy hand. And he gave him tithes of all.   Ge 24:27

21 And the king of Sodom said unto Abram, Give me the persons, and take the goods to thyself.

14:10 *slimepits.* These asphalt pits were so extensive that the Dead Sea was called the As-phalt Sea by early writers. They probably represented accumulations of organic debris from the flood, collecting in the unique basins of the Great Rift Valley which traverse the region.

14:15 *by night.* It is possible that this was in the nature of a commando raid on a rela-tively small contingent of the armies of the northern confederacy.

14:18 *Melchizedek.* The identity of Melchizedek is controversial, especially in view of the statements made concerning him in Psalm 110:4, and in Hebrews 5:6,10; 6:20; 7:1-21. "The Lord" is called by David "a priest for ever after the order of Melchizedek." The writer of He-brews says that Melchizedek was "without father, without mother, without descent (i.e., 'ge-nealogy'), having neither beginning of days, nor end of life; but made like unto the Son of God; abideth a priest continually" (He 7:3). The usual interpretation of these words is that he was made into a type of Christ since, as a "King of Righteousness" (the meaning of *Melchizedek*) and "King of Peace" (the meaning of Salem), he appears and leaves the record, suddenly, with no mention of either ancestry or death. This, however, is obviously a strained and naturalistic exegesis of exalted and supernaturalistic language. It seems better to take the words literally, in which case they could only be applicable to Christ Himself, appearing here to Abram in a theophany. This would also solve the problem of how such a godly king and priest as Melchizedek could be ruling a city in such an ungodly land as Canaan and, why, if he did, Abram would have had no other contact with him. The fact that He was "made like unto the Son of God" accords with one of Christ's *pre-incarnate* ap-pearances; at His human birth, He became the *incarnate* Son of God forever. Melchizedek was also said to be a man (He 7:4), but the same is true in the case of other theophanies, one of which was shown to Abram and Lot (18:2,22; 19:1-24). That Melchizedek's Salem could never have been Jerusalem is evident especially from Ezekiel 16:2–4 (see note on Eze 16:4).

22 And Abram ᴿsaid to the king of Sodom, I ᴿhave lift up mine hand unto the LORD, the most high God, ᴿthe possessor of heaven and earth,   Ge 14:2,8,10 • Da 12:7 • Ge 14:19

23 That I will not *take* from a thread even to a shoelatchet, and that I will not take any thing that *is* thine, lest thou shouldest say, I have made Abram rich:

24 Save only that which the young men have eaten, and the portion of the men which went with me, A'-ner, Esh'-col, and Mam'-re; let them take their portion.

CHAPTER 15

God Promises Abram an Heir

After these things the word of the LORD came unto Abram ᴿin a vision, saying, ᴿFear not, Abram: I *am* thy shield, *and* thy exceeding great reward.   Da 10:1 • Ge 21:17; 26:24

2 ᴿAnd Abram said, Lord GOD, what wilt thou give me, ᴿseeing I go childless, and the ᵀsteward of my house *is* this E-li-e'-zer of Damascus?   Ge 17:18 • Ac 7:5 • *heir*

3 And Abram said, Behold, to me thou hast given no seed: and, lo, ᴿone born in my house is mine heir.   Ge 14:14

4 And, behold, the word of the LORD *came* unto him, saying, This shall not be thine heir; but he that shall come forth out of thine own bowels shall be thine heir.

5 And he brought him forth abroad, and said, Look now toward heaven, and ᴿtellᵀ ᴿthe stars, if thou be able to number them: and he said unto him, ᴿSo shall thy ᴿseed be.   Ps 147:4 • Je 33:22 • Ex 32:13 • Ge 17:19 • *count*

6 And he believed in the LORD; and he counted it to him for righteousness.

7 And he said unto him, I *am* the LORD that brought thee out of Ur of the Chal'-dees, to give thee this land to inherit it.

8 And he said, Lord GOD, ᴿwhereby shall I know that I shall inherit it?   Lk 1:18

9 And he said unto him, Take me an heifer of three years old, and a ᵀshe goat of three years old, and a ram of three years old, and a turtledove, and a young pigeon.   *female*

10 And he took unto him all these, and ᴿdividedᵀ them in the midst, and laid each piece one against another: but ᴿthe birds divided he not.   Je 34:18 • Le 1:17 • *cut them in two*

11 And when the fowls came down upon the carcases, Abram drove them away.

15:1 *word of the LORD.* This is the first use of "word" in Scripture and, significantly, personifies the "word of the LORD." This verse also contains the first mentions of "vision," "fear not," "shield," "reward," and "I am." In effect, God comforts Abram after a most traumatic experience, urging him not to fear the words of men, since the word of the Lord assured him both full protection and abundant provision.

15:1 *I am thy shield.* Here is the first of the great "I am's" of Christ, and probably this incident was that to which He referred when He said, "Abraham rejoiced to see my day" (Jo 8:56), and then claimed "Before Abraham was, I am" (Jo 8:58). In fact, "I am" is the very name of the self-revealing God (Ex 3:14).

15:3 *mine heir.* The Nuzi tablets indicate that a childless couple could legally adopt a servant as their ostensible heir. Apparently Abraham had done this in the case of Eliezer.

15:6 *believed.* This is the first mention of "belief" or "faith" in the Bible, as well as the first mention of "counted" or "imputed." In Noah's case, "grace" preceded imputed righteousness (6:9—"just" means "righteous"); in Abraham's case, it was "faith." Both are essential for righteousness that satisfies God (Ep 2:8-10); one stresses the divine side, the other the human. This verse is quoted three times in the New Testament (Ro 4:3; Ga 3:6; Jam 2:23); in each case it is stressed that Abraham is a type of all who are saved, the principle always being that of salvation through faith (which is by grace) unto righteousness.

15:10 *in the midst.* God was to confirm the covenant to Abram in a most instructive manner. Though God's promise had been free and unconditional to Abram (premised only on his faith), it would be very costly to God, requiring the death of His incarnate Son. This was pictured by the death of one of each of the five kinds of clean animals acceptable for sacrificial purposes, with their remains divided into two rows. This was customary procedure at the time in establishing a solemn compact, with the contracting parties sealing it by passing

12 And when the sun was going down, a deep sleep fell upon Abram; and, lo, an horror of great darkness fell upon him.

13 And he said unto Abram, Know of a surety [R]that thy seed shall be a stranger in a land *that is* not theirs, and shall serve them; and [R]they shall afflict them four hundred years;   Ex 1:11 • Ex 12:40

14 And also that nation, whom they shall serve, [R]will I judge: and afterward [R]shall they come out with great substance. Ex 6:6 • Ex 12:36

15 And [R]thou shalt go [R]to thy fathers in peace; [R]thou shalt be buried in a good old age.   Job 5:26 • Ge 25:8; 47:30 • Ge 25:8

16 But [R]in the fourth generation they shall come hither again: for the iniquity of the Am'-or-ites *is* not yet full.   Ex 12:41

17 And it came to pass, that, when the sun went down, and it was dark, behold a smoking furnace, and a burning lamp that [R]passed between those pieces.   Je 34:18,19

18 In the same day the LORD [R]made a covenant with Abram, saying, [R]Unto thy [T]seed have I given this land, from the river of Egypt unto the great river, the river Euphra'-tes: Ge 24:7 • Ge 12:7; 17:8 • *descendants*

19 The Ken'-ites, and the Ken'-iz-zites, and the Kad'-mon-ites,

20 And the Hit'-tites, and the Per'-iz-zites, and the Reph'-a-ims,

---

between the two rows. Here, however, only God passed through, since it was a unilateral, unconditional commitment on His part.

15:12 *a deep sleep.* The whole procedure in this remarkable ritual was profoundly instructive to Abram. The long delay foreshadowed a long period that must elapse before God's promise would be fulfilled, during which the believer would have to guard against attacks of wicked men and evil spirits. The deep sleep could only symbolize death—a substitutionary death by One whom the sacrifices pictured, and in whose death Abram and all believers must share before the glory can follow.

15:13 *four hundred years.* Some writers take this as a round number, the more precise value being 430 years (Ex 12:40). But see note on Exodus 12:41.

15:16 *fourth generation.* It is not absolutely certain whether the 430-year term mentioned in the Abrahamic covenant begins with the coming of Abraham into Canaan or the descent of the children of Israel into Egypt. The former seems indicated by Galatians 3:16-17 in which case the "sojourning" mentioned in Exodus 12:40 and the "affliction" of Genesis 15:13 would apply to their total experience in both Canaan and Egypt. If this is the case, then the actual sojourn in Egypt would be only 215 years (from the time of Abram's entry into Canaan to the birth of Isaac was 25 years; Isaac was 60 years old at Jacob's birth; and Jacob was 130 years old when he and his children migrated to Egypt, a total of 215 years—see 12:4; 21:5; 25:26; 47:9). The "fourth generation" consisted of men whose great-grandfathers had been among the 70 Israelites who entered Egypt. Even if the children of Israel actually stayed 400 years in Egypt, the life span in those days was still around 100 or more (Moses died at 120), so it would have easily been possible for people of the fourth generation still to be living at the time of the exodus.

There is also the problem of whether 215 years could have been enough time for the Israelite population to grow from about 70 to about two million. Although this seems unlikely, it would have been possible if the average family size had been about eight children (remember that Jacob himself had 12) and the average life span still about 100 years, with parents living to see their great-grandchildren grow to maturity. In contrast, consider the notes at Exodus 6:17 and 12:41.

15:18 *covenant with Abram.* Although this is the first time God's promises to Abram are actually called a covenant, its terms merely confirm and clarify the initial promise in Genesis 12:7. Its ultimate fulfillment is yet future, although it received a partial fulfillment under Solomon (1 Ki 8:65) and possibly Jeroboam II (2 Ki 14:25).

15:20 *the Hittites.* The Hittites were descended from Heth (10:15), eventually becoming

21 And the Am′-or-ites, and the Ca′-naan-ites, and the Gir′-ga-shites, and the Jeb′-u-sites.

CHAPTER 16

A Carnal Plan for Children

Now Sa′-rai Abram′s wife bare him no children: and she had an handmaid, an Egyptian, whose name *was* Ha′-gar.

2 ᴿAnd Sa′-rai said unto Abram, Behold now, the Lᴏʀᴅ ᴿhath restrained me from bearing: I pray thee, ᴿgo in unto my maid; it may be that I may obtain children by her. And Abram ᴿhearkened to the voice of Sa′-rai.   Ge 30:3 • Ge 20:18 • Ge 30:3,9 • Ge 3:17

3 And Sa′-rai Abram′s wife took Ha′-gar her maid the Egyptian, after Abram ᴿhad dwelt ten years in the land of Canaan, and gave her to her husband Abram to be his wife.   Ge 12:4,5

4 And he went in unto Ha′-gar, and she conceived: and when she saw that she had conceived, her mistress was ᴿdespised in her ᵀeyes.   [Pr 30:21,23] • *sight*

5 And Sa′-rai said unto Abram, My wrong *be* upon thee: I have given my maid into thy bosom; and when she saw that she had conceived, I was despised in her eyes: the Lᴏʀᴅ judge between me and thee.

6 But Abram said unto Sa′-rai, Behold, thy maid *is* in thy hand; do to her as it pleaseth thee. And when Sa′-rai dealt hardly with her, she fled from her face.

7 And the angel of the Lᴏʀᴅ found her by a fountain of water in the wilderness, by the fountain in the way to ᴿShur.   Ex 15:22

8 And he said, Ha′-gar, Sa′-rai′s maid, whence camest thou? and whither wilt thou go? And she said, I flee from the face of my mistress Sa′-rai.

9 And the angel of the Lᴏʀᴅ said unto her, Return to thy mistress, and ᴿsubmit thyself under her hands.   [Tit 2:9]

10 And the angel of the Lᴏʀᴅ said unto her, I will multiply thy seed exceedingly, that it shall not be numbered for multitude.

11 And the angel of the Lᴏʀᴅ said unto her, Behold, thou *art* with child, ᴿand shalt bear a son, and shalt call his name ᵀIsh′-ma-el; because the Lᴏʀᴅ hath heard thy affliction.   Lk 1:13,31 • Lit. *God Hears*

12 ᴿAnd he will be a wild man; his hand *will be* against every man, and every man′s hand against him; ᴿand he shall dwell in the presence of all his brethren.   Ge 21:20 • Ge 25:18

13 And she called the name of the Lᴏʀᴅ that spake unto her, Thou God seest me: for she said, Have I also here ᵀlooked after him ᴿthat seeth me?   Ge 31:42 • *Seen the back of*

14 Wherefore the well was called ᴿBe′-er–la-hai′–roi; behold, *it is* ᴿbetween Ka′-desh and Be′-red.   Ge 24:62 • Nu 13:26

15 And ᴿHa′-gar bare Abram a son: and Abram called his son′s name, which Ha′-gar bare, Ish′-ma-el.   Ga 4:22

16 And Abram *was* fourscore and six years old, when Ha′-gar bare Ish′-ma-el to Abram.

---

a great empire. See notes on Genesis 23:20 and Joshua 1:4. There are some 40 references to them in the Bible.

16:2 *by her.* In the culture of the time, it was considered so essential for a wife to give her husband an heir that, if necessary, she could have a child by proxy, as it were, through her personal maid. Note also the similar arrangement for Jacob by his wives, Leah and Rachel (30:3,9). The famous Nuzi tablets, found in northern Syria, confirm that it was customary and legal in the nations of that time and place for a wife unable to produce children to provide her handmaid to be a surrogate wife to her husband, with any resulting child considered her own.

16:6 *as it pleaseth thee.* The Nuzi tablets mentioned above also allowed the wife, if she so chose, to order both the mistress and the child to leave.

16:7 *angel of the Lᴏʀᴅ.* This is the first specific reference to angels in Scripture (though angels are called "sons of God" in 6:2). Here it is "the angel of the LORD [Jehovah]," specifically identified (16:13) as Jehovah Himself. The term "*the* angel of the Lᴏʀᴅ," therefore, seems often to refer to Christ Himself in a theophany.

16:12 *wild man.* Literally, "a wild ass of a man," seemingly referring prophetically to a characteristic of the Arab peoples who are descendants of Ishmael, a character apparent even today in the modern Israeli-Arab conflict.

CHAPTER 17

Establishing the Covenant: Circumcision

And when Abram was ninety years old and nine, the LORD ᴿappeared to Abram, and said unto him, ᴿI *am* the Almighty God; ᴿwalk before me, and be thou ᴿperfect. Ge 12:7; 18:1 • Ge 28:3; 35:11 • 2 Ki 20:3 • De 18:13

2 And I will make my ᴿcovenant between me and thee, and ᴿwill multiply thee exceedingly. Ge 15:18 • Ge 12:2; 13:16; 15:5; 18:18

3 And Abram fell on his face: and God talked with him, saying,

4 As for me, behold, my covenant *is* with thee, and thou shalt be ᴿa father of ᵀmany nations. [Ro 4:11,12,16] • Lit. *multitude of nations*

5 ᵀNeither shall thy name any more be called Abram, but ᴿthy name shall be Abraham; ᴿfor a father of many nations have I made thee. Ne 9:7 • Ro 4:17 • *No longer*

6 And I will make thee exceeding fruitful, and I will make ᴿnations of thee, and ᴿkings shall come out of thee. Ge 17:16; 35:11 • Ma 1:6

7 And I will ᴿestablish my covenant between me and thee and thy seed after thee in their generations for an everlasting covenant, ᴿto be a God unto thee, and to thy seed after thee. [Ga 3:17] • Ge 26:24; 28:13

8 And I will give unto thee, and to thy seed after thee, the land wherein thou art a stranger, all the land of Canaan, for an everlasting possession; and I will be their God.

9 And God said unto Abraham, Thou shalt keep my covenant therefore, thou, and thy seed after thee in their generations.

10 This *is* my covenant, which ye shall keep, between me and you and thy seed after thee; ᴿEvery man child among you shall be circumcised. Ac 7:8

11 And ye shall circumcise the flesh of your foreskin; and it shall be ᴿa token of the covenant betwixt me and you. Ex 12:13,48

12 And he that is eight days old ᴿshall be circumcised among you, every ᵀman child in your generations, he that is born in the house, or bought with money of any stranger, which *is* not of thy seed. Le 12:3 • *male*

13 He that is born in thy house, and he that is bought with thy money, must needs be circumcised: and my covenant shall be in your flesh for an everlasting covenant.

14 And the uncircumcised man child whose flesh of his foreskin is not circumcised, that soul shall be cut off from his people; he hath broken my covenant.

15 And God said unto Abraham, As for Sa'-rai thy wife, thou shalt not call her name Sa'-rai, but ᵀSarah *shall* her name *be*. Lit. *Princess*

16 And I will bless her, ᴿand give thee a son also of her: yea, I will bless her, and she shall be *a mother* ᴿof nations; kings of people shall be of her. Ge 18:10 • Ge 35:11

17 Then Abraham fell upon his face, ᴿand laughed, and said in his heart, Shall *a child* be born unto him that is an hundred years old? and shall Sarah, that is ninety years old, bear? Ge 17:3; 18:12; 21:6

18 And Abraham ᴿsaid unto God, O that Ish'-ma-el might live before thee! Ge 18:23

17:1 *Almighty God.* This is the first of some 48 occurrences in the Old Testament of this distinctive name of God (Hebrew *El Shaddai*).

17:2 *my covenant.* God used the term "covenant" (Hebrew *berith*) no less than 13 times in Genesis 17. Although He gives instructions and commandments here to Abram, they are not given as conditions of God's covenant; His promises again were unconditional. Three times (17:7,13,19) God calls it an "everlasting" covenant, and He promises again the land to Abram's seed as an "everlasting" possession (17:8). His name is changed from Abram ("exalted father") to Abraham ("father of a multitude"). Not only would he be the father of multitudes of physical descendants (Jews, Arabs, etc.), but the spiritual father of all them that believe in the true God as He is.

17:11 *token.* As the rainbow encircling the whole earth was a token of God's covenant with all men (9:17), so circumcision, encircling the channel by which the human seed is preserved and transmitted, especially the promised Seed in the line of Abraham, is the token of God's covenant with His chosen nation. It was not a sign to be seen of all men, as was the rainbow, but a sign to be seen only by a man's parents and his wife, reminding them of their faith commitment to the God of Abraham, and His promise to them.

17:16 *bless her.* Sarah (with a new name meaning "princess") was blessed first by a mira-

19 And God said, RSarah thy wife shall bear thee a son indeed; and thou shalt call his name Isaac: and I will establish my covenant with him for an everlasting covenant, *and* with his seed after him.

20 And as for Ish'-ma-el, I have heard thee: Behold, I have blessed him, and will make him fruitful, and Rwill multiply him exceedingly; twelve princes shall he beget, and I will make him a great nation.　Ge 16:10

21 But my Rcovenant will I establish with Isaac, Rwhich Sarah shall bear unto thee at this set time in the next year.　Ge 26:2-5 • Ge 21:2

22 And he left off talking with him, and God went up from Abraham.

23 And Abraham took Ish'-ma-el his son, and all that were born in his house, and all that were bought with his money, every male among the men of Abraham's house; and circumcised the flesh of their foreskin in the selfsame day, as God had said unto him.

24 And Abraham *was* ninety years old and nine, when he was circumcised in the flesh of his foreskin.

25 And Ish'-ma-el his son *was* thirteen years old, when he was circumcised in the flesh of his foreskin.

26 In the selfsame day was Abraham circumcised, and Ish'-ma-el his son.

27 And Rall the men of his house, born in the house, and bought with money of the stranger, were circumcised with him.　Ge 18:19

CHAPTER 18

Sarah's Faith Is Tried

And the LORD appeared unto him in the Rplains of Mam'-re: and he sat in the tent door in the heat of the day;　Ge 13:18; 14:13

2 RAnd he lift up his eyes and looked, and, lo, three men stood by him: Rand when he saw *them*, he ran to meet them from the tent door, and bowed himself Ttoward the ground,　He 13:2 • Ge 19:1 • *to*

3 And said, My Lord, if now I have found favour in thy sight, pass not Taway, I pray thee, from thy servant:　*on by*

4 Let Ra little water, I pray you, be Tfetched, and wash your feet, and rest yourselves under the tree:　Ge 19:2; 24:32; 43:24 • *brought*

5 And RI will fetch a morsel of bread, and Rcomfort ye your hearts; after that ye shall pass on: Rfor therefore are ye come to your servant. And they said, So do, as thou hast said.　Ju 6:18,19; 13:15,16 • Ju 19:5 • Ge 19:8; 33:10

6 And Abraham hastened into the tent unto Sarah, and said, Make ready quickly three measures of fine meal, knead *it*, and make cakes upon the hearth.

7 And Abraham ran unto the herd, and fetcht a calf tender and good, and gave *it* unto a young man; and he hasted to Tdress it.　*prepare*

8 And Rhe took butter, and milk, and the calf which he had Tdressed, and set *it* before them; and he stood by them under the tree, and they did eat.　Ge 19:3 • *prepared*

---

cle (probably at the time of 18:14) that rejuvenated her body, enabling her to have a son long after it seemed biologically possible. As Isaac became a type of Christ, so she became a type of Mary, and is considered to be a spiritual mother of believers as Abraham was their spiritual father (note He 11:11-12; 1 Pe 3:6).

18:1 *the LORD appeared*. This remarkable theophany is highly instructive. The Lord Jesus in pre-incarnate form and two of His angels all appeared in the form of three men, even eating with Abraham. The writer of Hebrews refers to this event when he says that "some have entertained angels unawares" (He 13:2). Later the two angels move on to communicate with Lot in Sodom (18:22) while the Lord remained to talk further with Abraham. Thus both the angels and God Himself can, when necessary, assume fully human bodies. Similarly, in His resurrection body, Christ "did eat before them" (Lk 24:43) and He said that, in the resurrection, all believers will be "as the angels of God in heaven" (Ma 22:30). Our immortal bodies will be fully physical bodies, but, like the angels, not subject to the gravitational and electromagnetic forces which govern our present bodies.

18:8 *did eat*. It is significant that not only Abraham, but also the three visitors—two of whom were angels, the other being Christ Himself in a theophany—all ate the meat prepared by Sarah and the servant. Whatever nutritional merits vegetarian diets might or might not have, they are not required by biblical commandment. Note Genesis 9:3-4; 1 Timothy 4:3-4.

9 And they said unto him, Where *is* Sarah thy wife? And he said, Behold, in the tent.

10 And he said, I will certainly return unto thee Raccording to the time of life; and, lo, RSarah thy wife shall have a son. And Sarah heard *it* in the tent door, which *was* behind him. 2 Ki 4:16 • Ro 9:9

11 Now Abraham and Sarah *were* old *and* well stricken in age; *and* it ceased to be with Sarah after the manner of women.

12 Therefore Sarah laughed within herself, saying, After I am waxed old shall I have pleasure, my lord being old also?

13 And the LORD said unto Abraham, Wherefore did Sarah laugh, saying, Shall I of a surety bear a child, which am old?

14 RIs any thing too hard for the LORD? RAt the time appointed I will return unto thee, according to the time of life, and Sarah shall have a son. Je 32:17 • Ge 17:21; 18:10

15 Then Sarah denied, saying, I laughed not; for she was afraid. And he said, Nay; but thou didst laugh.

Abraham's Faith Is Tried

16 And the men rose up from thence, and looked toward Sodom: and Abraham went with them to bring them on the way.

17 And the LORD said, RShall I hide from Abraham that thing which I do; Ps 25:14

18 Seeing that Abraham shall surely become a great and mighty nation, and all the nations of the earth shall be Rblessed in him? [Ac 3:25,26]

19 For I know him, Rthat he will command his children and his household after him, and they shall keep the way of the LORD, to do justice and judgment; that the LORD may bring upon Abraham that which he hath spoken of him. [De 4:9,10; 6:6,7]

20 And the LORD said, Because Rthe cry of Sodom and Go-mor'-rah is great, and because their sin is very grievous; Ge 4:10; 19:13

21 RI will go down now, and see whether they have done altogether according to the cry of it, which is come unto me; and if not, RI will know. Ge 11:5 • De 8:2; 13:3

22 And the men turned their faces from thence, Rand went toward Sodom: but Abraham stood yet before the LORD. Ge 18:16; 19:1

23 And Abraham Rdrew near, and said, RWilt thou also Rdestroy the Rrighteous with the wicked? [He 10:22] • Nu 16:22 • Job 9:22 • Ge 20:4

24 TPeradventure there be fifty righteous within the city: wilt thou also destroy and not spare the place for the fifty righteous that *are* therein? *Suppose*

25 That be far from thee to do after this manner, to slay the righteous with the

---

18:14 *hard.* "Hard" is the same word as "wonderful," one of the terms used to describe the coming Messiah in Isaiah 9:6. God gave Sarah the faith to believe that He could accomplish this wonderful miracle of rejuvenating her body, partly by letting her know that He could hear her laugh even when she was out of His sight, and only laughed "within herself" (18:12).

18:19 *command his children.* This is the first specific reference in the Bible to the teaching of children, indicating that such instruction is the primary responsibility of the father and should take the form of commandments, centering first on the ways of the Lord, then on justice and judgment to fellowmen.

18:20 *very grievous.* The iniquity of the Amorites was not yet full (15:16), but these cities of the plain had reached God's limit, especially in view of their reversion to gross wickedness after the marvelous deliverance God gave them through Abraham and after seeing and hearing the testimony of Melchizedek, and even the witness of Lot.

18:23 *destroy the righteous.* This is the most remarkable passage of intercessory prayer in the Bible, also indicating how vitally important is the presence of even a tiny godly minority in an ungodly community. This model intercessory prayer continually appeals both to God's righteous character and His lovingkindness, as the basis for making the request. Abraham thought he knew of 10 righteous people in Sodom (Lot and his family of two unmarried sons, two unmarried daughters, two married daughters and their husbands), not realizing that most of Lot's family had been caught up in the city's wickedness, and so stopped his intercession at 10.

wicked: and ^Rthat the righteous should be as the wicked, that be far from thee: Shall not the Judge of all the earth do right?   Is 3:10,11

26 And the Lord said, ^RIf I find in Sodom fifty righteous within the city, then I will spare all the place for their sakes.   Je 5:1

27 And Abraham answered and said, Behold now, I have taken upon me to speak unto the Lord, which *am* ^R*but* dust and ashes: [Ge 3:19]

28 Peradventure there shall lack five of the fifty righteous: wilt thou destroy all the city for *lack of* five? And he said, If I find there forty and five, I will not destroy *it*.

29 And he spake unto him yet again, and said, Peradventure there shall be forty found there. And he said, I will not do *it* for forty's sake.

30 And he said *unto him*, Oh let not the Lord be angry, and I will speak: Peradventure there shall thirty be found there. And he said, I will not do *it*, if I find thirty there.

31 And he said, Behold now, I have taken upon me to speak unto the Lord: Peradventure there shall be twenty found there. And he said, I will not destroy *it* for twenty's sake.

32 And he said, Oh let not the Lord be angry, and I will speak yet but this once: Peradventure ten shall be found there. And he said, I will not destroy *it* for ten's sake.

33 And the Lord went his way, as soon as he had left communing with Abraham: and Abraham returned unto his place.

CHAPTER 19

The Destruction of Sodom and Gomorrah

And there ^Rcame two angels to Sodom ^Tat even; and ^RLot sat in the gate of Sodom: and Lot seeing *them* rose up to meet them; and he bowed himself with his face toward the ground;   Ge 18:2,16,22 • Ge 18:1-5 • *in the evening*

2 And he said, Behold now, my lords, ^Rturn in, I pray you, into your servant's house, and tarry all night, and wash your feet, and ye shall rise up early, and go on your ways. And they said, Nay; but we will abide in the street all night.   [He 13:2]

3 And he ^Tpressed upon them greatly; and they turned in unto him, and entered into his house; ^Rand he made them a feast, and did bake ^Runleavened bread, and they did eat.   Ge 18:6-8 • Ex 12:8 • *urged them*

4 But before they lay down, the men of the city, *even* the men of Sodom, compassed the house round, both old and young, all the people from every quarter:

5 ^RAnd they called unto Lot, and said unto him, Where *are* the men which came in to thee this night? ^Rbring them out unto us, that we may know them.   Is 3:9 • Ju 19:22

6 And ^RLot went out at the door unto them, and shut the door after him,   Ju 19:23

7 And said, I pray you, brethren, do not so wickedly.

8 ^RBehold now, I have two daughters which have not known man; let me, I pray you, bring them out unto you, and do ye to

---

18:25 *Judge of all the earth.* God is still the judge of all the earth, not only of the chosen nation, and Abraham recognized this.

19:1 *in the gate.* Archaeology has shown that it was customary in the Palestinian culture of the time for legal transactions, public proclamations, and general business to be carried on at the city gate (Ru 4:1-2; 2 Sa 18:24,33). Lot had become recognized by this time as a leading resident of the city, despite his faith in God. Possibly the other leaders knew of his relation to Abraham, who had saved the city from destruction by the northern confederacy.

19:4 *all the people.* The enormity of Sodom's wickedness is indicated by the eagerness with which not a few degenerates, but all the men of the city desired to commit the crime of homosexual rape, probably leading to murder, on two unknown visitors to their city. Lot's desire to protect them demonstrates his basically godly character (2 Pe 2:8) even though his carnality had led him into this compromising association.

19:8 *do ye to them.* Lot's willingness to sacrifice his daughters (the fact that they still were virgins in such a place indicates that he at least had some influence over his family) is hard to understand, but it may well be that, by this time, he knew or suspected the angelic identity of the guests.

them as *is* good in your eyes: only unto these men do nothing; for therefore came they under the shadow of my roof. Ju 19:24

9 And they said, Stand back. And they said *again*, This one *fellow* came in to sojourn, and he will needs be a judge: now will we deal worse with thee, than with them. And they pressed sore upon the man, *even* Lot, and came near to break the door.

10 But the men put forth their hand, and pulled Lot into the house to them, and shut to the door.

11 And they ᴿsmoteᵀ the men that *were* at the door of the house with blindness, both small and great: so that they wearied themselves to find the door. Ge 20:17 • *struck*

12 And the men said unto Lot, Hast thou here any besides? son in law, and thy sons, and thy daughters, and whatsoever thou hast in the city, ᴿbring *them* out of this place: 2 Pe 2:7,9

13 For we will destroy this place, because the ᴿcry of them ᵀis waxen great before the face of the Lᴏʀᴅ; and ᴿthe Lᴏʀᴅ hath sent us to destroy it. Ge 18:20 • 1 Ch 21:15 • *has grown*

14 And Lot went out, and spake unto his sons in law, ᴿwhich married his daughters, and said, ᴿUp, get you out of this place; for the Lᴏʀᴅ will destroy this city. ᴿBut he seemed as one that ᵀmocked unto his sons in law. Ma 1:18 • Nu 16:21,24,26,45 • Ex 9:21 • *joked*

15 And when the morning arose, then the angels ᵀhastened Lot, saying, ᴿArise, take thy wife, and thy two daughters, which are here; lest thou be consumed in the ᵀiniquity of the city. Re 18:4 • *urged Lot to hurry* • *punishment*

16 And while he lingered, the men ᴿlaid hold upon his hand, and upon the hand of his wife, and upon the hand of his two daughters; the ᴿLᴏʀᴅ being merciful unto him: ᴿand they brought him forth, and set him without the city. 2 Pe 2:7 • Lk 18:13 • Ps 34:22

17 And it came to pass, when they had brought them forth abroad, that ᵀhe said, Escape for thy life; ᴿlook not behind thee, neither stay thou in all the plain; escape to the mountain, lest thou be consumed. Je 48:6

18 And Lot said unto them, Oh, ᴿnot so, my Lord: Ac 10:14

19 Behold now, thy servant hath found grace in thy sight, and thou hast magnified thy mercy, which thou hast shewed unto me in saving my life; and I cannot escape to the mountain, lest some evil take me, and I die:

20 Behold now, this city *is* near to flee unto, and it *is* a little one: Oh, let me escape thither, (*is* it not a little one?) and my soul shall live.

21 And he said unto him, See, ᴿI have ᵀaccepted thee concerning this thing also, that I will not overthrow this city, for the which thou hast spoken. Job 42:8,9 • *favoured thee*

22 Haste thee, escape thither; for ᴿI cannot do any thing till thou ᵀbe come thither. Therefore ᴿthe name of the city was called Zo'-ar. Ex 32:10 • Ge 13:10; 14:2 • *arrive there*

23 The sun was risen upon the earth when Lot entered into Zo'-ar.

24 Then the Lᴏʀᴅ rained upon ᴿSodom and upon Go-mor'-rah brimstone and ᴿfire from the Lᴏʀᴅ out of heaven; De 29:23 • Le 10:2

25 And he ᵀoverthrew those cities, and all the plain, and all the inhabitants of the cities, and ᴿthat which grew upon the ground. Ps 107:34 • *devastated*

26 But his wife looked back from behind him, and she became ᴿa pillar of salt. Lk 17:32

27 And Abraham gat up early in the morning to the place where ᴿhe ᵀstood before the Lᴏʀᴅ: Ge 18:22 • *had stood*

19:11 blindness. This miracle, which probably produced a blindness of mental confusion in the mob, rather than of actual physical sight, now clearly identified the two "men" as supernatural messengers of God, but even so, Lot's family hesitated and his sons-in-law refused to follow their urgent instructions.

19:19 magnified thy mercy. This first reference in the Bible to God's "mercy" is described quite properly by Lot as "magnified." God's mercy is also said to be "from everlasting to everlasting" (Ps 103:17), and as great "as the heaven is high above the earth" (Ps 103:11). He is "rich in mercy" (Ep 2:4) and has shown "abundant mercy" (1 Pe 1:3) in saving us. God's mercy is appropriately described in superlatives!

19:22 escape thither. Lot had been instructed to go to the mountain (19:17), but he prevailed upon the angels to let him live in Zoar. He soon became unwelcome in Zoar, how-

28 And he looked toward Sodom and Go-mor′-rah, and toward all the land of the plain, and beheld, and, lo, ᴿthe smoke of the country went up as the smoke of a furnace.   Re 9:2; 18:9

29 And it came to pass, when God destroyed the cities of the plain, that God ᴿremembered Abraham, and sent Lot out of the midst of the overthrow, when he overthrew the cities in the which Lot dwelt. Ge 8:1; 18:23

Lot's Transgression

30 And Lot went up out of Zo′-ar, and ᴿdwelt in the mountain, and his two daughters with him; for he feared to dwell in Zo′-ar: and he dwelt in a cave, he and his two daughters.   Ge 19:17,19

31 And the firstborn said unto the younger, Our father *is* old, and *there is* not a man in the earth ᴿto come in unto us after the manner of all the earth: Ge 16:2,4; 38:8,9

32 Come, let us make our father drink wine, and we will lie with him, that we ᴿmay preserve seed of our father.   [Mk 12:19]

33 And they made their father drink wine that night: and the firstborn went in, and lay with her father; and he perceived not when she lay down, nor when she arose.

34 And it came to pass on the morrow,

---

ever, and went to the mountain after all (19:30). It is always better to follow God's instructions directly.

19:24 *brimstone and fire.* The precise nature of the physical agents used by God in the destruction of the five cities of the plain is uncertain. "Brimstone" is usually associated with sulfur, but the word may be used for any inflammable substance. The word "fire" is also used here for the first time in the Bible and could be understood either as a divine fire (as in Ju 6:21; 1 Ki 18:38) or as gases and other combustibles ignited in a volcanic explosion falling to earth after their eruption. The entire region gives abundant evidence of tremendous volcanic activity in the past, although most of this probably preceded Abraham, occurring in the later stages of the flood and in the early decades following the flood. The area is still very active tectonically, lying astride the "Great Rift Valley," extending all the way from the Jordan River Valley into southern Africa. Unless the judgment was entirely miraculous, in its physical nature as well as its timing, the most likely explanation seems to be the sudden release, by an earthquake and volcanic explosion of great quantities of gas, sulfur and bituminous materials that had accumulated from materials entrapped beneath the valley floor during the flood. These were ignited by a simultaneous electrical storm, so that it appeared to Abraham, watching from afar, that "the smoke of the country went up as the smoke of a furnace" (19:28).

19:26 *pillar of salt.* This remarkable happening is stated matter-of-factly, with no suggestion that it was a special miracle or divine judgment. Lot's wife "looked back" (the phrase might even be rendered "returned back" or "lagged back") seeking to cling to her luxurious life in Sodom (note Christ's reference to this in Lk 17:32-33), and was destroyed in the "overthrow" (19:25,29) of the city. There are many great deposits of rock salt in the region, formed probably by massive precipitation from thermal brines upwelling from the earth's deep mantle during the great flood. Possibly the overthrow buried her in a shower of these salt deposits blown skyward by the explosions. There is also the possibility that she was buried in a shower of volcanic ash, with her body gradually being converted into "salt" over the years following through the process of petrifaction, in a manner similar to that experienced by the inhabitants of Pompeii and Herculaneum in the famous eruption of Mount Vesuvius.

19:30 *dwelt in a cave.* There have been "cave-dwellers" all through history, not primitive ape-men, but true cultured humans, forced by circumstances into such habitations. This home was quite a comedown for a family accustomed to material luxuries. The caves of the Dead Sea region have been inhabited by many people over the centuries. In fact, the famous Dead Sea Scrolls were found in such caves, left by communities of the Essene sect. Note also Job 30:3-6.

that the firstborn said unto the younger, Behold, I lay yesternight with my father: let us make him drink wine this night also; and go thou in, *and* lie with him, that we may preserve ᵀseed of our father. *the lineage*

35 And they made their father drink wine that night also: and the younger arose, and lay with him; and he perceived not when she lay down, nor when she arose.

36 Thus were both the daughters of Lot with child by their father.

37 And the firstborn bare a son, and called his name Moab: ᴿthe same *is* the father of the Mo'-ab-ites unto this day. De 2:9

38 And the younger, she also bare a son, and called his name Ben–am'-mi: ᴿthe same *is* the father of the children of Ammon unto this day. De 2:19

CHAPTER 20

The Test of Abimelech

And Abraham journeyed from ᴿthence toward the south country, and dwelled between ᴿKa'-desh and Shur, and ᴿsojourned in Ge'-rar. Ge 18:1 • Ge 12:9; 16:7,14 • Ge 26:1,6

2 And Abraham said of Sarah his wife, ᴿShe *is* my sister: and A-bim'-e-lech king of Ge'-rar sent, and took Sarah. Ge 12:11-13; 26:7

3 But ᴿGod came to A-bim'-e-lech ᴿin a dream by night, and said to him, ᴿBehold, thou *art but* a dead man, for the woman which thou hast taken; for she *is* a man's wife. Ps 105:14 • Job 33:15 • Ge 20:7

4 But A-bim'-e-lech had not come near her: and he said, Lord, ᴿwilt thou slay also a righteous nation? Ge 18:23-25

5 Said he not unto me, She *is* my sister? and she, even she herself said, He *is* my brother: in the integrity of my heart and innocency of my hands have I done this.

6 And God said unto him in a dream, Yea, I know that thou didst this in the integrity of thy heart; for ᴿI also withheld thee from sinning ᴿagainst me: therefore suffered I thee not to touch her. 1 Sa 25:26,34 • Ge 39:9

7 Now therefore restore the man *his* wife; ᴿfor he *is* a prophet, and he shall pray for thee, and thou shalt live: and if thou restore *her* not, know thou that thou shalt surely die, thou, and all that *are* thine. 1 Sa 7:5

8 Therefore A-bim'-e-lech rose early in the morning, and called all his servants, and

---

19:36 *child by their father*. This case of incest is not specifically condemned in Scripture, presumably because the Mosaic laws against incest had not yet been given. Lot's daughters knew, for example, that their great uncle, Nahor, had married his niece, their own Aunt Milcah (11:27-29), and that Abraham's wife Sarah was his half-sister (20:12). Nevertheless, their particular act was unnatural, to say the least, and they knew that their father would not consent to it if he were sober. To their credit, they had remained virgins up to this time (19:8), even in a licentious city like Sodom and were not motivated by physical lust, but by their concern that their family not be left without descendants. They should have merely trusted God concerning this need, however. The people descended from them, the Moabites and Ammonites, were perpetual enemies of the Israelites.

20:1 *Gerar*. Gerar was capital of the Philistine colony on the seacoast. The Philistines were descendants of Ham through Mizraim, and apparently were originally from Crete. Some centuries later, they all migrated to Canaan and became a strong coastal nation, inveterate enemies of Israel. The name Palestine came from them. The title of their kings at this time was Abimelech, similar to Pharaoh in Egypt.

20:2 *my sister*. How Abraham and Sarah could have entered into the same type of deception for which they had long before been rebuked in Egypt (12:10-20) is hard to understand, but apparently the situation took them by surprise and they got trapped into the same old subterfuge before they realized it.

20:2 *Abimelech*. Abimelech was evidently a title, like Pharaoh in Egypt. Gerar was a prosperous Philistine settlement along the coast, near the Egyptian border, and Abraham must have journeyed there for business purposes.

20:7 *a prophet*. This is the first use of the word "prophet" or "prophecy" in Scripture. As the context indicates, its meaning is not primarily that of foretelling the future, but of being God's spokesman, conveying His words by divine inspiration to man (compare 2 Pe 1:19-

told all these things in their ears: and the men were ᵀsore afraid.   *very*

9 Then A-bim'-e-lech called Abraham, and said unto him, What hast thou done unto us? and what have I offended thee, that thou hast brought on me and on my kingdom a great sin? thou hast done deeds unto me ᴿthat ought not to be done.   Ge 34:7

10 And A-bim'-e-lech said unto Abraham, What sawest thou, that thou hast done this thing?

11 And Abraham said, Because I thought, Surely the fear of God *is* not in this place; and they will slay me for my wife's sake.

12 And yet indeed ᴿ*she is* my sister; she *is* the daughter of my father, but not the daughter of my mother; and she became my wife.   Ge 11:29

13 And it came to pass, when ᴿGod caused me to wander from my father's house, that I said unto her, This *is* thy kindness which thou shalt shew unto me; at every place whither we shall come, ᴿsay of me, He *is* my brother.   Ge 12:1-9,11 • Ge 12:13; 20:5

14 And A-bim'-e-lech ᴿtook sheep, and oxen, and menservants, and womenservants, and gave *them* unto Abraham, and restored him Sarah his wife.   Ge 12:16

15 And A-bim'-e-lech said, Behold, ᴿmy land *is* before thee: dwell where it pleaseth thee.   Ge 13:9; 34:10; 47:6

16 And unto Sarah he said, Behold, I have given thy brother a thousand *pieces* of silver: ᴿbehold, he *is* to thee a covering of the eyes, unto all that *are* with thee, and with all *other*: thus she was reproved.   Ge 26:11

17 So Abraham ᴿprayed unto God: and God ᴿhealed A-bim'-e-lech, and his wife, and his maidservants; and they bare *children*.   Job 42:9 • Ge 21:2

18 For the LORD ᴿhad fast closed up all the wombs of the house of A-bim'-e-lech, because of Sarah Abraham's wife.   Ge 12:17

CHAPTER 21

The Birth of Isaac

And the LORD ᴿvisited Sarah as he had said, and the LORD did unto Sarah ᴿas he had spoken.   1 Sa 2:21 • [Ga 4:23,28]

2 For Sarah ᴿconceived, and bare Abraham a son in his old age, at the set time of which God had spoken to him.   He 11:11,12

3 And Abraham called the name of his son that was born unto him, whom Sarah bare to him, ᴿIsaac.ᵀ   Ge 17:19,21 • Lit. *Laughter*

4 And Abraham ᴿcircumcised his son Isaac being eight days old, ᴿas God had commanded him.   Ac 7:8 • Ge 17:10,12

5 And Abraham was an hundred years old, when his son Isaac was born unto him.

6 And Sarah said, ᴿGod hath ᵀmade me

---

21). God exacts strong punishment on any who harm His prophets, even when they themselves are blameworthy (Ps 105:15).

20:11 *will slay me.* The fact that Abimelech did not deny Abraham's expressed charge indicates that his fears may well have been justified.

20:12 *my sister.* Sarah was Abraham's half-sister. In the early centuries after the dispersion, close marriages were often necessary, with very small tribal populations. This may have been especially desirable in godly families, in order to preserve faithfulness to God's revelation and His purposes. As noted before, this situation was not harmful genetically until many harmful mutations could have accumulated in the nation's genetic pool. By the time of Moses, this had apparently become a problem, and laws against incest were established.

21:1 *as he had said.* Despite their age—Abraham was 100 and Sarah was 90 (17:17)—God miraculously fulfilled His promise, made 25 years earlier (12:4,7), to give them a son. Furthermore, the promise was fulfilled at the "time appointed" (18:14).

21:4 *eight days old.* The act of circumcision was not only the sign of the Abrahamic covenant (see note on 17:11), but was also a significant contribution to health, of both husband and wife, as modern medical knowledge confirms. It is also well established that, as far as the health of the infant is concerned, the eighth day is the optimum time for performing the operation.

to laugh, *so that* all that hear ᴿwill laugh with me.   Is 54:1 • Lk 1:58 • Lit. *made laughter for me*

7 And she said, Who would have said unto Abraham, that Sarah should ᵀhave given children suck? ᴿfor I have born *him* a son in his old age.   Ge 18:11,12 • *nurse children*

8 And the child grew, and was weaned: and Abraham made a great feast the *same* day that Isaac was weaned.

9 And Sarah saw the son of Ha'-gar ᴿthe Egyptian, which she had born unto Abraham, ᴿmocking.   Ge 16:1,4,15 • [Ga 4:29]

10 Wherefore she said unto Abraham, ᴿCast out this bondwoman and her son: for the son of this bondwoman shall not be heir with my son, *even* with Isaac. Ga 3:18; 4:30

11 And the thing was very grievous in Abraham's sight ᴿbecause of his son. Ge 17:18

12 And God said unto Abraham, Let it not be grievous in thy sight because of the lad, and because of thy bondwoman; in all that Sarah hath said unto thee, hearken unto her voice; for ᴿin Isaac shall thy seed be called.   [Ro 9:7,8]

13 And also of the son of the bondwoman will I make ᴿa nation, because he *is* thy ᵀseed.   Ge 16:10; 17:20; 21:18; 25:12-18 • *descendant*

14 And Abraham rose up early in the morning, and took bread, and a ᵀbottle of water, and gave *it* unto Ha'-gar, putting *it* on her shoulder, and the child, and ᴿsent her

away: and she departed, and wandered in the wilderness of Be'-er–she'-ba.   Jo 8:35 • *skin*

15 And the water was ᵀspent in the bottle, and she ᵀcast the child under one of the shrubs.   *used up • placed*

16 And she went, and sat her down ᵀover against *him* a good way off, as it were a bowshot: for she said, Let me not see the death of the child. And she sat over against *him*, and lift up her voice, and wept.   *opposite*

17 And ᴿGod heard the voice of the lad; and the ᴿangel of God called to Ha'-gar out of heaven, and said unto her, What aileth thee, Ha'-gar? fear not; for God hath heard the voice of the lad where he *is*. Ex 3:7 • Ge 22:11

18 Arise, lift up the lad, and hold him ᵀin thine hand; for ᴿI will make him a great nation.   Ge 16:10; 21:13; 25:12-16 • *with*

19 And ᴿGod opened her eyes, and she saw a well of water; and she went, and filled the ᵀbottle with water, and gave the lad drink.   Nu 22:31 • *skin*

20 And God ᴿwas with the lad; and he grew, and dwelt in the wilderness, ᴿand became an archer.   Ge 28:15; 39:2,3,21 • Ge 16:12

21 And he dwelt in the wilderness of Pa'-ran: and his mother ᴿtook him a wife out of the land of Egypt.   Ge 24:4

22 And it came to pass at that time, that A-bim'-e-lech and Phi'-chol the chief captain of his host spake unto Abraham, say-

---

21:7 *his old age.* When God heals miraculously, he does it instantly and completely. Sarah's body was so rejuvenated that although she was 90 years old, she was able both to bear a child and even to nurse him. Abraham was so "young" again that even at 100 years of age he could father six more sons of Keturah many years later, after Sarah's death.

21:11 *very grievous.* Sarah's insistence that Hagar and Ishmael be cast out was very grievous to Abraham, not only because of his personal concern for them, but because it was expected of a man in those days (according to the Nuzi tablets) to provide support for a surrogate wife and her children, even if the true wife should later be able to have a child of her own. The latter would legally be the heir, but the former would still be considered in the family.

21:14 *bottle of water.* This provision, considering his sincere concern for Hagar and Ishmael, can best be understood as a sure confidence that God, who had instructed him to send them away, would care for them. Hagar also needed to learn this.

21:17 *the lad.* Ishmael, who was now about 16 years old, and his mother were praying. He perhaps had given her his own bread and water to sustain her in the desert.

21:17 *angel of God.* The "angel of God [*Elohim*]" had before been called the "angel of the Lord [*Jehovah*]" (16:7). Previously, Hagar was under the Abrahamic covenant while still in Abraham's household. Now she was on her own and the divine being is identified by His majestic name instead of His redemptive name.

ing, God *is* with thee in all that thou doest:

23 Now therefore ᴿswearᵀ unto me here by God that thou wilt not deal falsely with me, nor with my son, nor with my son's son: *but* according to the kindness that I have done unto thee, thou shalt do unto me, and to the land wherein thou hast sojourned. Jos 2:12 • *take an oath*

24 And Abraham said, I will swear.

25 And Abraham reproved A-bim'-e-lech because of a well of water, which A-bim'-e-lech's servants had violently taken away.

26 And A-bim'-e-lech said, I ᵀwot not who hath done this thing: neither didst thou tell me, neither yet heard I *of it*, but to day. *know*

27 And Abraham took sheep and oxen, and gave them unto A-bim'-e-lech; and both of them ᴿmade a ᵀcovenant. Ge 26:31; 31:44 • *treaty*

28 And Abraham set seven ewe lambs of the flock by themselves.

29 And A-bim'-e-lech said unto Abraham, ᴿWhat *mean* these seven ewe lambs which thou hast set by themselves? Ge 33:8

30 And he said, For *these* seven ewe lambs shalt thou take of my hand, that ᴿthey may be a witness unto me, that I have digged this well. Ge 31:48,52

31 Wherefore he ᴿcalled that place Be'-er-she'-ba; because there they sware both of them. Ge 21:14; 26:33

32 Thus they made a covenant at Be'-er-she'-ba: then A-bim'-e-lech rose up, and Phi'-chol the chief captain of his host, and they returned into the land of the Phi-lis'-tines.

33 And *Abraham* planted a grove in Be'-er-she'-ba, and called there on the name of the Lᴏʀᴅ, ᴿthe everlasting God. De 32:40; 33:27

34 And Abraham sojourned in the Phi-lis'-tines' land many days.

CHAPTER 22

The Offering of Isaac

And it came to pass after these things, that ᴿGod did ᵀtempt Abraham, and said unto him, Abraham: and he said, Behold, *here* I *am*. He 11:17 • *test*

2 And he said, Take now thy son, thine

21:31 *Beer-sheba.* "Beer-sheba" means both "well of the oath" and "well of the seven." Even though it was on land claimed by the Philistines, it was commonly understood at the time that the man who dug a well was its owner.

21:33 *everlasting God.* This is the first time this particular name of God is used ("*Jehovah, El Olam,*" meaning "Jehovah is the eternal God"). Abraham realized that, though he had made a covenant with a temporal king, he was really the recipient of the covenant promises of an eternal king. He had granted Abimelech tentative possession of a portion of the promised land, but Jehovah's covenant promised his own seed its eternal possession.

21:34 *many days.* As far as the record goes, Abraham had never returned from "sojourning" (note 21:23) in the land of the Philistines since the time he and Sarah had moved there before Isaac was born (20:1) and Abimelech had granted him freedom to dwell anywhere in his land (20:15).

22:1 *God did tempt.* This is the first occurrence of the word "tempt" (Hebrew *nacah*). It does not mean tempt to do evil (Jam 1:13), but is usually translated "prove." Although God knew what Abraham would do, it must be "proven" to all (including even Abraham himself) that he loved God more than anyone else and that his faith in God's Word was absolute, thus demonstrating the validity of God's selection of him as father of the chosen nation.

22:2 *whom thou lovest.* It is providentially significant that this is the first occurrence of the word "love" in the Bible, referring as it does to the love of a father for his son. The New Testament makes it clear that this story of Abraham and Isaac is not only true historically but is also a type of the heavenly Father and His only begotten Son, depicting the coming sacrifice on Mount Calvary. In a beautiful design (no doubt Spirit-inspired), it is appropriate that the first use of "love" in each of the three Synoptic Gospels (Ma 3:17; Mk 1:11; Lk 3:22) shows the Father calling out from heaven that "this is my beloved Son," at the bap-

only *son* Isaac, whom thou lovest, and get thee into the land of Mo-ri'-ah; and offer him there for a burnt offering upon one of the mountains which I will tell thee of.

3 And Abraham rose up early in the morning, and saddled his ᵀass, and took two of his young men with him, and Isaac his son, and ᵀclave the wood for the burnt offering, and rose up, and went unto the place of which God had told him.   *donkey • split*

4 Then on the third day Abraham lifted up his eyes, and saw the place afar off.

5 And Abraham said unto his young men, Abide ye here with the ass; and I and the ᵀlad will go yonder and worship, and ᴿcome again to you.   [He 11:19] • Lit. *young man*

6 And Abraham took the wood of the burnt offering, and laid *it* upon Isaac his son; and he took the fire in his hand, and a knife; and they went both of them together.

7 And Isaac spake unto Abraham his father, and said, My father: and he said, Here *am* I, my son. And he said, Behold the fire and the wood: but where *is* the ᵀlamb for a burnt offering?   *goat*

8 And Abraham said, My son, God will provide himself a lamb for a burnt offering: so they went both of them together.

9 And they came to the place which God had told him of; and Abraham built an altar there, and laid the wood in order, and bound Isaac his son, and ᴿlaid him on the altar upon the wood.   [He 11:17-19]

10 And Abraham stretched forth his hand, and took the knife to slay his son.

11 And the angel of the LORD called unto him out of heaven, and said, Abraham, Abraham: and he said, Here *am* I.

12 And he said, ᴿLay not thine hand upon the lad, neither do thou any thing unto him: for now I know that thou fearest God, seeing thou hast not withheld thy son, thine only *son* from me.   1 Sa 15:22

13 And Abraham lifted up his eyes, and looked, and behold behind *him* a ram caught in a thicket by his horns: and Abraham went and took the ram, and offered him up for a burnt offering in the stead of his son.

14 And Abraham called the name of that place ᵀJe-ho'-vah–ji'-reh: as it is said *to* this

---

tism of Jesus (which, of course, also speaks of death and resurrection). In the Gospel of John, on the other hand, where the word "love" occurs more than in any other book of the Bible, its first occurrence is at John 3:16: "God so loved the world" that He, like Abraham, was willing to sacrifice His beloved Son.

22:2 *offer him there.* Note that God did not actually tell Abraham to slay his son, though it was natural that he would so understand it, but to *offer* him (compare Ro 12:1).

22:3 *young men.* The Hebrew word for "young men" is the same as "lad," referring to Isaac, in Genesis 22:5,12. Thus Isaac was not a little boy at this time, and was undoubtedly acquainted with the Canaanite practice of sacrificing their firstborn sons to their gods. He could surely have escaped from his aged father had he not been willing himself to obey God's command.

22:4 *the place.* Moriah was about 30 miles away, and was the place where David would later plan the temple (2 Ch 3:1), and where Christ Himself would one day be offered as the Lamb of God.

22:4 *third day.* The "third day" speaks also of the period of Christ's burial.

22:5 *worship.* The word for "worship" (Hebrew *shachah*) means simply "bow down"— that is, submit to God's will. This is what Christ did, perfectly, on the cross.

22:5 *come again.* Note Abraham's great faith. At a time when no one had ever come back from the dead, Abraham so strongly believed that God would keep His word concerning Isaac that he believed God would raise him from the dead after he had obeyed God in slaying him (He 11:17-19).

22:8 *a lamb.* Though Abraham was fully prepared to slay Isaac, he evidently comprehended the ultimate meaning of the divinely-ordained principle of substitutionary sacrifice practiced ever since God shed the blood of the first sacrificial lamb to provide a covering for Adam and Eve. He knew that, one day, the "Lamb of God" must be offered by God to "take

day, In the mount of the LORD it shall be ᵀseen.   Lit. *The LORD Will Provide* or *See* • *provided*

15 And the angel of the LORD called unto Abraham out of heaven the second time,

16 And said, ᴿBy myself have I sworn, saith the LORD, for because thou hast done this thing, and hast not withheld thy son, thine only *son:*   Ps 105:9

17 That in blessing I will bless thee, and in multiplying I will multiply thy seed as the stars of the heaven, and as the sand which *is* upon the sea shore; and ᴿthy seed shall possess the gate of his enemies; Ge 24:60

18 ᴿAnd in thy seed shall all the nations of the earth be blessed; because thou hast obeyed my voice.   Ge 12:3; 18:18; 26:4

19 So Abraham returned unto his young men, and they rose up and went together to ᴿBe'-er–she'-ba; and Abraham dwelt at Be'-er–she'-ba.   Ge 21:31

20 And it came to pass after these things, that it was told Abraham, saying, Behold, ᴿMil'-cah, she hath also born children unto thy brother Na'-hor;   Ge 11:29; 24:15

21 Huz his firstborn, and Buz his brother, and Kem'-u-el the father of Ar'-am,

22 And Che'-sed, and Ha'-zo, and Pil'-dash, and Jid'-laph, and Be-thu'-el.

23 And ᴿBe-thu'-el begat ᵀRebekah: these eight Mil'-cah did bear to Na'-hor, Abraham's brother.   Ge 24:15 • *Rebecca,* Ro 9:10

24 And his concubine, whose name *was* Reu'-mah, she bare also Te'-bah, and Ga'-ham, and Tha'-hash, and Ma'-a-chah.

CHAPTER 23

The Death of Sarah

And Sarah was an hundred and seven and twenty years old: *these were* the years of the life of Sarah.

2 And Sarah died in ᴿKir'-jath–ar'-ba; the same *is* ᴿHe'-bron in the land of Canaan: and Abraham came to mourn for Sarah, and to weep for her.   Jos 14:15; 15:13; 21:11 • Ge 13:18; 23:19

3 And Abraham stood up from before his dead, and spake unto the sons of ᴿHeth, saying,   Ge 10:15; 15:20

4 ᴿI *am* a stranger and a sojourner with you: ᴿgive me ᵀa possession of a burying-place with you, that I may bury my dead out of my sight.   [Ge 17:8] • Ac 7:5,16 • *property for*

5 And the children of Heth answered Abraham, saying unto him,

6 Hear us, my lord: thou *art* ᴿa mighty prince among us: in the choice of our sepulchres bury thy dead; none of us shall withhold from thee his sepulchre, but that thou mayest bury thy dead.   Ge 13:2; 14:14; 24:35

7 And Abraham stood up, and bowed himself to the people of the land, *even* to the children of Heth.

8 And he ᵀcommuned with them, saying, If it be your mind that I should bury my dead out of my sight; hear me, and intreat for me to E'-phron the son of Zo'-har,   *spoke*

9 That he may give me the cave of ᴿMach-pe'-lah, which he hath, which *is* in the end of his field; for as much money as it is worth he shall give it me for a possession of a buryingplace amongst you.   Ge 25:9

10 And E'-phron dwelt among the children of Heth: and E'-phron the Hit'-tite answered Abraham in the audience of the children of Heth, *even* of all that ᴿwent in at the gate of his city, saying,   Ge 23:18; 34:20,24

11 ᴿNay, my lord, hear me: the field give I thee, and the cave that *is* therein, I give it thee; in the presence of the sons of my people give I it thee: bury thy dead.   2 Sa 24:21-24

12 And Abraham bowed down himself before the people of the land.

---

away the sin of the world" (Jo 1:29) and thus to make possible the fulfillment of all His eternal promises.

22:15 *the angel of the LORD.* It is certain that this angel is actually the Lord Himself—that is, Christ in a pre-incarnate theophany—because of His ability to personally promise the blessings in Genesis 22:16-18. Also note Genesis 22:11-12.

22:17 *as the sand.* Here the number of stars (of which only about 3,000 can be seen with the naked eye) is compared to the number of sand grains. Both can now be calculated as of the order of 10^{25}, a remarkable anticipation of modern science.

22:17 *thy seed.* In Genesis 22:17-18, three times God used the word "seed" in the singular, instead of "seeds" in the plural. Paul claimed that this verse is a prophecy of Christ (Ga 3:16), instead of a prophecy of all the children of Abraham. This argument is predicated on

13 And he spake unto E'-phron in the audience of the people of the land, saying, But if thou *wilt give it*, I pray thee, hear me: I will give thee money for the field; take *it* of me, and I will bury my dead there.

14 And E'-phron answered Abraham, saying unto him,

15 My lord, hearken unto me: the land *is worth* four hundred ᴿshek'-els of silver; what *is* that ᵀbetwixt me and thee? bury therefore thy dead.   Ex 30:13 • *between*

16 And Abraham hearkened unto E'-phron; and Abraham ᴿweighed to E'-phron the silver, which he had named in the ᵀaudience of the sons of Heth, four hundred shek'-els of silver, current *money* with the merchant.   Je 32:9,10 • *hearing*

17 And ᴿthe field of E'-phron, which *was* in Mach-pe'-lah, which *was* before Mam'-re, the field, and the cave which *was* therein, and all the trees that *were* in the field, that *were* in all the borders round about, were ᵀmade sure   Ge 25:9; 49:29-32; 50:13 • *deeded*

18 Unto Abraham for a possession in the presence of the children of Heth, before all that went in at the gate of his city.

19 And after this, Abraham buried Sarah his wife in the cave of the field of Mach-pe'-lah before Mam'-re: the same *is* He'-bron in the land of Canaan.

20 And the field, and the cave that *is* therein, ᴿwere ᵀmade sure unto Abraham for a possession of a buryingplace by the sons of Heth.   Je 32:10,11 • *deeded to*

CHAPTER 24

Isaac Takes a Wife

And Abraham ᴿwas old, *and* well stricken in age: and the Lᴏʀᴅ ᴿhad blessed Abraham in all things. Ge 18:11; 21:5 • Ge 12:2; 13:2; 24:35

2 And Abraham said ᴿunto his eldest servant of his house, that ᴿruled over all that he had, ᴿPut, I pray thee, thy hand under my thigh: Ge 15:2 • Ge 24:10; 39:4-6 • Ge 47:29

3 And I will make thee ᴿswear by the Lᴏʀᴅ, the God of heaven, and the God of the earth, that thou shalt not take a wife

---

the truth of verbal inspiration, which even makes a fine distinction between singular and plural.

23:15 *shekels of silver*. At this time, the shekel was not a coin as such, but rather a specified weight, probably about two-fifths of an ounce.

23:17 *Machpelah*. There is a seeming discrepancy between this passage and the statement of Stephen (Ac 7:16) that Abraham's purchased sepulcher was in Shechem. A possible explanation is that he bought the latter for his later family born of Keturah (23:1; 25:1). These children then eventually lost it to the Hivites, from whom Jacob repurchased it for an altar 85 years after Abraham's death (33:20). It was later given to Joseph, and he and probably his brothers were eventually buried in it (Jos 24:32; Ac 7:15-16).

23:19 *Sarah his wife*. Sarah is the only woman in the Bible whose age at death is given (23:1). Isaac was 37 when she died. As Abraham is called the father of all believers, so Sarah is considered mother of all believing women (1 Pe 3:5-6), and she died in faith (He 11:13).

23:20 *a possession*. Although God had promised Abraham a vast nation, the only land he ever owned in Canaan was this burial ground. Later, he, as well as Isaac and Jacob, Leah and Rebekah, would also be buried here (25:9; 35:27,29; 49:30-31; 50:13). Today there is a Muslim mosque over the alleged site of this cave.

23:20 *sons of Heth*. This entire transaction has been illuminated by archaeology, and there is little doubt that it reflects accurately the customs of that period (around 1900 B.C.), especially among the Hittites, an early colony of which had settled in Canaan by then. Ephron, from whom Abraham purchased the cave, was a Hittite (23:10), and the Hittites (known on the monuments as Hatti) were "sons of Heth," who was a son of Canaan (10:15). The great Hittite Empire was centered in what is now Turkey, but had colonies in various places. This covenant between Abraham and Ephron contains a number of words and concepts now known to be typical of Hittite documents.

unto my son of the daughters of the Ca'-naan-ites, among whom I dwell: Ge 14:19,22

4 ᴿBut thou shalt go ᴿunto my country, and to my kindred, and take a wife unto my son Isaac.   Ge 28:2 • Ge 12:1

5 And the servant said unto him, ᵀPeradventure the woman will not be willing to follow me unto this land: must I ᵀneeds bring thy son again unto the land from whence thou camest?   *Perhaps • take*

6 And Abraham said unto him, Beware thou that thou ᵀbring not my son thither again.   *take*

7 The Lᴏʀᴅ God of heaven, which ᴿtook me from my father's house, and from the land of my kindred, and which spake unto me, and that sware unto me, saying, Unto thy seed will I give this land; he shall send his angel before thee, and thou shalt take a wife unto my son from thence.   Ge 12:1; 24:3

8 And if the woman will not be willing to follow thee, then ᴿthou shalt be clear from this my oath: only ᵀbring not my son thither again.   Jos 2:17-20 • *take*

9 And the servant put his hand under the thigh of Abraham his master, and sware to him concerning that matter.

10 And the servant took ten camels of the camels of his master, and departed; ᴿfor all the goods of his master *were* in his hand: and he arose, and went to Mes-o-po-ta'-mi-a, unto the city of Na'-hor.   Ge 24:2,22

11 And he made his camels to kneel down without the city by a well of water at the time of the evening, *even* the time ᴿthat women go out to draw *water*.   Ex 2:16

12 And he ᴿsaid, O Lᴏʀᴅ God of my master Abraham, I pray thee, ᴿsendᵀ me good speed this day, and shew kindness unto my master Abraham.   Ex 3:6,15 • Ne 1:11 • *give me success*

13 Behold, ᴿI stand *here* by the well of water; and ᴿthe daughters of the men of the city come out to draw water: Ge 24:43 • Ex 2:16

14 And let it come to pass, that the damsel to whom I shall say, Let down thy pitcher, I pray thee, that I may drink; and she shall say, Drink, and I will give thy camels drink also: *let the same be* she *that* thou hast appointed for thy servant Isaac; and ᴿthereby shall I know that thou hast shewed kindness unto my master.   Ju 6:17,37

15 And it came to pass, before he had done speaking, that, behold, Rebekah came out, who was born to Be-thu'-el, son of Mil'-cah, the wife of Na'-hor, Abraham's brother, with her pitcher upon her shoulder.

16 And the damsel *was* very ᵀfair to look upon, a virgin, neither had any man known her: and she went down to the well, and filled her pitcher, and came up.   *beautiful*

17 And the servant ran to meet her, and said, Let me, I pray thee, drink a little water of thy pitcher.

18 ᴿAnd she said, Drink, my lord: and she hasted, and let down her pitcher upon her hand, and gave him drink.   [1 Pe 3:8,9]

24:4 *my country*. Abraham had learned the hard way that the heir of the promises should not leave the promised land. Nevertheless, a suitable wife through whom the promised seed could be born and trained could not be found among the people then in the land. Consequently, the father must send a trusted servant to find a suitable bride for his son, far away and among a small remnant who still served the true God. A typological parallel with the Heavenly Father sending the Holy Spirit to claim a bride for His Son seems well warranted in this case (note Jo 14:26; 16:13-14; Ac 15:14; 2 Co 11:2).

24:7 *his angel*. Angels perform many services on behalf of God's people (He 1:14). This passage indicates that one such service is guiding the steps of the believer and preparing the way before him in answer to prayer.

24:9 *under the thigh*. This is a euphemistic reference to the genital organ, in symbolic reference (like that of circumcision) to the vital importance of maintaining the purity and integrity of the seed in whom God's purposes were to be accomplished.

24:12 *I pray thee*. This prayer is a model prayer for determining God's leading. It involved requesting a specific evidence which would be, in itself, beautifully consistent with the purpose of the guidance being sought (a suitable young woman who was both strong enough and considerate enough to volunteer to provide water for 10 thirsty camels) and yet would require a combination of characteristics bound to be rare under the circumstances. Although not mentioned specifically, his prayers presupposed that she would be a godly virgin and from Abraham's people.

19 And when she had done giving him drink, she said, I will draw *water* for thy camels also, until they have done drinking.

20 And she hasted, and emptied her pitcher into the trough, and ran again unto the well to draw *water,* and drew for all his camels.

21 And the man wondering at her held his peace, to wit whether the LORD had made his journey prosperous or not.

22 And it came to pass, as the camels had done drinking, that the man took a golden ᴿearring^T of half a shek′-el weight, and two bracelets for her hands of ten *shek′-els* weight of gold; Ex 32:2,3 • *nose ring*

23 And said, Whose daughter *art* thou? tell me, I pray thee: is there room *in* thy father′s house for us to lodge in?

24 And she said unto him, ᴿI *am* the daughter of Be-thu′-el the son of Mil′-cah, which she bare unto Na′-hor. Ge 22:23; 24:15

25 She said moreover unto him, We have both straw and ᵀprovender enough, and room to lodge in. *food*

26 And the man ᴿbowed down his head, and worshipped the LORD. Ex 4:31

27 And he said, ᴿBlessed *be* the LORD God of my master Abraham, who hath not left destitute my master of his ᵀmercy and his truth: I *being* in the way, the LORD led me to the house of my master′s brethren. Ex 18:10

28 And the damsel ran, and told *them of* her mother′s house these things.

29 And Rebekah had a brother, and his name *was* ᴿLaban: and Laban ran out unto the man, unto the well. Ge 29:5,13

30 And it came to pass, when he saw the earring and bracelets upon his sister′s hands, and when he heard the words of Rebekah his sister, saying, Thus spake the man unto me; that he came unto the man; and, behold, he stood by the camels at the well.

31 And he said, Come in, ᴿthou blessed of the LORD; wherefore standest thou ᵀwithout? for I have prepared the house, and ᵀroom for the camels. Ju 17:2 • *outside* • *a place*

32 And the man came into the house: and he ᵀungirded his camels, and ᴿgave straw and provender for the camels, and water to ᴿwash his feet, and the men′s feet that *were* with him. Ge 43:24 • Ge 19:2 • *unloaded*

33 And there was set *meat* before him to eat: but he said, I will not eat, until I have told mine errand. And he said, Speak on.

34 And he said, I *am* Abraham′s servant.

35 And the LORD ᴿhath blessed my master greatly; and he is become great: and he hath given him flocks, and herds, and silver, and gold, and menservants, and maidservants, and camels, and asses. Ge 13:2; 24:1

36 And Sarah my master′s wife bare a son to my master when she was old: and unto him hath he given all that he hath.

37 And my master ᴿmade me swear, saying, Thou shalt not take a wife to my son of the daughters of the Ca′-naan-ites, in whose land I dwell: Ge 24:2-4

38 ᴿBut thou shalt go unto my father′s house, and to my kindred, and take a wife unto my son. Ge 24:4

39 And I said unto my master, Peradventure the woman will not follow me.

40 ᴿAnd he said unto me, The LORD, ᴿbefore whom I walk, will send his angel with thee, and prosper thy way; and thou shalt take a wife for my son of my kindred, and of my father′s house: Ge 24:7 • Ge 5:22,24; 17:1

41 ᴿThen shalt thou be clear from *this* my oath, when thou comest to my kindred; and if they give not thee *one,* thou shalt be clear from my oath. Ge 24:8

42 And I came this day unto the well, and said, ᴿO LORD God of my master Abraham, if now thou do prosper my way which I go: Ge 24:12

43 ᴿBehold, I stand by the well of water; and it shall come to pass, that when the virgin cometh forth to draw *water,* and I say to her, Give me, I pray thee, a little water of thy pitcher to drink; Ge 24:13

44 And she say to me, Both drink thou, and I will also draw for thy camels: *let* the same *be* the woman whom the LORD hath appointed out for my master′s son.

24:22 *golden earring.* Large golden earrings and intricate golden necklaces and bracelets have been found at Ur, dating well before Abraham′s time. Ancient craftsmen were highly skilled artisans.

24:36 *all that he hath.* The servant′s recitation of Isaac′s soon-to-be-inherited wealth (24:35) no doubt appealed to Laban′s cupidity, which was later so clearly manifested in his dealings with Isaac′s son (ch. 29–31).

45 ᴿAnd before I had ᵀdone ᴿspeaking in mine heart, behold, Rebekah came forth with her pitcher on her shoulder; and she went down unto the well, and drew *water*: and I said unto her, Let me drink, I pray thee.   Ge 24:15 • 1 Sa 1:13 • *finished*

46 And she made haste, and let down her pitcher from her *shoulder*, and said, Drink, and I will give thy camels drink also: so I drank, and she made the camels drink also.

47 And I asked her, and said, Whose daughter *art* thou? And she said, The daughter of Be-thu'-el, Na'-hor's son, whom Mil'-cah bare unto him: and I put the ᵀearring upon her face, and the bracelets upon her hands.   *nose ring on her nose*

48 ᴿAnd I bowed down my head, and worshipped the Lᴏʀᴅ, and blessed the Lᴏʀᴅ God of my master Abraham, which had led me in the right way to take my master's brother's daughter unto his son.   Ge 24:26,52

49 And now if ye will ᴿdeal kindly and truly with my master, tell me: and if not, tell me; that I may turn to the right hand, or to the left.   Jos 2:14

50 Then Laban and Be-thu'-el answered and said, ᴿThe thing proceedeth from the Lᴏʀᴅ: we cannot ᴿspeak unto thee bad or good.   Ps 118:23 • Ge 31:24,29

51 Behold, Rebekah ᴿ*is* before thee, take *her*, and go, and let her be thy master's son's wife, as the Lᴏʀᴅ hath spoken.   Ge 20:15

52 And it came to pass, that, when Abraham's servant heard their words, ᴿhe worshipped the Lᴏʀᴅ, *bowing himself* to the earth.   Ge 24:26,48

53 And the servant brought forth ᴿjewelsᵀ of silver, and jewels of gold, and ᵀraiment, and gave *them* to Rebekah: he gave also to her brother and to her mother ᴿprecious things.   Ex 3:22; 11:2; 12:35 • 2 Ch 21:3 • *jewelry* • *clothing*

54 And they did eat and drink, he and the men that *were* with him, and tarried all night; and they rose up in the morning, and he said, Send me away unto my master.

55 And her brother and her mother said, Let the damsel ᵀabide with us *a few* days, at the least ten; after that she shall go.   *stay*

56 And he said unto them, ᵀHinder me not, seeing the Lᴏʀᴅ hath prospered my way; send me away that I may go to my master.   *delay*

57 And they said, We will call the damsel, and ᵀenquire at her mouth.   *ask her personally*

58 And they called Rebekah, and said unto her, Wilt thou go with this man? And she said, I will go.

59 And they sent away Rebekah their sister, ᴿand her nurse, and Abraham's servant, and his men.   Ge 35:8

60 And they blessed Rebekah, and said unto her, Thou *art* our sister, be thou ᴿ*the mother* of thousands of ᵀmillions, and ᴿlet thy seed possess the gate of those which hate them.   Ge 17:16 • Ge 22:17; 28:14 • *ten thousands*

61 And Rebekah arose, and her damsels, and they rode upon the camels, and followed the man: and the servant took Rebekah, and went his way.

62 And Isaac came from the way of the ᴿwell La-hai'–roi; for he dwelt in the south country.   Ge 16:14; 25:11

63 And Isaac went out ᴿto meditate in the field at the eventide: and he lifted up his eyes, and saw, and, behold, the camels *were* coming.   Jos 1:8

64 And Rebekah lifted up her eyes, and when she saw Isaac, ᴿshe ᵀlighted off the camel.   Jos 15:18 • *dismounted from*

65 For she *had* said unto the servant, What man *is* this that walketh in the field to meet us? And the servant *had* said, It *is* my master: therefore she took a vail, and covered herself.

24:56 Hinder me not. This response might seem at first to indicate an unfeeling attitude on the part of the servant. However, once the Lᴏʀᴅ's will is clearly revealed, as it had been here, any delay is dangerous, providing opportunity for second thoughts and even satanic diversions.

24:58 Wilt thou go. According to the customs of the times, as indicated in the Nuzi tablets, the father had the obligation to find a wife for his sons, as Abraham had done for Isaac, and also to approve an offer of marriage made for his daughter. If the father was dead or incapacitated, however, the eldest son and heir was supposed to approve any marriage offer for his sister. In this case, however, the sister also had the right to accept or reject the offer, as Laban and Rebekah did.

66 And the servant told Isaac all things that he had done.

67 And Isaac brought her into his mother Sarah's tent, and took Rebekah, and she became his wife; and he loved her: and Isaac was comforted after his mother's *death*.

CHAPTER 25
The Death of Abraham 1 Ch 1:28-33

Then again Abraham took a wife, and her name *was* RKe-tu'-rah.   1 Ch 1:32,33

2 And Rshe bare him Zim'-ran, and Jok'-shan, and Me'-dan, and Mid'-i-an, and Ish'-bak, and Shu'-ah.   1 Ch 1:32,33

3 And Jok'-shan begat She'-ba, and De'-dan. And the sons of De'-dan were As-shu'-rim, and Le-tu'-shim, and Le-um'-mim.

4 And the sons of Mid'-i-an; E'-phah, and E'-pher, and Ha'-noch, and A-bi'-dah, and El-da'-ah. All these *were* the children of Ke-tu'-rah.

5 And RAbraham gave all that he had unto Isaac.   Ge 24:35,36

6 But unto the sons of the concubines, which Abraham had, Abraham gave gifts, and Rsent them away from Isaac his son, while he yet lived, eastward, unto Rthe east country.   Ge 21:14 • Ju 6:3

7 And these *are* the days of the years of Abraham's life which he lived, an hundred threescore and fifteen years.

8 Then Abraham gave up the ghost, and Rdied in a good old age, an old man, and

---

24:67 *he loved her.* Although the New Testament does not specifically say that Isaac and Rebekah constitute a "type" of Christ and His church, the numerous parallels are more than coincidental, and do follow naturally from the clear identification of Isaac himself as a type of Christ (note Ga 3:16; He 11:17-19). In the symbolic parallel, the servant sent by Abraham to seek a bride for his son becomes the Holy Spirit, sent by the Heavenly Father to find and bring the heavenly bride, the church, to His Son (Jo 14:26; 16:13-14; Ac 15:14). After she accepts the invitation, the Spirit, like Abraham's servant, guides the bride through the wilderness to join the Bridegroom when He comes out to meet her at the end of the journey. There are numerous detailed parallels one can discern as the passage is studied in depth.

25:1 *Keturah.* The home and background of Keturah are unknown. Like Hagar, she is called a concubine (25:6; 1 Ch 1:32) to emphasize that her sons were not to inherit the promises centered in Isaac. However, God had also promised (17:4) that Abraham would be a father of many nations. When his body was miraculously rejuvenated at age 100 to father Isaac, he remained "young" for many more years, eventually begetting six more sons of the younger Keturah.

25:2 *Midian.* Of Keturah's six sons (all probably born early in Abraham's 35-year period with her), Midian is the only one whose descendants, the Midianites, are adequately identified. The others probably mixed with the various descendants of Ishmael, Lot and Esau to become the modern Arabic peoples. Abraham sent them "eastward" (25:6) with adequate gifts to begin their own tribes, and this would correspond to Arabia.

25:3 *Sheba and Dedan.* These two grandsons of Abraham by Keturah seem to have been named after two grandsons of Cush (10:7), although Shem also had a great-grandson named Sheba (10:22,24-25,28). One of these, probably the Cushite, evidently became the ancestor of the Sabaeans, and the Queen of Sheba (1 Ki 10:1; Job 1:15). The Sabaeans have been well identified on the monuments as a kingdom in southwest Arabia, near modern Yemen.

25:8 *good old age.* Abraham died at 175 years of age (25:7), which, by this time, was considered a very great age, even though his father Terah had lived to 205. Human longevity had greatly declined since the flood but was still significantly greater than in the modern world.

25:8 *to his people.* Since none of his people had been buried in this location, this phrase clearly indicates the belief that "his people" were still alive somewhere. This place of departed spirits was later, in fact, called "Abraham's bosom" (Lk 16:22).

full *of years;* and ᴿwas gathered to his people. Ge 15:15; 47:8,9 • Ge 25:17; 35:29; 49:29,33

9 And his sons Isaac and Ish'-ma-el buried him in the cave of Mach-pe'-lah, in the field of E'-phron the son of Zo'-har the Hit'-tite, which *is* before Mam'-re;

10 ᴿThe field which Abraham purchased of the sons of Heth: ᴿthere was Abraham buried, and Sarah his wife. Ge 23:3-16 • Ge 49:31

11 And it came to pass after the death of Abraham, that God blessed his son Isaac; and Isaac dwelt by the ᴿwell La-hai'–roi. Ge 16:14

12 Now ᵀthese *are* the ᴿgenerations of Ish'-ma-el, Abraham's son, whom Ha'-gar the Egyptian, Sarah's handmaid, bare unto Abraham: Ge 11:10,27; 16:15 • *this is the genealogy*

13 And ᴿthese *are* the names of the sons of Ish'-ma-el, by their names, according to their generations: the firstborn of Ish'-ma-el, Ne-ba'-joth; and Ke'-dar, and Ad'-be-el, and Mib'-sam, 1 Ch 1:29-31

14 And Mish'-ma, and Du'-mah, and Mas'-sa,

15 ᵀHa'-dar, and Te'-ma, Je'-tur, Na'-phish, and Ked'-e-mah: MT *Hadad*

16 These *are* the sons of Ish'-ma-el, and these *are* their names, by their towns, and by their ᵀcastles; ᴿtwelve princes according to their nations. Ge 17:20 • *settlements* or *camps*

17 And these *are* the years of the life of Ish'-ma-el, an hundred and thirty and seven years: and he gave up the ghost and died; and was gathered unto his people.

18 ᴿAnd they dwelt from Hav'-i-lah unto Shur, that *is* before Egypt, as thou goest toward Assyria: *and* he ᵀdied ᴿin the presence of all his brethren. 1 Sa 15:7 • Ge 16:12 • Lit. *fell*

The Generations of Isaac

19 And these *are* the generations of Isaac, Abraham's son: Abraham begat Isaac:

20 And Isaac was forty years old when he took Rebekah to wife, ᴿthe daughter of Be-thu'-el the Syrian of Pa'-dan–a'-ram, the sister to Laban the Syrian. Ge 22:23; 24:15,29,67

21 And Isaac ᵀintreated the Lᴏʀᴅ for his wife, because she *was* barren: ᴿand the Lᴏʀᴅ was intreated of him, and ᴿRebekah his wife conceived. 1 Ch 5:2 • Ro 9:10-13 • *pleaded with*

22 And the children struggled together within her; and she said, If *it be* ᵀso, why *am* I thus? ᴿAnd she went to enquire of the Lᴏʀᴅ. 1 Sa 1:15; 9:9; 10:22 • *well*

23 And the Lᴏʀᴅ said unto her, ᴿTwo nations *are* in thy womb, and two manner of

---

25:9 *Isaac and Ishmael.* Isaac and Ishmael were thus reconciled by this time. Perhaps it was their father's death which reunited them.

25:12 *generations of Ishmael.* Genesis 25:12-16 seem to represent the *toledoth* of Ishmael, quite possibly a record kept by Ishmael which he gave to Isaac at the time of their reunion at Abraham's funeral. At this time, Ishmael would have been 90 years old, with his 12 sons each now established in small "nations" of their own, as "princes" of those tribes. After Ishmael's death, Isaac then added his own comments concerning them (25:17-18), before terminating his own *toledoth* with his signature at Genesis 25:19. Ishmael died 58 years before Isaac died; and, like Abraham, was "gathered unto his people" (25:17), indicating that he died in faith. Ishmael's "nations," though not all clearly identified historically, undoubtedly dwelt mainly in northern Arabia.

25:19 *generations of Isaac.* Genesis 25:19a terminates the long record kept by Isaac, which apparently began at Genesis 11:27 where Terah's record left off. Much of the narrative of Genesis 12–22, of course, would have been told to Isaac by his father Abraham. At this point (25:19b), it seems that Jacob took over the task, finally terminating his *toledoth* at Genesis 37:2.

25:20 *Syrian.* In Hebrew, "Syria" is *Aram,* from which came the Aramaic language. Aram was a son of Shem, thus related to Isaac.

25:22 *struggled together within her.* Babies have real feelings, thoughts, and personalities even before birth. This is clear biblically (Ps 139:14-16; Ec 11:5; Lk 1:44), and is being increasingly confirmed by modern scientific monitoring of embryonic children growing in the womb.

25:23 *serve the younger.* This prenatal revelation to Rebekah clearly instructed her that, contrary to custom, the youngest of her twin sons was to be spiritual leader of the

people shall be separated from thy bowels; and ^R the one people shall be stronger than *the other* people; and ^R the elder shall serve the younger. Ge 17:4-6,16; 24:60 • 2 Sa 8:14 • Ro 9:12

24 And when her days to be delivered were fulfilled, behold, *there were* twins in her womb.

25 And the first came out red, ^R all over like an hairy garment; and they called his name ^T Esau. Ge 27:11,16,23 • Lit. *Hairy*

26 And after that came his brother out, and his hand took hold on Esau's heel; and his name was called Jacob: and Isaac *was* threescore years old when she bare them.

27 And the boys grew: and Esau was a cunning hunter, a man of the field; and Jacob *was* a plain man, dwelling in tents.

28 And Isaac loved Esau, because he did ^R eat of *his* venison: ^R but Rebekah loved Jacob. Ge 27:4,19,25,31 • Ge 27:6-10

29 And Jacob sod pottage: and Esau came from the field, and he *was* faint:

30 And Esau said to Jacob, Feed me, I pray thee, with that same red *pottage*; for I *am* faint: therefore was his name called ^T E'-dom. Lit. *Red*

31 And Jacob said, Sell me this day thy birthright.

32 And Esau said, Behold, I *am* at the point to die: and ^R what profit shall this birthright do to me? Mk 8:36,37

---

family. His task was to transmit the divine promises to future generations. This information surely was shared with Isaac and, later, with Esau and Jacob. Yet both Isaac and Esau seem to have rejected this revelation and determined to convey these privileges to Esau.

25:25 *Esau*. The newborn infants were given names corresponding to their remarkable appearance at birth, Esau meaning "hairy" and Jacob "heel-catcher" (perhaps, by extension—"supplanter").

25:26 *Esau's heel*. The prophet Hosea interprets Jacob's odd name as an evidence of his strength and power with God (Ho 12:3), overtaking his older and more outwardly impressive brother because of his strength before God.

25:27 *cunning hunter*. The only hunters mentioned in the Bible are Nimrod (10:9) and Esau, and both were rebels against the will and revelation of God. Although God permits the eating of meat, the hunting of animals for sport is questionable at best. God cares even when a sparrow dies (Ma 10:29). The family did not need game for meat, since Isaac had great flocks and herds; neither did they need protection from wild animals, as Esau had to be a "cunning" hunter to find any to slay. He was simply a carnal, profane, licentious playboy (He 12:16).

25:27 *plain man*. The word "plain" (Hebrew *tam*) actually means "perfect" (as used in Job 1:1,8; 2:3) or mature. Jacob worked at home, while Esau played in the fields. Jacob took God's promises reverently and seriously; Esau "despised his birthright" (25:34).

25:28 *Isaac loved Esau*. In spite of God's commandment (25:23) and Jacob's merits (25:27), Isaac showed strong partiality to Esau, and for the most carnal of reasons. He loved the venison Esau would bring home from his hunt. But God said: "Jacob have I loved" (Mal 1:1-3; Ro 9:10-13).

25:29 *sod pottage*. That is, "boiled stew" or "soup."

25:31 *birthright*. The birthright customarily involved a double portion of the inheritance (De 21:17), but this privilege also involved the spiritual leadership of the family. Esau desired the first but not the second. In any case, the father was responsible to transfer the birthright to a more deserving son if necessary (1 Ch 5:1-2), and Isaac should have long since made it clear that it was to go to Jacob. The latter, appalled at the thought of a carnal profligate like Esau having the spiritual responsibilities of the birthright, offered to purchase it from him, perhaps initially in jest. However, Esau agreed to the absurd bargain, thus making it still clearer that he was unqualified.

25:32 *at the point to die*. It would have taken Esau only a few minutes to fix himself something to eat. He probably meant, however, that he would die some day, and the

33 And Jacob said, Swear to me this day; and he sware unto him: and ᴿhe sold his birthright unto Jacob.　　　　He 12:16

34 Then Jacob gave Esau bread and ᵀpottage of lentiles; and ᴿhe did eat and drink, and rose up, and went his way: thus Esau ᴿdespised *his* birthright. Ec 8:15 • He 12:16,17 • *stew*

CHAPTER 26

Strife with the People of Gerar

And there was a famine in the land, beside ᴿthe first famine that was in the days of Abraham. And Isaac went unto ᴿA-bim'-e-lech king of the Phi-lis'-tines unto Ge'-rar.　　　　Ge 12:10 • Ge 20:1,2

2 And the LORD appeared unto him, and said, Go not down into Egypt; dwell in ᴿthe land which I shall tell thee of:　　Ge 12:1

3 Sojourn in this land, and I will be with thee, and will bless thee; for unto thee, and unto thy seed, I will give all these countries, and I will perform the oath which I sware unto Abraham thy father;

4 And I will make thy seed to multiply as the stars of heaven, and will give unto thy seed all these countries; and in thy seed shall all the nations of the earth be blessed;

5 ᴿBecause that Abraham obeyed my voice, and kept my charge, my commandments, my statutes, and my laws.　Ge 22:16,18

6 And Isaac dwelt in Ge'-rar:

7 And the men of the place asked *him* of his wife; and he said, She *is* my sister: for he feared to say, *She is* my wife; lest, *said he*, the men of the place should kill me for Rebekah; because she *was* fair to look upon.

8 And it came to pass, when he had been there a long time, that A-bim'-e-lech king of the Phi-lis'-tines looked out at a window, and saw, and, behold, Isaac *was* ᵀsporting with Rebekah his wife.　　*caressing*

9 And A-bim'-e-lech called Isaac, and said, Behold, ᵀof a surety she *is* thy wife: and

---

birthright would be worthless to him then. He knew that Isaac might well (indeed should) decide eventually to give it to Jacob. This way, he would at least get a good meal out of it! Esau, literally, "despised his birthright" (25:34). The amazing thing is that most modern Christians, like Isaac, tend to "love Esau," and regard Jacob as the culprit in this transaction. Jacob, of course, should have simply trusted God to work things out according to His will and promise, rather than trying to devise his own means for getting this accomplished. Jacob's sin, however, was that of insufficient faith and patience.

25:33 *sold his birthright.* Legal tablets found at Nuzi in Syria stipulate that an heir could sell any or all of his inheritance to a brother.

26:2 *the LORD appeared.* This is apparently the first time in over 50 years that God had appeared to Isaac; here He confirmed the covenant made with Abraham and Isaac on Mount Moriah. It was also the first famine in the land of promise since Abram had gone down to Egypt over a century earlier. Isaac, unused to such testings, now needed special assurance.

26:5 *my laws.* Long before Moses, there were divine commandments and laws, and Abraham obeyed them. Certain law codes found among the Babylonians, the Hittites and others also pre-date Moses and agree in many respects with the Mosaic laws, perhaps reflecting a primeval system given by God (possibly only verbally) that disappeared after Babel except for those, like Abraham, who retained and obeyed the truth. Note also the same implication in Job 23:12.

26:7 *my sister.* Critics allege that this is merely another version of the story of Abraham's experience in Gerar (20:1-8). This is not possible; the scribal "redactors" whom these same critics think brought the different components of Genesis together would have been far too shrewd to deliberately create such an obvious barrier to its acceptance by their readers. The event must have taken place as described. Isaac and Rebekah repeated the same fabrication that Abraham and Sarah had attempted over a century earlier, for essentially the same reasons, and with essentially the same results—human rebuke for their deception, but God's protection in spite of this.

26:9 *she is thy wife.* The Nuzi tablets, from northern Mesopotamia and describing life and customs in the patriarchal age, indicate that it was possible for a man to adopt a

how saidst thou, She *is* my sister? And Isaac said unto him, Because I said, Lest I die ᵀfor her. *obviously • on account of*

10 And A-bim'-e-lech said, What *is* this thou hast done unto us? one of the people might ᵀlightly have lien with thy wife, and ᴿthou shouldest have brought guiltiness upon us. Ge 20:9 • *soon*

11 And A-bim'-e-lech charged all *his* people, saying, He that ᴿtoucheth this man or his wife shall surely be put to death. Ps 105:15

12 Then Isaac sowed in that land, and received in the same year ᴿan hundredfold: and the LORD blessed him. Ma 13:8,23

13 And the man ᴿwaxedᵀ great, and ᵀwent forward, and grew until he became very great: [Pr 10:22] • *grew* • *continued prospering until*

14 For he had possession of flocks, and possession of herds, and great store of servants: and the Phi-lis'-tines envied him.

15 For all the wells ᴿwhich his father's servants had digged in the days of Abraham his father, the Phi-lis'-tines had stopped them, and filled them with earth. Ge 21:25,30

16 And A-bim'-e-lech said unto Isaac, Go from us; for ᴿthou art much mightier than we. Ex 1:9

17 And Isaac departed thence, and ᵀpitched his tent in the valley of Ge'-rar, and dwelt there. *camped*

18 And Isaac digged again the wells of water, which they had digged in the days of Abraham his father; for the Phi-lis'-tines had stopped them after the death of Abraham: ᴿand he called their names after the names by which his father had called them. Ge 21:31

19 And Isaac's servants digged in the valley, and found there a well of ᵀspringing water. *running*

20 And the herdmen of Ge'-rar did strive with Isaac's herdmen, saying, The water *is* ours: and he called the name of the well E'-sek; because they strove with him.

21 And they digged another well, and strove for that also: and he called the name of it ᵀSit'-nah. Lit. *Enmity*

22 And he ᵀremoved from thence, and digged another well; and for that they strove not: and he called the name of it ᵀRe-ho'-both; and he said, For now the LORD hath made room for us, and we shall ᴿbe fruitful in the land. Ge 17:6; 28:3; 41:52 • *moved* • Lit. *Spaciousness*

23 And he went up from thence to Be'-er–she'-ba.

24 And the LORD ᴿappeared unto him the same night, and said, I *am* the God of Abraham thy father: fear not, for I *am* with thee, and will bless thee, and multiply thy seed for my servant Abraham's sake. Ge 26:2

25 And he ᴿbuilded an altar there, and called upon the name of the LORD, and pitched his tent there: and there Isaac's servants digged a well. Ge 12:7,8; 13:4,18; 22:9; 33:20

26 Then A-bim'-e-lech went to him from Ge'-rar, and A-huz'-zath one of his friends, and Phi'-chol the chief captain of his army.

27 And Isaac said unto them, Wherefore come ye to me, ᴿseeing ye hate me, and have ᴿsent me away from you? Ju 11:7 • Ge 26:16

28 And they said, We saw certainly that the LORD ᴿwas with thee: and we said, Let there be now an oath betwixt us, *even* betwixt us and thee, and let us make a ᵀcovenant with thee; Ge 21:22,23 • *treaty*

29 That thou wilt do us no ᵀhurt, as we have not touched thee, and as we have done unto thee nothing but good, and have sent thee away in peace: ᴿthou *art* now the blessed of the LORD. Ge 24:31 • *harm*

---

woman as his sister, then later also take her as his wife. It is thus at least possible that Rebekah was both wife and sister to Isaac—the same for Abraham and Sarah.

26:12 hundredfold. This is the first mention of seed-sowing in the Bible. Throughout the Bible, seed-sowing is commonly symbolic of Christian witnessing, and this aspect is paramount in the first mention of seed-sowing in the New Testament (Ma 13:23). In both cases, it is providentially significant that the good seed brought forth a hundredfold.

26:25 builded an altar. According to records, this is the only altar built by Isaac. God appeared to him again after he was back at Beer-sheba ("well of the covenant"), where he had lived in his closest fellowship with God. The well had belonged to Abraham, and it was accepted as such by the Philistines (still a relatively small body of settlers that had come from their own homeland in Crete), so Isaac knew that he was now justified in staying there. The

30 ᴿAnd he made them a feast, and they did eat and drink.   Ge 19:3

31 And they rose up ᵀbetimes in the morning, and ᴿsware one to another: and Isaac sent them away, and they departed from him in peace.   Ge 21:31 • early

32 And it came to pass the same day, that Isaac's servants came, and told him concerning the well which they had digged, and said unto him, We have found water.

33 And he called it ᵀShe'-bah: ᴿtherefore the name of the city is Be'-er–she'-ba unto this day.   Ge 21:31; 28:10 • Lit. Oath or Seven

Esau Grieves His Parents

34 ᴿAnd Esau was forty years old when he took to wife Judith the daughter of Be-e'-ri the Hit'-tite, and Bash'-e-math the daughter of E'-lon the Hit'-tite: Ge 28:8; 36:2

35 Which ᴿwere a grief of mind unto Isaac and to Rebekah.   Ge 27:46; 28:1,8

CHAPTER 27

Jacob Takes Esau's Blessing

And it came to pass, that when Isaac was ᴿold, and ᴿhis eyes were dim, so that he could not see, he called Esau his eldest son, and said unto him, My son: and he said unto him, Behold, here am I.   Ge 35:28 • Ge 48:10

2 And he said, Behold now, I am old, I ᴿknow not the day of my death: [Pr 27:1]

3 Now therefore take, I pray thee, thy weapons, thy quiver and thy bow, and go out to the field, and take me some venison;

4 And make me savoury meat, such as I love, and bring it to me, that I may eat; that my soul ᴿmay bless thee before I die.   De 33:1

5 And Rebekah heard when Isaac spake to Esau his son. And Esau went to the field to hunt for venison, and to bring it.

6 And Rebekah spake unto Jacob her son, saying, Behold, I heard thy father speak unto Esau thy brother, saying,

7 Bring me ᵀvenison, and make me ᵀsavoury meat, that I may eat, and bless thee before the LORD before my death.   game • tasty food

8 Now therefore, my son, obey my voice according to that which I command thee.

9 Go now to the flock, and fetch me from thence two good kids of the goats; and I will make them ᴿsavoury meat for thy father, such as he loveth: Ge 27:4

10 And thou shalt bring it to thy father, that he may eat, and that he ᴿmay bless thee before his death.   Ge 27:4; 48:16

11 And Jacob said to Rebekah his mother, Behold, ᴿEsau my brother is a hairy man, and I am a ᵀsmooth man: Ge 25:25 • smooth-skinned

---

ancient town of Beer-sheba has been partially excavated, and visitors today are shown a well claimed to be that of Abraham and Isaac.

26:31 betimes. An archaic expression meaning "promptly."

26:35 grief of mind. Here is further proof of God's wisdom in choosing Jacob. Esau disregarded both God's primeval principle of monogamy and the need to marry a wife who believed in the true God. Instead he married two pagan Hittite women, whose idolatry and ungodliness grieved his parents. Even more tragically, Isaac seems to have made no attempt to prevent this, and was still resolved to give Esau his patriarchal blessing.

27:5 Rebekah heard. Isaac, knowing that he was wrong in deciding to transmit the blessing to Esau, was secretive about his plans. His actions would wrongly award Esau the place of both physical and spiritual preeminence in the family (27:29). The blessing was intended by God for the line of the promised Seed. Rebekah just happened to overhear Isaac's plans. At this time, Jacob and Esau were probably about 75 years old, and Isaac 135.

27:9 meat for thy father. Although Isaac professed to "love" Esau's venison (27:4), Rebekah could prepare goat meat to taste exactly the same. Thus, it must have been his son's physical exploits, shared vicariously by Isaac, that he really loved.

27:10 bless thee. Rebekah was so resolved that Isaac should not sin against God in blessing Esau (thus bringing almost certain divine retribution upon both Isaac and Esau) that she was willing to risk everything to prevent it. She knew that her stratagem, even if successful, would be discovered as soon as Esau returned, with possibly tragic consequences. However, she apparently felt that God's wrathful judgment upon her husband and her eldest son, if they persisted in trifling with God's most solemn covenants and commandments in this fashion, was to be feared even more. Lest Jacob should refuse to push himself forward

12 My father ᵀperadventure will ᴿfeel me, and I shall seem to him as a deceiver; and I shall bring ᴿa curse upon me, and not a blessing.　　　Ge 27:21,22 • De 27:18 • *perhaps*

13 And his mother said unto him, ᴿUpon me *be* thy curse, my son: only obey my voice, and go fetch me *them*.　　　Ge 43:9

14 And he went, and fetched, and brought *them* to his mother: and his mother ᴿmade ᵀsavoury meat, such as his father loved.　　　Pr 23:3 • *tasty food*

15 And Rebekah took ᴿgoodlyᵀ raiment of her eldest son Esau, which *were* with her in the house, and put them upon Jacob her younger son:　　　Ge 27:27 • *choice clothes*

16 And she put the skins of the kids of the goats upon his hands, and upon the ᵀsmooth of his neck:　　　*smooth* part

17 And she gave the savoury meat and the bread, which she had prepared, into the hand of her son Jacob.

18 And he came unto his father, and said, My father: and he said, Here *am* I; who *art* thou, my son?

19 And Jacob said unto his father, I *am* Esau thy firstborn; I have done according as thou ᵀbadest me: arise, I pray thee, sit and eat of my ᵀvenison, ᴿthat thy soul may bless me.　　　Ge 27:4 • *told* • *game*

20 And Isaac said unto his son, How *is it* that thou hast found *it* so quickly, my son? And he said, Because the Lᴏʀᴅ thy God brought *it* to me.

21 And Isaac said unto Jacob, Come near, I pray thee, that I may feel thee, my son, whether thou *be* my very son Esau or not.

22 And Jacob went near unto Isaac his father; and he felt him, and said, The voice *is* Jacob's voice, but the hands *are* the hands of Esau.

23 And he ᵀdiscerned him not, because ᴿhis hands were hairy, as his brother Esau's hands: so he blessed him.　　　Ge 27:16 • *recognized*

24 And he said, *Art* thou ᵀmy very son Esau? And he said, I *am*.　　　*really my son*

25 And he said, Bring *it* near to me, and I will eat of my son's venison, ᴿthat my soul may bless thee. And he brought *it* near to him, and he did eat: and he brought him wine, and he drank.　　　Ge 27:4,10,19,31

26 And his father Isaac said unto him, Come near now, and kiss me, my son.

27 And he came near, and ᴿkissed him: and he smelled the smell of his ᵀraiment, and blessed him, and said, See, ᴿthe smell of my son *is* as the smell of a field which the Lᴏʀᴅ hath blessed:　　　Ge 29:13 • Song 4:11 • *clothing*

28 Therefore ᴿGod give thee of the dew of heaven, and ᴿthe fatness of the earth, and plenty of corn and wine:　　　He 11:20 • Ge 45:18

---

like this, Rebekah invoked her right to filial obedience in commanding him to do so (27:8). Confronted with this forced choice between two divine commandments (obedience or truthfulness), Jacob chose the course more in line with God's ultimate purpose.

27:12 deceiver. "Deceiver" is better translated "mocker." At this point, Jacob hoped that he would not actually have to lie verbally to his father, but he did fear that he might seem to be mocking his blindness by dressing and smelling and feeling like Esau. Rebekah assured him that she would take the blame.

27:20 brought it to me. Jacob no doubt hoped that Isaac would not question him at all. But Isaac did, and so there was no way of accomplishing Rebekah's plan now except by overt lying and even by taking God's name in vain. Jacob and Rebekah were godly and sensitive people, and it must have grieved them greatly to break God's commandments like this, especially knowing that it could only be a matter of an hour or so before it would all be exposed, with all the wrath and recriminations that would follow. The whole episode can only really be understood in light of their hope that Isaac's sudden knowledge that his beloved wife and faithful son would go to such lengths to prevent him from blaspheming God and His will might shock him to his senses—as, indeed, it did! It is significant that God never spoke to either Rebekah or Jacob by way of rebuke over this incident. In fact, God later explicitly confirmed Isaac's blessing to Jacob (28:13-15). The rebuke was solely for Esau, and the repentance was Isaac's, not Jacob's.

27:29 curseth thee. Isaac's presumption in blessing Esau like this is obvious when con-

29 ᴿLet people serve thee, and nations bow down to thee: be lord over thy brethren, and ᴿlet thy mother's sons bow down to thee: ᴿcursed *be* every one that curseth thee, and blessed *be* he that blesseth thee. Ge 9:25; 25:23 • Ge 37:7,10; 49:8 • Ge 12:2,3

30 And it came to pass, as soon as Isaac had made an end of blessing Jacob, and Jacob ᵀwas yet scarce gone out from the presence of Isaac his father, that Esau his brother came in from his hunting. *had scarcely*

31 And he also had made ᵀsavoury meat, and brought it unto his father, and said unto his father, Let my father arise, and ᴿeat of his son's venison, that thy soul may bless me. Ge 27:4 • *tasty food*

32 And Isaac his father said unto him, Who *art* thou? And he said, I *am* thy son, thy firstborn Esau.

33 And Isaac trembled very exceedingly, and said, Who? where *is* he that hath taken venison, and brought *it* me, and I have eaten of all before thou camest, and have blessed him? yea, *and* he shall be blessed.

34 And when Esau heard the words of his father, ᴿhe cried with a great and exceeding bitter cry, and said unto his father, Bless me, *even* me also, O my father. [He 12:17]

35 And he said, Thy brother came with subtilty, and hath taken away thy blessing.

36 And he said, ᴿIs not he rightly named ᵀJacob? for he hath supplanted me these two times: he took away my birthright; and, behold, now he hath taken away my bless-ing. And he said, Hast thou not reserved a blessing for me? Ge 25:26,32-34 • Lit. *Supplanter*

37 And Isaac answered and said unto Esau, ᴿBehold, I have made him thy ᵀlord, and all his brethren have I given to him for servants; and ᴿwith corn and wine have I sustained him: and what shall I do now unto thee, my son? 2 Sa 8:14 • Ge 27:28,29 • *master*

38 And Esau said unto his father, Hast thou but one blessing, my father? bless me, *even* me also, O my father. And Esau lifted up his voice, ᴿand wept. He 12:17

39 And Isaac his father answered and said unto him, Behold, ᴿthy dwelling shall be ᵀthe fatness of the earth, and of the dew of heaven from above; He 11:20 • *of the fertility*

40 And by thy sword shalt thou live, and ᴿshalt serve thy brother; and ᴿit shall come to pass when thou shalt have ᵀthe dominion, that thou shalt break his yoke from off thy neck. Ge 25:23; 27:29 • 2 Ki 8:20-22 • *become restless*

41 And Esau hated Jacob because of the blessing wherewith his father blessed him: and Esau said in his heart, ᴿThe days of mourning for my father are at hand; then will I slay my brother Jacob. Ge 50:2-4,10

42 And these words of Esau her elder son were told to Rebekah: and she sent and called Jacob her younger son, and said unto him, Behold, thy brother Esau, ᵀas touching thee, doth ᴿcomfort himself, ᵀpurposing to kill thee. Ps 64:5 • *concerning you* • *by intending*

43 Now therefore, my son, obey my

---

trasted with God's specific instruction given before they were born that Jacob should have this position (25:23).

27:29 blesseth thee. Here Isaac repeats God's own original promise to Abraham (12:3), again in flagrant disregard of God's will.

27:33 trembled very exceedingly. Literally, "most excessively with a great trembling." A violent complex of emotions overwhelmed Isaac, as he suddenly realized all that had happened, and the reasons behind it all.

27:33 he shall be blessed. Isaac's anger and resentment were overshadowed by his realization that God Himself had intervened. God was going to bless Jacob and there was no way Isaac could change this. In fact, the blessing would have gone to Jacob even if Isaac had succeeded in pronouncing it upon Esau. Man's will cannot thwart God's purposes.

27:39 fatness of the earth. "Thy dwelling shall be the fatness" should read, "shall be away from the fatness of the earth."

27:40 have the dominion. "Have the dominion" is better rendered "shake thyself." Whether this prophecy concerning Esau was actually from God, or simply Isaac's personal prediction, is open to question.

voice; and arise, flee thou to Laban my brother ᴿto Ha'-ran; Ge 11:31; 25:20; 28:2,5

44 And ᵀtarry with him a ᴿfew days, until thy brother's fury turn away; Ge 31:41 • *stay*

45 Until thy brother's anger turn away from thee, and he forget *that* which thou hast done to him: then I will send, and fetch thee from thence: why should I be ᵀdeprived also of you both in one day? *bereaved*

46 And Rebekah said to Isaac, ᴿI am weary of my life because of the daughters of Heth: ᴿif Jacob take a wife of the daughters of Heth, such as these *which are* of the daughters of the land, what good shall my life do me? Ge 26:34,35; 28:8 • Ge 24:3

CHAPTER 28

And Isaac called Jacob, and ᴿblessed him, and ᵀcharged him, and said unto him, ᴿThou shalt not take a wife of the daughters of Canaan. Ge 27:33 • Ge 24:3 • *commanded*

2 ᴿArise, go to Pa'-dan-a'-ram, to the house of Be-thu'-el thy mother's father; and take thee a wife from thence of the daughters of Laban thy mother's brother. Ho 12:12

3 And God Almighty bless thee, and make thee fruitful, and multiply thee, that thou mayest be a multitude of people;

4 And give thee ᴿthe blessing of Abraham, to thee, and to thy seed with thee; that thou mayest inherit the land ᴿwherein thou art a stranger, which God gave unto Abraham. Ge 12:2,3; 22:17 • Ge 17:8; 23:4; 36:7

5 And Isaac sent away Jacob: and he went to Pa'-dan-a'-ram unto Laban, son of Be-thu'-el the Syrian, the brother of Rebekah, Jacob's and Esau's mother.

6 When Esau saw that Isaac had blessed Jacob, and sent him away to Pa'-dan-a'-ram, to take him a wife from thence; and that as he blessed him he gave him a charge, saying, Thou shalt not take a wife of the daughters of Canaan;

7 And that Jacob obeyed his father and his mother, and was gone to Pa'-dan-a'-ram;

8 And Esau seeing that the daughters of Canaan pleased not Isaac his father;

9 Then went Esau unto Ish'-ma-el, and ᴿtook ᵀunto the wives which he had ᴿMa'-ha-lath the daughter of Ish'-ma-el Abraham's son, ᴿthe sister of Ne-ba'-joth, to be his wife. Ge 26:34,35 • Ge 36:2,3 • Ge 25:13 • *in addition to*

Jacob's Dream

10 And Jacob ᴿwent out from Be'-er-she'-ba, and went toward Ha'-ran. Ho 12:12

11 And he ᵀlighted upon a certain place, and ᵀtarried there all night, because the sun was set; and he took ᵀof the stones of that place, and put *them for* his pillows, and lay down in that place to sleep. *came to* • *stayed* • *one of*

12 And he dreamed, and behold a ladder set up on the earth, and the top of it reached to heaven: and behold the angels of God ascending and descending on it.

28:1 blessed him. At this point, Isaac repeated and expanded his blessing to Jacob, indicating his full realization that God's will had been accomplished.

28:1 daughters of Canaan. Jacob was probably 75 years old, and Isaac had been inexcusably negligent in not attempting long before this (as Abraham had done for him) to find suitable wives among his home countrymen for his sons. Esau's bigamous marriage to two Hittite women had been one tragic consequence of his negligence.

28:9 unto Ishmael. Esau, finally realizing that his troubles were of his own doing, and realizing that his father no longer supported his position, was belatedly trying to help matters by marrying an Ishmaelite woman. Even Ishmael, however, was outside the scope of God's promises regarding the Seed.

28:9 Mahalath. There is an apparent contradiction between the names of Esau's wives in Genesis 26:34 and 28:9. The probable resolution of this problem is discussed in the note on Genesis 36:3.

28:12 reached to heaven. This was a theophany, the first of about eight Jacob would experience. It happened in the form of a remarkable dream. Jacob was assured of God's intense interest and of his own key role in God's plan. The great ladder with ascending and descending angels, bridging the gulf between earth and heaven, symbolized Christ Himself (Jo 1:51; 3:13; Ep 4:8-10), as well of assuring Jacob of his own access to God through prayer and obedience.

13 RAnd, behold, the LORD stood above it, and said, RI *am* the LORD God of Abraham thy father, and the God of Isaac: the land whereon thou liest, to thee will I give it, and to thy Tseed; Ge 35:1; 48:3 • Ge 26:24 • *descendants*

14 And thy Rseed T shall be as the dust of the earth, and thou shalt spread abroad Rto the west, and to the east, and to the north, and to the south: and in thee and in thy seed shall all the families of the earth be blessed. Ge 13:16; 22:17 • Ge 13:14,15 • *descendants*

15 And, behold, RI *am* with thee, and will keep thee in all *places* whither thou goest, and will bring thee again into this land; for I will not leave thee, until I have done *that* which I have spoken to thee of. Ge 26:3,24; 31:3

16 And Jacob awaked out of his sleep, and he said, Surely the LORD is in Rthis place; and I knew *it* not. Ex 3:5

17 And he was afraid, and said, How Tdreadful *is* this place! this *is* none other but the house of God, and this *is* the gate of heaven. *awesome*

18 And Jacob rose up early in the morning, and took the stone that he had put *for* his pillows, and Rset it up *for* a pillar, and poured oil upon the top of it. Ge 31:13,45

19 And he called the name of Rthat place TBeth'–el: but the name of that city *was* called Luz at the first. Ju 1:23,26 • Lit. *House of God*

20 RAnd Jacob vowed a vow, saying, If God will be with me, and will keep me in this way that I go, and will give me Rbread to eat, and raiment to put on, Ju 11:30 • 1 Ti 6:8

21 So that RI come again to my father's house in peace; Rthen shall the LORD be my God: Ju 11:31 • De 26:17

22 And this stone, which I have set *for* a pillar, Rshall be God's house: Rand of all that thou shalt give me I will surely give Tthe tenth unto thee. Ge 35:7,14 • Ge 14:20 • *a tithe*

CHAPTER 29

Jacob's Labors

Then Jacob went on his journey, Rand came into the land of the people of the east. Nu 23:7

2 And he looked, and behold a Rwell in the field, and, lo, there *were* three flocks of sheep lying by it; for out of that well they watered the flocks: and a great stone *was* upon the well's mouth. Ge 24:10,11

3 And thither were all the flocks gathered: and they rolled the stone from the well's mouth, and watered the sheep, and put the stone again upon the well's mouth in his place.

4 And Jacob said unto them, My brethren, whence *be* ye? And they said, Of RHa'–ran *are* we. Ge 11:31; 28:10

5 And he said unto them, Know ye RLaban the son of Na'–hor? And they said, We know *him*. Ge 24:24,29; 28:2

6 And he said unto them, *Is* he well? And they said, *He is* well: and, behold, Ra'–chel his daughter cometh with the sheep.

7 And he said, Lo, *it is* yet Thigh day, neither *is it* time that the cattle should be gathered together: water ye the sheep, and go and feed *them*. Early in the day

8 And they said, We cannot, until all the flocks be gathered together, and *till* they roll the stone from the well's mouth; then we water the sheep.

9 And while he yet spake with them, RRa'–chel came with her father's sheep: for she kept them. Ex 2:16

10 And it came to pass, when Jacob saw Ra'–chel the daughter of Laban his mother's brother, and the sheep of Laban his mother's brother, that Jacob went near, and Rrolled the stone from the well's mouth, and

---

28:20 If God. The word "if" here should be read with the connotation of "since." Jacob was not bargaining with God, as some think, but gratefully accepting God's promised blessing as just outlined by Him (28:13-15). He was reciprocating by vowing that the Lord would always be his God and that he would serve Him.

28:22 the tenth. This is the second reference to tithing in the Bible. Abraham had given tithes to Melchizedek, as God's priest (14:20), and Jacob evidently intended to do the same, although it is not clear at this stage in history just how this could be done, since the Aaronic priesthood had not yet been established. Jacob had built an altar here at Bethel ("the house of God") as his first effort in this direction.

watered the flock of Laban his mother's brother.   Ex 2:17

11 And Jacob ^Rkissed Ra'-chel, and lifted up his voice, and wept.   Ge 33:4; 45:14,15

12 And Jacob told Ra'-chel that he *was* ^Rher father's ^Tbrother, and that he *was* Rebekah's son: ^Rand she ran and told her father.   Ge 13:8; 14:14,16; 28:5 • Ge 24:28 • *relative*

13 And it came to pass, when Laban heard the tidings of Jacob his sister's son, that ^Rhe ran to meet him, and embraced him, and kissed him, and brought him to his house. And he told Laban all these things.   Ge 24:29-31

14 And Laban said to him, ^RSurely thou *art* my bone and my flesh. And he abode with him the space of a month.   Ge 2:23; 37:27

15 And Laban said unto Jacob, Because thou *art* my brother, shouldest thou therefore serve me for ^Tnought? tell me, ^Rwhat *shall* thy wages *be*?   Ge 30:28; 31:41 • *nothing*

16 And Laban had two daughters: the name of the elder *was* Leah, and the name of the younger *was* Ra'-chel.

17 Leah *was* ^Ttender eyed; but Ra'-chel was beautiful and well favoured.   *delicate or soft*

18 And Jacob loved Ra'-chel; and said, ^RI will serve thee seven years for Ra'-chel thy younger daughter.   Ge 31:41

19 And Laban said, *It is* better that I give her to thee, than that I should give her to another man: abide with me.

20 And Jacob ^Rserved seven years for Ra'-chel; and they seemed unto him *but* a few days, for the love he had to her.   Ge 30:26

21 And Jacob said unto Laban, Give *me* my wife, for my days are fulfilled, that I may ^Rgo in unto her.   Ju 15:1

22 And Laban gathered together all the men of the place, and ^Rmade a feast.   Jo 2:1,2

23 And it came to pass in the evening, that he took Leah his daughter, and brought her to him; and he went in unto her.

24 And Laban gave unto his daughter Leah Zil'-pah his maid *for* an handmaid.

25 And it came to pass, that in the morning, behold, it *was* Leah: and he said to Laban, What *is* this thou hast done unto me? did not I serve with thee for Ra'-chel? wherefore then hast thou beguiled me?

26 And Laban said, It must not be so done in our ^Tcountry, to give the younger before the firstborn.   Lit. *place*

27 ^RFulfil her week, and we will give thee this also for the service which thou shalt serve with me yet seven other years.   Ju 14:2

28 And Jacob did so, and fulfilled her week: and he gave him Ra'-chel his daughter ^Tto wife also.   *as*

29 And Laban gave to Ra'-chel his daughter Bil'-hah his handmaid to be her maid.

30 And he went in also unto Ra'-chel, and he loved also Ra'-chel more than Leah, and served with him yet seven other years.

29:14 my bone and my flesh. Jacob was the son of Laban's sister (Rebekah) and of Laban's father's cousin (Isaac). Thus he and Laban did, indeed, have the same basic genetic controls, which specify the characteristics of the individual's flesh and bones.

29:23 brought her to him. This cruel deception on Laban's part was not God's retribution for Jacob's deception of Isaac, as many have suggested. Leah was destined to be the mother of Judah, through whom Christ would come. Leah was less attractive than Rachel and had found no husband as yet, thus inhibiting her younger sister also from marrying (29:26), so that both were well past the normal age for marrying (as was Jacob). Laban was afraid that no suitable husband would ever be found for Leah, and so used this trick to force Jacob into marrying both. This would, he hoped, tie Jacob (a productive worker with a substantial future inheritance) permanently to Laban and his family. Leah also had come to love Jacob and, although her father's device must have been difficult and embarrassing for her, as well as for Rachel, she went along with the plan in obedience to her father.

29:27 her week. Crafty Laban elicited 14 years of free and fruitful labor from Jacob because of Jacob's unselfish love for Rachel. After Jacob had served seven years and then was forced to marry Leah first, Laban finally gave Rachel to Jacob also, for another seven years of service. However, he had only to wait seven days (Leah's festive week, in accord with custom) before receiving Rachel too. Note, incidentally, that time was being measured in weeks (even in Syria) almost 500 years before the giving of the Sabbath com-

31 And when the LORD Rsaw that Leah *was* That ed, he Ropened her womb: but Ra'-chel *was* barren. Ps 127:3 • Ge 30:1 • *unloved*

32 And Leah conceived, and bare a son, and she called his name TReuben: for she said, Surely the LORD hath Rlooked upon my affliction; now therefore my husband will love me. De 26:7 • Lit. *See, a Son*

33 And she conceived again, and bare a son; and said, Because the LORD hath heard that I *was* Thated, he hath therefore given me this *son* also: and she called his name TSimeon. *unloved* • Lit. *Heard*

34 And she conceived again, and bare a son; and said, Now this time will my husband Tbe joined unto me, because I have born him three sons: therefore was his name called TLevi. *become attached to* • Lit. *Attached*

35 And she conceived again, and bare a son: and she said, Now will I praise the LORD: therefore she called his name RJudah;T and Tleft bearing. Ma 1:2 • Lit. *Praise* • *stopped*

CHAPTER 30

And when Ra'-chel saw that Rshe bare Ja-cob no children, Ra'-chel Renvied her sis-ter; and said unto Jacob, Give me children, Ror else I die. Ge 16:1,2; 29:31 • Ge 37:11 • [Job 5:2]

2 And Jacob's anger was kindled against Ra'-chel: and he said, RAm I in God's stead, who hath withheld from thee the fruit of the womb? 1 Sa 1:5

3 And she said, Behold Rmy maid Bil'-hah, go in unto her; Rand she shall bear Tupon my knees, Rthat I may also have chil-dren by her. Ge 16:2 • Ge 50:23 • Ge 16:2,3 • *to be* upon

4 And she gave him Bil'-hah her hand-maid to wife: and Jacob went in unto her.

5 And Bil'-hah conceived, and bare Jacob a son.

6 And Ra'-chel said, God hath Rjudged Tme, and hath also heard my voice, and hath given me a son: therefore called she his name TDan. La 3:59 • *my case* • Lit. *Judge*

7 And Bil'-hah Ra'-chel's maid conceived again, and bare Jacob a second son.

8 And Ra'-chel said, With Tgreat wres-tlings have I wrestled with my sister, and I have prevailed: and she called his name Naph'-ta-li. Lit. *wrestlings of God*

9 When Leah saw that she had left bear-ing, she took Zil'-pah her maid, and Rgave her Jacob Tto wife. Ge 30:4 • *as*

10 And Zil'-pah Leah's maid bare Jacob a son.

11 And Leah said, A Ttroop cometh: and she called his name Gad. *fortune*

12 And Zil'-pah Leah's maid bare Jacob a second son.

13 And Leah said, Happy am I, for the daughters Rwill call me blessed: and she called his name TAsher. Lk 1:48 • Lit. *Happy*

14 And Reuben went in the days of wheat harvest, and found mandrakes in the field,

---

mandment on Mount Sinai. This is incidental testimony that the nations of the world had been (perhaps inadvertently) commemorating the literal creation week ever since the beginning.

29:31 hated. The word is better rendered "slighted." Jacob loved Rachel *more* than he loved Leah (29:30), but he surely loved Leah, too.

29:35 I praise the LORD. The Lord in grace not only gave Leah (the "slighted" wife—not "hated," as wrongly rendered in 29:31) more sons than Rachel, but one of these was Judah, who was destined to produce the kingly tribe—including David and, eventually, Christ. It is thus significant that this is the first occurrence of the word here translated "praise," and more commonly rendered "give thanks."

30:3 go in unto her. In accordance with the customs of the time, which allowed both polygamy and concubinage, Laban had provided maids for his daughters as insurance that they would not be childless. Any children borne by their personal maids would legally be recognized as theirs. Even though this kind of arrangement was legal, it was not in accord with God's original plan for the marriage relation. The Bible tells of many polygamous marriages that God allowed, but of none which were happy marriages.

30:3 children by her. See note on Genesis 16:2.

30:14 mandrakes. The mandrake is in the potato family with a berrylike fruit. Its root was prized in ancient times as an aphrodisiac and inducer of fertility. Rachel did eventually have two sons, but it was not because of the mandrakes.

and brought them unto his mother Leah. Then Ra'-chel said to Leah, ᴿGive me, I pray thee, of thy son's mandrakes. Ge 25:30

15 And she said unto her, ᴿ*Is it* a small matter that thou hast taken my husband? and wouldest thou take away my son's mandrakes also? And Ra'-chel said, Therefore he shall lie with thee to night for thy son's mandrakes. [Nu 16:9,13]

16 And Jacob came out of the field in the evening, and Leah went out to meet him, and said, Thou must come in unto me; for surely I have hired thee with my son's mandrakes. And he lay with her that night.

17 And God hearkened unto Leah, and she conceived, and bare Jacob the fifth son.

18 And Leah said, God hath given me my hire, because I have given my maiden to my husband: and she called his name ᵀIs'-sa-char. Lit. *Hire*

19 And Leah conceived again, and bare Jacob the sixth son.

20 And Leah said, God hath endued me *with* a good dowry; now will my husband dwell with me, because I have born him six sons: and she called his name Zeb'-u-lun.

21 And afterwards she bare a ᴿdaughter, and called her name Dinah. Ge 34:1

22 And God ᴿremembered Ra'-chel, and God hearkened to her, and ᴿopened her womb. 1 Sa 1:19,20 • Ge 29:31

23 And she conceived, and bare a son; and said, God hath taken away ᴿmy reproach: Lk 1:25

24 And she called his name ᵀJoseph; and said, ᴿThe Lᴏʀᴅ shall add to me another son. Ge 35:16-18 • Lit. *He Will Add*

25 And it came to pass, when Ra'-chel had born Joseph, that Jacob said unto La-ban, Send me away, that I may go unto ᴿmine own place, and to my country. Ge 18:33

26 Give *me* my wives and my children, ᴿfor whom I have served thee, and let me go: for thou knowest my service which I have done thee. Ge 29:18-20,27,30

27 And Laban said unto him, I pray thee, if I have found favour in thine eyes, *tarry: for* ᴿI have learned by experience that the Lᴏʀᴅ hath blessed me for thy sake. Ge 26:24; 39:3

28 And he said, ᴿAppointᵀ me thy wages, and I will give *it.* Ge 29:15; 31:7,41 • *Name me*

29 And ᵀhe said unto him, ᴿThou knowest how I have served thee, and how thy ᵀcattle was with me. Ge 31:6,38-40 • Jacob • *livestock*

30 For *it was* little which thou hadst before I *came,* and it is *now* increased unto a multitude; and the Lᴏʀᴅ hath blessed thee since my coming: and now when shall I ᴿprovide for mine own house also? [1 Ti 5:8]

31 And he said, What shall I give thee? And Jacob said, Thou shalt not give me any thing: if thou wilt do this thing for me, I will again feed *and* keep thy flock.

32 I will pass through all thy flock to day, removing from thence all the speckled and spotted ᵀcattle, and all the brown cattle among the sheep, and the spotted and speckled among the goats: and ᴿofᵀ such shall be my hire. Ge 31:8 • *sheep* • these *shall be my wages*

30:27 *by experience.* The words "by experience" should be translated "by enchantments." Though he knew God after a fashion, Laban had become a sort of pagan mystic. God had overruled even in this, however, and Laban learned that the unusual prosperity he was experiencing was because of Jacob's abilities and faithfulness.

30:28 *I will give it.* Laban gave Jacob *carte blanche* to set up his own terms. Thus, Jacob by no means took advantage of Laban, as many teach. Rather, the terms proposed by Jacob were heavily weighted in Laban's favor.

30:32 *speckled and spotted cattle.* Laban had received 14 years of free labor from Jacob, and had prospered greatly as a result. Therefore he, in effect, told Jacob that he would pay whatever Jacob wanted, if Jacob would continue. Jacob responded with a proposal which Laban quickly accepted, recognizing it as highly beneficial to himself. Jacob's wages would be the spotted and off-color animals which the flocks might produce in the future—first, however, removing all such animals in the existing flocks so they could not be used in breeding. Thus, Jacob would get only the off-colored and speckled animals which might be born to a flock containing only solid-colored, dominant-colored animals. These terms, apart from God's intervention, would have enormously favored Laban. Jacob did know, from long experience as a shepherd and stock breeder that some "heterozygous" animals

33 So shall my ᴿrighteousness answer for me in time to come, when it shall come ᵀfor my hire before thy face: every one that *is* not speckled and spotted among the goats, and brown among the sheep, that shall be counted stolen with me.   Ps 37:6 • *about my wages*

34 And Laban said, Behold, I would it might be according to thy word.

35 And he removed that day the he goats that were ᴿringstraked and spotted, and all the she goats that were speckled and spotted, *and* every one that had *some* white in it, and all the brown among the sheep, and gave *them* into the hand of his sons. Ge 31:9-12

36 And he set three days' journey ᵀbetwixt himself and Jacob: and Jacob fed the rest of Laban's flocks.   *between*

37 And ᴿJacob took him rods of green poplar, and of the hazel and chesnut tree; and ᵀpilled white ᵀstrakes in them, and made the white appear which *was* in the rods.   Ge 31:9-12 • *peeled* • *strips*

38 And he set the rods which he had ᵀpilled before the flocks in the gutters in the watering troughs when the flocks came to drink, that they should conceive when they came to drink.   *peeled*

39 And the flocks conceived before the rods, and brought forth cattle ᵀringstraked, speckled, and spotted.   *streaked*

40 And Jacob did separate the lambs, and set the faces of the flocks toward the ᵀringstraked, and all the brown in the flock of Laban; and he put his own flocks by themselves, and put them not ᵀunto Laban's cattle.   *streaked* • *with*

41 And it came to pass, whensoever the stronger ᵀcattle did conceive, that Jacob laid the rods before the eyes of the cattle in the gutters, that they might conceive among the rods.   *livestock*

42 But when the cattle were feeble, he put *them* not in: so the feebler were Laban's, and the stronger Jacob's.

43 And the man increased exceedingly, and had much cattle, and maidservants, and menservants, and camels, and asses.

CHAPTER 31
Jacob's Flight

And he heard the words of Laban's sons, saying, Jacob hath taken away all that *was* our father's; and of *that* which *was* our father's hath he gotten all this ᴿglory. Ps 49:16

2 And Jacob beheld the ᴿcountenance of Laban, and, behold, it *was* ᵀnot ᴿtoward him as before.   Ge 4:5 • De 28:54 • *not favourable*

3 And the LORD said unto Jacob, Return unto the land of thy fathers, and to thy kindred; and I will ᴿbe with thee.   Ge 46:4

4 And Jacob sent and called Ra′-chel and Leah to the field unto his flock,

5 And said unto them, ᴿI see your father's ᵀcountenance, that it *is* ᵀnot toward me as before; but the God of my father ᴿhath been with me.   Ge 31:2,3 • Is 41:10 • Lit. *faces* • *not favourable*

6 And ᴿye know that with all my ᵀpower I have served your father.   Ge 30:29; 31:38-41 • *might*

7 And your father hath deceived me, and ᴿchanged my wages ten times; but God suffered him not to hurt me.   Ge 29:25; 31:41

8 If he said thus, The speckled shall be thy wages; then all the cattle bare speckled: and if he said thus, The ringstraked shall be thy hire; then bare all the cattle ringstraked.

9 Thus God hath taken away the cattle of your father, and given *them* to me.

---

would be in the flock even though all appeared to be "homozygous," so that at least a few animals would be born spotted and speckled, even from Laban's solid-colored animals. He trusted the Lord to determine how many.

30:35 ringstraked. That is, "having streaks of color around the body."

30:37 pilled white strakes. That is, "pealed white streaks."

30:38 rods which he had pilled. These striped rods were not for the purpose of inducing some "prenatal influence" on the animals, as critics have scoffed. With his 70 years or more of practical experience with large flocks, Jacob knew better than that. Either the chemicals from the wood or the sight of the streaked rods must have served as an aphrodisiac for the animals, inducing them to mate as they came to the troughs. Jacob only used the rods with the stronger animals, so that the progeny would also be strong. Under usual conditions, this stratagem should have greatly benefited Laban's flocks.

30:39 conceived. The word for "conceived" can mean "were in heat."

10 And it came to pass at the time that the Tcattle conceived, that I lifted up mine eyes, and saw in a dream, and, behold, the rams which leaped upon the cattle *were* ringstraked, speckled, and grisled. *flocks*

11 And Rthe angel of God spake unto me in a dream, *saying*, Jacob: And I said, Here *am* I. Ge 16:7-11; 22:11,15; 31:13; 48:16

12 And he said, Lift up now thine eyes, and see, all the rams which leap upon the cattle *are* Tringstraked, speckled, and Tgrisled: for RI have seen all that Laban doeth unto thee. Ex 3:7 • *streaked* • *gray-spotted*

13 I *am* the God of Beth'-el, Rwhere thou anointedst the pillar, *and* where thou vowedst a vow unto me: now Rarise, get thee out from this land, and return unto the land of thy kindred. Ge 28:16-22; 35:1,6,15 • Ge 31:3; 32:9

14 And Ra'-chel and Leah answered and said unto him, *Is there* yet any portion or inheritance for us in our father's house?

15 Are we not counted of him strangers? for Rhe hath sold us, and hath quite devoured also our money. Ge 29:15,20,23,27

16 For all the riches which God hath taken from our father, that *is* ours, and our children's: now then, whatsoever God hath said unto thee, do.

17 Then Jacob rose up, and set his sons and his wives upon camels;

18 And he carried away all his Tcattle, and all his goods which he had gotten, the cattle of his getting, which he had gotten in Pa'-dan-a'-ram, for to go to Isaac his father in the land of RCanaan. Ge 17:8; 33:18; 35:27 • *livestock*

19 And Laban went to shear his sheep: and Ra'-chel had stolen the Rimages T that *were* her father's. Ju 17:5 • *household idols*, He *teraphim*

20 And Jacob stole away unawares to La-ban the Syrian, in that he told him not that he Tfled. *was fleeing*

21 So he fled with all that he had; and he rose up, and passed over the river, and Rset his face *toward* the mount Gil'-e-ad. 2 Ki 12:17

22 And it was told Laban on the third day that Jacob was fled.

23 And he took Rhis brethren with him, and pursued after him seven days' journey; and they overtook him in the Tmount Gil'-e-ad. Ge 13:8 • *mountains of*

24 And God Rcame to Laban the Syrian in a dream by night, and said unto him, Take heed that thou speak not to Jacob either good or bad. Ge 20:3; 31:29; 46:2-4

25 Then Laban overtook Jacob. Now Ja-cob had pitched his tent in the mount: and Laban with his brethren pitched in the mount of Gil'-e-ad.

26 And Laban said to Jacob, What hast thou done, that thou hast stolen away un-awares to me, and Rcarried away my daugh-ters, as captives *taken* with the sword? 1 Sa 30:2

27 Wherefore didst thou flee away se-cretly, and steal away from me; and didst not tell me, that I might have sent thee away with Tmirth, and with songs, with Ttabret, and with harp? *joy* • *timbrel*

28 And hast not suffered me Rto kiss my sons and my daughters? Rthou hast now done foolishly in *so* doing. Ge 31:55 • 1 Sa 13:13

29 It is in the power of my hand to do you hurt: but the RGod of your father spake unto me Ryesternight, saying, Take thou heed that thou speak not to Jacob either good or bad. Ge 28:13; 31:5,24,42,53 • Ge 31:24

30 And now, *though* thou wouldest needs

31:10 *saw in a dream.* God revealed to Jacob in this dream that, even though the cattle all *seemed* to be of the dominantly solid colors, those which actually were mating were geneti-cally heterozygous, thus producing an abnormal proportion of spotted offspring to aug-ment Jacob's flock. God thus providentially honored Jacob's faith and punished Laban's cu-pidity.

31:11 *the angel of God.* This "angel of God" claimed to be "the God of Beth-el" (31:13). This clearly indicates a theophany, with God the Son appearing in pre-incarnate form.

31:15 *he hath sold us.* Leah and Rachel revealed here that they had long resented the way their father had "sold" them to Jacob. The exorbitant price extracted from Jacob—14 years' free labor—made them love Jacob but resent Laban. Furthermore, instead of using this pay-ment like a dowry, to provide a base for his daughters' future financial security, he had given nothing to them personally.

31:23 *pursued after him.* Laban not only had repeatedly tried to defraud Jacob, but fully

be gone, because thou ᵀsore longedst after thy father's house, *yet* wherefore hast thou ᴿstolen my gods? Ju 17:5; 18:24 • *greatly long for*

31 And Jacob answered and said to Laban, Because I was ᴿafraid: for I said, ᵀPeradventure thou wouldest take by force thy daughters from me. Ge 26:7; 32:7,11 • *Perhaps*

32 With whomsoever thou findest thy gods, ᴿlet him not live: before our brethren ᵀdiscern thou what *is* thine with me, and take *it* ᵀto thee. For Jacob knew not that Ra'-chel had stolen them. Ge 44:9 • *identify* • *with*

33 And Laban went into Jacob's tent, and into Leah's tent, and into the two maidservants' tents; but he found *them* not. Then went he out of Leah's tent, and entered into Ra'-chel's tent.

34 Now Ra'-chel had taken the ᵀimages, and put them in the camel's furniture, and sat upon them. And Laban searched all the tent, but found *them* not. *household idols,* He *teraphim*

35 And she said to her father, Let it not displease my lord that I cannot ᴿrise up before thee; for the custom of women *is* upon me. And he searched, but found not the ᵀimages. Le 19:32 • *household idols,* He *teraphim*

36 And Jacob was wroth, and chode with Laban: and Jacob answered and said to Laban, What *is* my trespass? what *is* my sin, that thou hast so hotly pursued after me?

37 Whereas thou hast searched all my stuff, what hast thou found of all thy household stuff? set *it* here before my brethren and thy brethren, that they may judge betwixt us both.

38 This twenty years *have* I *been* with thee; thy ewes and thy she goats have not cast their young, and the rams of thy flock have I not eaten.

39 ᴿThat which was torn *of beasts* I brought not unto thee; I bare the loss of it; of my hand didst thou require it, *whether* stolen by day, or stolen by night. Ex 22:10

40 *Thus* I was; in the day the drought consumed me, and the frost by night; and my sleep departed from mine eyes.

41 Thus have I been twenty years in thy house; I served thee fourteen years for thy two daughters, and six years for thy cattle: and thou hast changed my wages ten times.

42 ᴿExcept the God of my father, the God of Abraham, and ᴿthe fear of Isaac, had been with me, surely thou hadst sent me away now empty. ᴿGod hath seen mine affliction and the labour of my hands, and rebuked *thee* yesternight. Ps 124:1,2 • Is 8:13 • Ex 3:7

43 And Laban answered and said unto Jacob, *These* daughters *are* my daughters, and *these* children *are* my children, and ᵀ*these* cattle *are* my cattle, and all that thou seest *is* mine: and what can I do this day unto these my daughters, or unto their children which they have born? *flock*

44 Now therefore come thou, let us make a covenant, I ᴿand thou; and let it be for a witness between me and thee. Jos 24:27

45 And Jacob ᴿtook a stone, and set it up *for* a pillar. Ge 28:18; 35:14

46 And Jacob said unto his brethren, Gather stones; and they took stones, and made an heap: and they did eat there upon the heap.

47 And Laban called it Je'-gar–sa-ha-du'-tha: but Jacob called it Gal'-e-ed.

48 And Laban said, This heap *is* a witness between me and thee this day. Therefore was the name of it called Gal'-e-ed;

49 And ᴿMiz'-pah;ᵀ for he said, The LORD watch between me and thee, when we are absent one from another. Ju 10:17; 11:29 • Lit. *Watch*

---

intended to take Jacob's flocks and herds back by force, probably slaying Jacob in the process. However, God intervened to prevent it.

31:32 *thy gods.* These "gods" were small household images (or *teraphim*), used both in religious observances (evidently Laban, though he knew about the true God, had been influenced to a degree by the paganism around him) and also as tokens of ownership of the real estate where their possessor lived. As such, it was considered a capital crime to steal them. Rachel, however, took this risk presumably because Laban had not given either her or Leah "any portion or inheritance for us in our father's house" (31:14). Laban did not find them in Jacob's possessions (Rachel had hidden them well), but we do not know whether this loss ever caused any commercial problem for him. In any case, because of their idolatrous associations, Jacob later buried all these pagan mementos at Bethel (35:4).

31:49 *Mizpah.* "Mizpah" means "watchtower." This has been called the "Mizpah Benediction," but Laban obviously did not mean it as any kind of blessing!

50 If thou shalt afflict my daughters, or if thou shalt take *other* wives beside my daughters, ᵀno man *is* with us; see, God *is* witness betwixt me and thee. *although no man*

51 And Laban said to Jacob, Behold this heap, and behold *this* pillar, which I have cast betwixt me and thee;

52 This heap *be* witness, and *this* pillar *be* witness, that I will not pass over this heap to thee, and that thou shalt not pass over this heap and this pillar unto me, for harm.

53 The God of Abraham, and the God of Na'-hor, the God of their father, ᴿjudge betwixt us. And Jacob ᴿsware by ᴿthe fear of his father Isaac. Ge 16:5 • Ge 21:23 • Ge 31:42

54 Then Jacob offered sacrifice upon the mount, and called his brethren to eat bread: and they did eat bread, and tarried all night in the mount.

55 And early in the morning Laban rose up, and kissed his sons and his daughters, and ᴿblessed them: and Laban departed, and ᴿreturned unto his place. Ge 28:1 • Nu 24:25

CHAPTER 32

Jacob Wrestles with the Angel

And Jacob went on his way, and ᴿthe angels of God met him. Nu 22:31

2 And when Jacob saw them, he said, This *is* God's ᴿhost:ᵀ and he called the name of that place Ma-ha-na'-im. Jos 5:14 • *camp*

3 And Jacob sent messengers before him to Esau his brother ᴿunto the land of Se'-ir, the country of E'-dom. Ge 14:6; 33:14,16

4 And he commanded them, saying, Thus shall ye speak unto my lord Esau; Thy servant Jacob saith thus, I have sojourned with Laban, and stayed there until now:

5 And ᴿI have oxen, and ᵀasses, flocks, and menservants, and womenservants: and I have sent to tell my lord, that ᴿI may find grace in thy sight. Ge 30:43 • Ge 33:8,15 • *donkeys*

6 And the messengers returned to Jacob, saying, We came to thy brother Esau, and also ᴿhe cometh to meet thee, and four hundred men with him. Ge 33:1

7 Then Jacob was greatly afraid and ᴿdistressed: and he divided the people that *was* with him, and the flocks, and herds, and the camels, into two ᵀbands; Ge 32:11; 35:3 • *companies*

8 And said, If Esau come to the one company, and ᵀsmite it, then the other company which is left shall escape. *attacks*

9 ᴿAnd Jacob said, ᴿO God of my father Abraham, and God of my father Isaac, the Lᴏʀᴅ which saidst unto me, Return unto thy country, and to thy kindred, and I will deal well with thee: [Ps 50:15] • Ge 28:13; 31:42

10 I am not worthy of the least of all the ᴿmercies, and of all the truth, which thou hast shewed unto thy servant; for with ᴿmy staff I passed over this Jordan; and now I am become two bands. Ge 24:27 • Job 8:7

11 Deliver me, I pray thee, from the hand of my brother, from the hand of Esau: for I fear him, lest he will come and smite me, *and* the mother with the children.

12 And ᴿthou saidst, I will surely do thee good, and make thy ᵀseed as the ᴿsand of the sea, which cannot be numbered for multitude. Ge 28:13-15 • Ge 22:17 • *descendants*

13 And he lodged there that same night; and took of that which came to his hand ᴿa present for Esau his brother; Ge 43:11

14 Two hundred she goats, and twenty he goats, two hundred ewes, and twenty rams,

---

32:1 *angels of God.* This is Jacob's second encounter with angels; the first, 20 years earlier, was as he left the promised land. He encounters them again as he returns. In both cases, whether facing the external dangers of the material world (typified by Laban) or the internal dangers of the religious world (typified by Esau), Jacob could rely on the help of God's invisible army of ministering spirits (He 1:14); the same is true for faithful men of God today.

32:2 *Mahanaim.* "Mahanaim" means "two hosts," referring to the small visible company of faithful followers and the vastly superior invisible host of mighty angels.

32:6 *to meet thee.* Esau was probably as fearful as Jacob, since he had not heard from him in 20 years and well remembered God's prophecy of Jacob's ruling.

32:9 *Jacob said, O God.* This prayer of Jacob's (32:9-12) is a beautiful model of effectual praying after sincerely following God's will and having done all he humanly could with his own resources and opportunities. Acknowledging that all of God's blessings were only by

15 Thirty ^Tmilch camels with their colts, forty ^Tkine, and ten bulls, twenty ^Tshe asses, and ten foals.　　　*milk • cows • female donkeys*

16 And he delivered *them* into the hand of his servants, every drove by themselves; and said unto his servants, Pass over before me, and put a ^Tspace betwixt drove and drove.　　　*distance between successive droves*

17 And he commanded the foremost, saying, When Esau my brother meeteth thee, and asketh thee, saying, Whose *art* thou? and whither goest thou? and whose *are* these before thee?

18 Then thou shalt say, *They be* thy servant Jacob's; it *is* a present sent unto my lord Esau: and, behold, also he *is* behind us.

19 And so commanded he the second, and the third, and all that followed the droves, saying, On this manner shall ye speak unto Esau, when ye find him.

20 And say ye moreover, Behold, thy servant Jacob *is* behind us. For he said, I will ^Rappease him with the present that goeth before me, and afterward I will see his face; peradventure he will accept of me.　　[Pr 21:14]

21 So went the present over before him: and himself lodged that night in the ^Tcompany.　　　*camp*

22 And he rose up that night, and took his two wives, and his two womenservants, and his eleven sons, ^Rand passed over the ford Jab'-bok.　　　De 3:16

23 And he took them, and sent them over the brook, and sent over that he had.

24 And Jacob was left alone; and there ^Rwrestled a man with him until the ^Tbreaking of the day.　　　Ho 12:2-4 • *dawn*

25 And when he saw that he prevailed not against him, he ^Ttouched the ^Thollow of his ^Tthigh; and ^Rthe hollow of Jacob's thigh was out of joint, as he wrestled with him.　　2 Co 12:7 • *struck • socket • hip*

26 And ^Rhe said, Let me go, for the day breaketh. And he said, ^RI will not let thee go, except thou bless me.　　Lk 24:28 • Ho 12:4

27 And he said unto him, What *is* thy name? And he said, Jacob.

28 And he said, ^RThy name shall be called no more Jacob, but Israel: for as a prince hast thou power with God and ^Rwith men, and hast prevailed.　　　Ge 35:10

29 And Jacob asked *him,* and said, Tell *me,* I pray thee, thy name. And he said, ^RWherefore *is* it *that* thou dost ask after my name? And he blessed him there.　　Ju 13:17,18

30 And Jacob called the name of the place Pe-ni'-el: for ^RI have seen God face to face, and my life is preserved.　　Ge 16:13

31 And as he passed over ^TPe-nu'-el the sun rose upon him, and he ^Thalted upon his thigh.　　Lit. *Face of God • limped on his hip*

His grace, Jacob then simply asks God to fulfill His Word, even though the outward circumstances seemed almost hopeless. No prayer can be truly efficacious unless it is in full harmony with God's revealed Word.

32:18 *a present.* Esau feared that Jacob was coming to claim the promised sovereignty over him and to take his possessions from him. By his language, Jacob allayed the first fear, and by his generous gifts, the second. Jacob was more concerned with God's sovereignty and God's provision.

32:24 *wrestled a man.* This "man" was actually an angel (Ho 12:4)—in fact, *the* angel, the pre-incarnate Christ, for Jacob recognized that he had seen God face to face (32:30), and this is impossible except through Christ (Jo 1:18). The intensity of Jacob's prayer, as he "wrestled" in his intercession (the word *Jabbok* means "wrestler," the river being named for the unique event that occurred there), was such that God actually deigned to appear to him in human form as an antagonist over whom he must prevail for the blessing. As he had held on to Esau's heel at birth, so he now held on to God, so earnest was his desire for God's purpose to be accomplished in and through him.

32:28 *Israel.* "Israel" can mean either "one who fights victoriously with God" or "a prevailing prince with God." This constitutes God's permanent testimony to Jacob's character, an opinion quite different from that of many modern Bible teachers. The "Supplanter" is now the "Prevailer." God delights in the faith of those who cling tenaciously to His promises and who claim them in prevailing prayer (see Lk 18:1,7).

32 Therefore the children of Israel eat not *of* the ᵀsinew which shrank, which *is* upon the ᵀhollow of the ᵀthigh, unto this day: because he ᵀtouched the hollow of Jacob's thigh in the sinew that shrank.　*muscle • socket • hip • struck*

CHAPTER 33

Jacob Makes Peace with Esau

And Jacob lifted up his eyes, and looked, and, behold, ᴿEsau came, and with him four hundred men. And he divided the children unto Leah, and unto Ra'-chel, and unto the two ᵀhandmaids.　Ge 32:6 • *maidservants*

2 And he put the handmaids and their children foremost, and Leah and her children after, and Ra'-chel and Joseph ᵀhindermost.　*last*

3 And he passed over before them, and ᴿbowed himself to the ground seven times, until he came near to his brother.　Ge 18:2; 42:6

4 ᴿAnd Esau ran to meet him, and embraced him, ᴿand fell on his neck, and kissed him: and they wept. Ge 32:28 • Ge 45:14,15

5 And he lifted up his eyes, and saw the women and the children; and said, Who *are* those with thee? And he said, The children ᴿwhich God hath graciously given thy servant.　Ge 48:9

6 Then the ᵀhandmaidens came near, they and their children, and they bowed themselves.　*maidservants*

7 And Leah also with her children came near, and bowed themselves: and after came Joseph near and Ra'-chel, and they bowed themselves.

8 And he said, What *meanest* thou by all this drove which I met? And he said, *These are* to find grace in the sight of my lord.

9 And Esau said, I have enough, my brother; keep that thou hast unto thyself.

10 And Jacob said, Nay, I pray thee, if now I have found ᵀgrace in thy sight, then receive my present at my hand: for therefore I ᴿhave seen thy face, as though I had seen the face of God, and thou wast pleased with me.　Ge 43:3 • *favour*

11 Take, I pray thee, ᴿmy blessing that is brought to thee; because God hath dealt ᴿgraciously with me, and because I have ᵀenough. ᴿAnd he urged him, and he took *it.*　1 Sa 25:27; 30:26 • Ex 33:19 • 2 Ki 5:23 • Lit. *all*

12 And he said, Let us take our journey, and let us go, and I will go before thee.

13 And he said unto him, My lord knoweth that the children *are* ᵀtender, and the flocks and herds ᵀwith young *are* with me: and if men should overdrive them one day, all the flock will die.　*weak • which are nursing*

14 Let my lord, I pray thee, pass over before his servant: and I will lead on softly, according as the cattle that goeth before me and the children be able to endure, until I come unto my lord ᴿunto Se'-ir.　Ge 32:3; 36:8

15 And Esau said, Let me now leave with thee *some* of the ᵀfolk that *are* with me. And he said, What needeth it? ᴿlet me find grace in the sight of my lord.　Ru 2:13 • *people*

32:32 *the sinew which shrank.* This sentence is apparently an editorial insertion by Moses in Jacob's *toledoth*, noting a custom by the Israelites commemorating the great experience of their founder. In order that Jacob should know forever that it was God who had actually *allowed* him to prevail, and not his own strength, a muscle in the ball-and-socket joint in the thigh, probably containing the sciatic nerve, shrank, resulting in a permanent limp and perpetual reminder of the experience.

33:11 *I have enough.* Esau likewise said, "I have enough" (33:9), hesitating to accept Jacob's generous gift. Quite probably, Esau's possessions were much greater than those of Jacob. He had defeated the Horites, conquered the land of Seir, and possessed a large retinue and large family by this time (36:1-8). The acceptance of a gift was evidence of reconciliation between estranged parties, but Esau felt it was unnecessary to accept it in Jacob's case, since both brothers were overjoyed at their restored fellowship. However, when Esau said, "I have enough," he used the word *rab*, meaning "much." Jacob said, "I have *kol* (meaning "everything!")." Jacob knew that his resources were inexhaustible, so he insisted that Esau receive his gift as a token of his love and concern for his welfare.

16 So Esau returned that day on his way unto Se'-ir.

17 And Jacob journeyed to ᴿSuc'-coth, and built him an house, and made ᵀbooths for his cattle: therefore the name of the place is called Suc'-coth.   Jos 13:27 • *shelters*

18 And Jacob came to Sha'-lem, a city of She'-chem, which *is* in the land of Canaan, when he came from Pa'-dan-a'-ram; and pitched his tent before the city.

19 And ᴿhe bought a parcel of a field, where he had spread his tent, at the hand of the children of Ha'-mor, She'-chem's father, for an hundred pieces of money.   Jo 4:5

20 And he erected there an altar, and ᴿcalled it El–e-lo'–he–Is'–ra-el.   Ge 35:7

CHAPTER 34

Dinah Is Defiled

And ᴿDinah the daughter of Leah, which she bare unto Jacob, went out to see the daughters of the land.   Ge 30:21

2 And when She'-chem the son of Ha'-mor the Hi'-vite, prince of the country, saw her, he ᴿtook her, and lay with her, and ᵀdefiled her.   Ge 20:2 • *violated*

3 And his soul clave unto Dinah the daughter of Jacob, and he loved the damsel, and spake kindly unto the ᵀdamsel. *young woman*

4 And She'-chem ᴿspake unto his father Ha'-mor, saying, Get me this damsel ᵀto wife.   Ju 14:2 • *as a wife*

5 And Jacob heard that he had defiled Dinah his daughter: now his sons were with his ᵀcattle in the field: and Jacob ᴿheld his peace until they were come.   2 Sa 13:22 • *livestock*

6 And Ha'-mor the father of She'-chem went out unto Jacob to ᵀcommune with him.   *speak*

7 And the sons of Jacob came out of the field when they heard *it:* and the men were grieved, and they were very ᵀwroth, because he ᴿhad wrought folly in Israel in lying with Jacob's daughter; ᴿwhich thing ought not to be done.   Ju 20:6 • 2 Sa 13:12 • *angry*

8 And Ha'-mor communed with them, saying, The soul of my son She'-chem longeth for your daughter: I pray you give her him to wife.

9 And make ye marriages with us, *and* give your daughters unto us, and take our daughters unto you.

10 And ye shall dwell with us: and the land shall be before you; dwell and trade ye therein, and get you possessions therein.

11 And She'-chem said unto her father and unto her brethren, Let me find ᵀgrace in your eyes, and what ye shall say unto me I will give.   *favour*

12 Ask me never so much dowry and gift, and I will give according as ye shall say unto me: but give me the damsel to wife.

13 And the sons of Jacob answered She'-chem and Ha'-mor his father ᴿdeceitfully, and said, because he had defiled Dinah their sister: Ge 31:7

14 And they said unto them, We cannot do this thing, to give our sister to one that is ᴿuncircumcised; for ᴿthat *were* a reproach unto us: Ex 12:48 • Jos 5:2-9

15 But in this will we consent unto you: If ye will be as we *be,* that every male of you be circumcised;

33:16 *Esau returned.* Despite Jacob's joy at the happy reunion, he knew that it would be essential in the fulfilling of God's purposes for his family and that of Esau to continue their separate ways.

33:20 *El-elohe-Israel.* On his initial entrance into Canaan, the promised land (the family had spent some time in Succoth, still east of the Jordan), Jacob desired both to own some of the land (as a token of his eventual possession of all of it) and to build an altar to his God, which he named—"The God who was the God of Israel."

34:1 *Dinah.* Dinah must have been at least in her teens by this time, so that Jacob and his family must have lived in Succoth and Shechem almost ten years. Her older brothers—Reuben, Simeon, Levi and Judah—were thus at least in their twenties.

34:5 *Jacob held his peace.* Jacob apparently took no part in the subsequent negotiations and plans, perhaps so grieved and distressed that he went off by himself. Probably he suddenly realized his dreadful mistake in settling so close and so long to such a callously immoral pagan city as Shechem. However, he compounded his mistake by being so indecisive in this crisis, abdicating his responsibility to Dinah's two hot-headed older brothers.

16 Then will we give our daughters unto you, and we will take your daughters to us, and we will dwell with you, and we will become one people.

17 But if ye will not hearken unto us, to be circumcised; then will we take our daughter, and we will be gone.

18 And their words pleased Ha'-mor, and She'-chem Ha'-mor's son.

19 And the young man deferred not to do the thing, because he had delight in Jacob's daughter: and he *was* more honourable than all the house of his father.

20 And Ha'-mor and She'-chem his son came unto the gate of their city, and communed with the men of their city, saying,

21 These men *are* peaceable with us; therefore let them dwell in the land, and trade therein; for the land, behold, *it is* large enough for them; let us take their daughters to us for wives, and let us give them our daughters.

22 Only ^Therein will the men consent unto us for to dwell with us, to be one people, if every male among us be circumcised, as they *are* circumcised. *on this condition*

23 *Shall* not their ^Tcattle and their ^Tsubstance and every ^Tbeast of theirs *be* ours? only let us consent unto them, and they will dwell with us. *livestock • property • animal*

24 And unto Ha'-mor and unto She'-chem his son hearkened all that ^Rwent out of the gate of his city; and every male was circumcised, all that went out of the gate of his city. Ge 23:10,18

25 And it came to pass on the third day, when they were ^Tsore, that two of the sons of Jacob, ^RSimeon and Levi, Dinah's brethren, took each man his sword, and came upon the city boldly, and slew all the males. Ge 29:33,34; 42:24; 49:5-7 • *in pain*

26 And they ^Rslew Ha'-mor and She'-chem his son with the edge of the sword, and took Dinah out of She'-chem's house, and went out. Ge 49:5,6

27 The sons of Jacob came upon the slain, and ^Tspoiled the city, because they had defiled their sister. *plundered*

28 They took their sheep, and their oxen, and their ^Tasses, and that which *was* in the city, and that which *was* in the field, *donkeys*

29 And all their wealth, and all their little ones, and their wives took they captive, and spoiled even all that *was* in the house.

30 And Jacob said to Simeon and Levi, ^RYe have ^Rtroubled me ^Rto make me ^Tto stink among the inhabitants of the land, among the Ca'-naan-ites and the Per'-iz-zites: ^Rand I *being* few in number, they shall gather themselves together against me, and slay me; and I shall be destroyed, I and my house. Ge 49:6 • Jos 7:25 • Ex 5:21 • De 4:27 • *obnoxious*

31 And they said, Should he deal with our sister as with an harlot?

34:19 *more honourable.* That is, Shechem was "honored" more than anyone else. Because of the high esteem in which he was held by the others, and by his willingness to be circumcised, the other men agreed to submit to a religious rite which they knew would be painful and questionable.

34:25 *slew all the males.* This act of murderous revenge, preceded by deception and blasphemy, was no doubt reconciled in the minds of Simeon and Levi as a case of the end justifying the means. The name of Israel had been tarnished severely (34:7), their beloved sister not only raped but bargained for like a harlot, and the whole affair treated as a matter-of-fact commercial arrangement by the city's king. The crime could not be ignored, but they could not take vengeance on Shechem only, since the rest of the men were as guilty as he in their attitudes about it (these men would themselves have defiled Dinah if they had had the opportunity, but they had to defer to their "honored" prince). Also, if the other men would have been spared, they would immediately have responded with a vendetta against all the Israelites. Jacob, by God's wisdom, could surely have found a better solution, but in his grief had withdrawn from the whole situation.

34:29 *wives took they captive.* Critics have alleged that the women were taken by the sons of Israel for their own sexual purposes, but this is certainly an unwarranted assumption. They took the women and children "captive" (they at least spared their lives and provided for their future sustenance), evidently using them as servants thereafter. Jacob already had a significant retinue of servants, and they probably joined them.

CHAPTER 35
The Altar at Beth-el

And God said unto Jacob, Arise, go up to ᴿBeth'-el, and dwell there: and make there an altar unto God, ᴿthat appeared unto thee when thou fleddest from the face of Esau thy brother.   *Ge 28:19; 31:13 • Ge 28:13*

2 Then Jacob said unto his ᴿhousehold, and to all that *were* with him, Put away the strange gods that *are* among you, and be clean, and change your garments: *Jos 24:15*

3 And let us arise, and go up to Beth'-el; and I will make there an altar unto God, who answered me in the day of my distress, and was with me in the way which I went.

4 And they gave unto Jacob all the ᵀstrange gods which *were* in their hand, and *all their* ᴿearrings which *were* in their ears; and Jacob hid them under ᴿthe oak which *was* by She'-chem.   *Ho 2:13 • Jos 24:26 • foreign*

5 And they journeyed: and ᴿthe terror of God was upon the cities that *were* round about them, and they did not pursue after the sons of Jacob.   *Ex 15:16; 23:27*

6 So Jacob came to ᴿLuz, which *is* in the land of Canaan, that *is*, Beth'-el, he and all the people that *were* with him.   *Ge 28:19,22; 48:3*

7 And he ᴿbuilt there an altar, and called the place El-beth'-el: because ᴿthere God appeared unto him, when he fled from the face of his brother.   *Ec 5:4 • Ge 28:13*

8 But ᴿDeb'-o-rah Rebekah's nurse died, and she was buried ᵀbeneath Beth'-el under an ᵀoak: and the name of it was called Al'-lon-bach'-uth.   *Ge 24:59 • below • terebinth tree*

9 And ᴿGod appeared unto Jacob again, when he came out of Pa'-dan-a'-ram, and ᴿblessed him.   *Jos 5:13 • Ge 32:29*

10 And God said unto him, Thy name *is* Jacob: ᴿthy name shall not be called any more Jacob, ᴿbut Israel shall be thy name: and he called his name Israel.   *Ge 17:5 • Ge 32:28*

11 And God said unto him, I *am* God Almighty: be fruitful and multiply; a nation and a company of nations shall be of thee, and kings shall come out of thy loins;

12 And the land which I gave Abraham and Isaac, to thee I will give it, and to thy ᵀseed after thee will I give the land.   *descendants*

13 And God ᴿwent up from him in the place where he talked with him.   *Ge 17:22; 18:33*

14 And Jacob set up a pillar in the place where he talked with him, *even* a pillar of stone: and he poured a drink offering thereon, and he poured oil thereon.

15 And Jacob called the name of the place where God spake with him, Beth'-el.

The Deaths of Rachel and Isaac

16 And they journeyed from Beth'-el; and there was but a little way to come to Eph'-rath: and Ra'-chel ᵀtravailed, and she had hard labour.   *travailed in childbirth*

17 And it came to pass, when she was in hard labour, that the midwife said unto her, Fear not; thou shalt have this son also.

18 And it came to pass, as her soul was in departing, (for she died) that she called his name ᵀBen-o'-ni: but his father called him ᵀBenjamin.   *Lit. Son of My Sorrow • Lit. Son of the Right Hand*

35:1 *go up to Beth-el.* It is strange that during all the 10 years or so that Jacob had been back in Canaan he had never yet gone back to nearby Bethel to build his altar, as he had promised God he would do when he was leaving Canaan (28:20-22). He may have been spiritually uncomfortable with how content he allowed his family to become in their compromising and worldly prosperity at Shechem.

35:2 *the strange gods.* His family and servants still had some of the pagan images and charms they had brought from Syria, not to mention the spoils of Shechem. These spoils had to be buried before they could really meet God at Bethel (like many modern believers who try to retain many of the accoutrements of ungodliness from which they had been once delivered).

35:8 *Allon-bachuth.* Allon-bachuth means "The Oak of Weeping." Deborah was Rebekah's nurse and accompanied her when she left her home to marry Isaac. Deborah no doubt stayed with Rebekah until Rebekah's death. She had known and loved Jacob ever since he was born, and evidently had gone to live with him on the occasion of one of his trips home from Shechem to Hebron to visit his aged father Isaac. Her aged body finally yielded up its spirit after the trauma of Shechem and the arduous climb up to Bethel.

19 And ᴿRa'-chel died, and was buried in the way to ᴿEph'-rath, which *is* Beth'-le-hem.　Ge 48:7 • Mi 5:2

20 And Jacob set a pillar upon her grave: that *is* the pillar of Ra'-chel's grave ᴿunto this day.　1 Sa 10:2

21 And Israel journeyed, and spread his tent beyond ᴿthe tower of E'-dar.　Mi 4:8

22 And it came to pass, when Israel dwelt in that land, that Reuben went and lay with Bil'-hah his father's concubine: and Israel heard *it*. Now the sons of Jacob were twelve:

23 The sons of Leah; ᴿReuben, Jacob's firstborn, and Simeon, and Levi, and Judah, and Is'-sa-char, and Zeb'-u-lun:　Ex 1:1-4

24 The sons of Ra'-chel; Joseph, and Benjamin:

25 And the sons of Bil'-hah, Ra'-chel's handmaid; Dan, and Naph'-ta-li:

26 And the sons of Zil'-pah, Leah's handmaid; Gad, and Asher: these *are* the sons of Jacob, which were born to him in Pa'-dan–a'-ram.

27 And Jacob came unto Isaac his father unto ᴿMam'-re, unto the ᴿcity of Ar'-bah, which *is* He'-bron, where Abraham and Isaac sojourned.　Ge 13:18; 18:1; 23:19 • Jos 14:15

28 And the days of Isaac were an hundred and fourscore years.

29 And Isaac gave up the ghost, and died, and ᴿwas gathered unto his people, *being* old and full of days: and his sons Esau and Jacob buried him.　Ge 15:15; 25:8; 49:33

CHAPTER 36

The Generations of Esau 1 Ch 1:35-42

Now ᵀthese *are* the generations of Esau, ᴿwho *is* E'-dom.　Ge 25:30 • *this is the genealogy*

2 ᴿEsau took his wives of the daughters of Canaan; A'-dah the daughter of E'-lon the ᴿHit'-tite, and ᴿA-hol-i-ba'-mah the daughter of A'-nah the daughter of Zib'-e-on the Hi'-vite;　Ge 26:34; 28:9 • 2 Ki 7:6 • Ge 36:25

3 And ᴿBash'-e-mathᵀ Ish'-ma-el's daughter, sister of Ne-ba'-joth.　Ge 28:9 • He *Basemath*

4 And ᴿA'-dah bare to Esau El'-i-phaz; and Bash'-e-math bare Reu'-el;　1 Ch 1:35

5 And ᵀA-hol-i-ba'-mah bare Je'-ush, and Ja-a'-lam, and Ko'-rah: these *are* the sons of Esau, which were born unto him in the land of Canaan.　Or *Oholibamah*

6 And Esau took his wives, and his sons, and his daughters, and all the persons of his house, and his cattle, and all his ᵀbeasts, and all his substance, which he had got in the land of Canaan; and went into the country from the face of his brother Jacob.　*animals*

7 ᴿFor their riches were more than that they might dwell together; and the land wherein they were strangers could not ᵀbear them because of their cattle.　Ge 13:6,11 • *support*

8 Thus dwelt Esau in ᴿmount Se'-ir: ᴿEsau *is* E'-dom.　Ge 32:3 • Ge 36:1,19

9 And these *are* the generations of Esau the father of the E'-dom-ites in mount Se'-ir:

10 These *are* the names of Esau's sons;

35:19 Ephrath, which is Beth-lehem. It was here that Rachel died and here that Jesus was born, as prophesied in Micah 5:2. Rachel's son Benjamin ("son of my right hand," first named by Rachel, Benoni, "son of pain") was the progenitor of the tribe that would eventually inhabit this portion of the promised land. Hence the phrase, "Rachel weeping for her children" (Je 31:15; Ma 2:18), when Herod sought to slay the male children of Bethlehem. Note also the reference to Ephratah in Psalm 132:6.

36:1 generations of Esau. This *toledoth* of Esau was probably acquired by Jacob when he and Esau came together for their father's burial. He appended it to his own *toledoth* just before he affixed his closing signature at Genesis 37:2.

36:3 sister of Nebajoth. The names of Esau's wives here seem to conflict with those at Genesis 26:34 and Genesis 28:9. However, it was not uncommon for a person to be known by one name early in life and another later in life (e.g., Abram: Abraham, Sarai: Sarah, Jacob: Israel). Possibly women were called by new names after marriage. Therefore, probably Adah, Aholibamah and Bashemath (in this record) were the same women as Bashemath and Judith (in 26:34) and Mahalath (in 28:9), respectively. Another explanation may be that Esau actually had six wives. A final possibility is that the names in one case are those in the native tongues of the women, and in the other case are their Hebrew names.

RE1'-i-phaz the son of A'-dah the wife of Esau, Reu'-el the son of TBash'-e-math the wife of Esau.   *1 Ch 1:35 • He Basemath*

11 And the sons of El'-i-phaz were Te'-man, Omar, TZe'-pho, and Ga'-tam, and Ke'-naz.   *Zephi, 1 Ch 1:36*

12 And Tim'-na was concubine to El'-i-phaz Esau's son; and she bare to El'-i-phaz RAm'-a-lek: these *were* the sons of A'-dah Esau's wife.   *Nu 24:20*

13 And these *are* the sons of Reu'-el; Na'-hath, and Ze'-rah, Sham'-mah, and Miz'-zah: these were the sons of TBash'-e-math Esau's wife.   *He Basemath*

14 And these were the sons of A-hol-i-ba'-mah, the daughter of A'-nah the daughter of Zib'-e-on, Esau's wife: and she bare to Esau Je'-ush, and Ja-a'-lam, and Ko'-rah.

15 These *were* Tdukes of the sons of Esau: the sons of El'-i-phaz the firstborn *son* of Esau; Tduke Te'-man, duke Omar, duke Ze'-pho, duke Ke'-naz,   *chiefs • chief*

16 Duke Ko'-rah, duke Ga'-tam, *and* duke Am'-a-lek: these *are* the dukes *that came* of El'-i-phaz in the land of E'-dom; these *were* the sons of A'-dah.

17 And these *are* the sons of Reu'-el Esau's son; duke Na'-hath, duke Ze'-rah, duke Sham'-mah, duke Miz'-zah: these *are* the dukes *that came* of Reu'-el in the land of E'-dom; these *are* the sons of Bash'-e-math Esau's wife.

18 And these *are* the sons of TA-hol-i-ba'-mah Esau's wife; duke Je'-ush, duke Ja-a'-lam, duke Ko'-rah: these *were* the dukes *that came* of A-hol-i-ba'-mah the daughter of A'-nah, Esau's wife.   *Or Oholibamah*

19 These *are* the sons of Esau, who *is* E'-dom, and these *are* their dukes.

20 These *are* the sons of Se'-ir Rthe Ho'-rite, who inhabited the land; Lo'-tan, and Sho'-bal, and Zib'-e-on, and A'-nah,   *Ge 14:6*

21 And Di'-shon, and E'-zer, and Di'-shan: these *are* the dukes of the Ho'-rites, the children of Se'-ir in the land of E'-dom.

22 And the children of Lo'-tan were Ho'-ri and THe'-mam; and Lo'-tan's sister *was* Tim'-na.   *Homam, 1 Ch 1:39*

23 And the children of Sho'-bal *were* these; TAl'-van, and Ma-na'-hath, and E'-bal, She'-pho, and O'-nam.   *Alian, 1 Ch 1:40*

24 And these *are* the children of Zib'-e-on; both A'-jah, and A'-nah: this *was that* A'-nah that found Rthe Tmules in the wilderness, as he fed the Tasses of Zib'-e-on his father.   *Le 19:19 • water • donkeys*

25 And the children of A'-nah *were* these; Di'-shon, and TA-hol-i-ba'-mah the daughter of A'-nah.   *Or Oholibamah*

26 And these *are* the children of TDi'-shon; THem'-dan, and Esh'-ban, and Ith'-ran, and Che'-ran.   *He Dishan • Amram, 1 Ch 1:41*

27 The children of E'-zer *are* these; Bil'-han, and Za'-a-van, and A'-kan.

28 The children of Di'-shan *are* these; RUz, and A'-ran.   *Job 1:1*

29 These *are* the Tdukes *that came* of the Ho'-rites; Tduke Lo'-tan, duke Sho'-bal, duke Zib'-e-on, duke A'-nah,   *chiefs • chief*

30 Duke Di'-shon, duke E'-zer, duke Di'-shan: these *are* the dukes *that came* of Ho'-ri, among their dukes in the land of Se'-ir.

31 And Rthese *are* the kings that reigned in the land of E'-dom, before there reigned any king over the children of Israel.   *1 Ch 1:43*

32 And Be'-la the son of Be'-or reigned in E'-dom: and the name of his city *was* Din'-ha-bah.

33 And Be'-la died, and Jo'-bab the son of Ze'-rah of Boz'-rah reigned in his stead.

34 And Jo'-bab died, and Hu'-sham of the land of Tem'-a-ni reigned in his stead.

35 And Hu'-sham died, and Ha'-dad the son of Be'-dad, who smote Mid'-i-an in

---

36:15 *dukes.* These "dukes," or chieftains, had all risen to prominence by the time of Isaac's death. Since Esau had married 40 years before Jacob did, he had one more generation of descendants than Jacob. Fourteen such dukes are listed in Genesis 36:15-19.

36:20 *sons of Seir.* The Mount Seir region, later known as Edom (meaning "red," another name for Esau), was originally settled by Horites, or Hurrians. The descendants of Esau had partially conquered these settlers by this time.

36:31 *the land of Edom.* The rest of Genesis 36 seems to have been inserted by Moses, at the time of the exodus, since he knew that the Israelites would be encountering the Edomites when they left the wilderness. Moses knew that the Israelites would eventually have a king (De 17:14-20), even though they still did not have one in his day.

the field of Moab, reigned in his stead: and the name of his city *was* A'-vith.

36 And Ha'-dad died, and Sam'-lah of Mas-re'-kah reigned in his stead.

37 And Sam'-lah died, and Saul of Re-ho'-both *by* the river reigned in his stead.

38 And Saul died, and Ba'-al–ha'-nan the son of Ach'-bor reigned in his stead.

39 And Ba'-al–ha'-nan the son of Ach'-bor died, and Ha'-dar reigned in his stead: and the name of his city *was* Pa'-u; and his wife's name *was* Me-het'-a-bel, the daughter of Ma'-tred, the daughter of Mez'-a-hab.

40 And these *are* the names of the ᵀdukes *that came* of Esau, according to their families, after their places, by their names; duke Tim'-nah, duke Al'-vah, duke Je'-theth, *chiefs*

41 Duke ᵀA-hol-i-ba'-mah, duke E'-lah, duke Pi'-non, Or *Oholibamah*

42 Duke Ke'-naz, duke Te'-man, duke Mib'-zar,

43 Duke Mag'-di-el, duke I'-ram: these *be* the dukes of E'-dom, according to their habitations in the land of their possession: he *is* Esau the father of the E'-dom-ites.

CHAPTER 37

Joseph's Brethren Sin against Him

And Jacob dwelt in the land ᴿwherein his father was a stranger, in the land of Canaan. Ge 17:8; 23:4; 28:4; 36:7

2 ᵀThese *are* the generations of Jacob. Joseph, *being* seventeen years old, was feed-ing the flock with his brethren; and the lad *was* with the sons of Bil'-hah, and with the sons of Zil'-pah, his father's wives: and Joseph brought unto his father ᴿtheir evil report. 1 Sa 2:22-24 • *This is the genealogy*

3 Now Israel loved Joseph more than all his children, because he *was* ᴿthe son of his old age: and he ᴿmade him a ᵀcoat of *many* colours. Ge 44:20 • Ge 37:23,32 • *tunic*

4 And when his brethren saw that their father loved him more than all his brethren, they ᴿhated him, and could not speak peaceably unto him. Ge 27:41; 49:23

5 And Joseph dreamed a dream, and he told *it* his brethren: and they hated him yet the more.

6 And he said unto them, Hear, I pray you, this dream which I have dreamed:

7 For, ᴿbehold, we *were* binding sheaves in the field, and, lo, my sheaf arose, and also stood upright; and, behold, your sheaves stood round about, and made obeisance to my sheaf. Ge 42:6,9; 43:26; 44:14

8 And his brethren said to him, Shalt thou indeed reign over us? or shalt thou indeed have dominion over us? And they hated him yet the more for his dreams, and for his words.

9 And he dreamed yet another dream, and told it his brethren, and said, Behold, I have dreamed a dream more; and, behold, ᴿthe sun and the moon and the eleven stars made obeisance to me. Ge 46:29; 47:25

10 And he told *it* to his father, and to his

37:1 *Jacob dwelt in the land.* This is the termination of the long record of Jacob, which began at Genesis 25:19, and ends with Genesis 37:2: "These are the generations of Jacob." He had evidently continued the account up to the burial of his father Isaac (35:28-29). His brother Esau joined with him in the burial service, and evidently gave Jacob his own records at this time. Jacob incorporated these "generations of Esau" (ch. 36) in his own record before he closed it.

37:2 *generations of Jacob.* This is the last time the formula, "these are the generations of…," is used in Genesis. This verse probably represents the signature of Jacob at the conclusion of the section originally written by Jacob (beginning at 25:19b). The information in the rest of Genesis must have come originally from Joseph and the other sons of Jacob. Possibly Moses recognized this by affixing a similar formula at its conclusion, in Exodus 1:1.

37:2 *feeding the flock.* Literally, "was shepherd over the flock." Though he was slightly younger than the four brothers with him, he was very capable and had been placed in charge by his father. In this capacity, he was expected by his father to make full reports, and these necessarily included a record of the poor work of his brothers. Evidently the six sons of Leah had been assigned other duties in another place. Benjamin, his younger brother, was still a child, at home with his father.

brethren: and his father rebuked him, and said unto him, What *is* this dream that thou hast dreamed? Shall I and thy mother and ᴿthy brethren indeed come to bow down ourselves to thee to the earth?   Ge 27:29

11 And ᴿhis brethren envied him; but his father ᴿobserved the saying.   Ac 7:9 • Da 7:28

12 And his brethren went to feed their father's flock in ᴿShe'-chem.   Ge 33:18-20

13 And Israel said unto Joseph, Do not thy brethren feed *the flock* in She'-chem? come, and I will send thee unto them. And he said to him, Here *am* I.

14 And he said to him, Go, I pray thee, see whether it be well with thy brethren, and well with the flocks; and bring me word again. So he sent him out of the vale of He'-bron, and he came to She'-chem.

15 And a certain man found him, and, behold, *he was* wandering in the field: and the man asked him, saying, What seekest thou?

16 And he said, I seek my brethren: tell me, I pray thee, where they feed *their flocks.*

17 And the man said, They are departed hence; for I heard them say, Let us go to Do'-than. And Joseph went after his brethren, and found them in Do'-than.

18 And when they saw him afar off, even before he came near unto them, ᴿthey conspired against him to slay him.   Mk 14:1

19 And they said one to another, Behold, this ᵀdreamer cometh.   Lit. *master of dreams*

20 ᴿCome now therefore, and let us slay him, and cast him into some pit, and we will say, Some ᵀevil beast hath devoured him: and we shall see what will become of his dreams.   Pr 1:11 • *wild*

21 And ᴿReuben heard *it,* and he delivered him out of their hands; and said, Let us not kill him.   Ge 42:22

22 And Reuben said unto them, Shed no blood, *but* cast him into this pit that *is* in the wilderness, and lay no hand upon him; that he might ᵀrid him out of their hands, to deliver him to his father again.   *deliver*

23 And it came to pass, when Joseph was come unto his brethren, that they ᴿstript Joseph out of his ᵀcoat, *his* coat of *many* colours that *was* on him;   Ma 27:28 • *tunic*

24 And they took him, and cast him into a pit: and the pit *was* empty, *there was* no water in it.

25 ᴿAnd they sat down to eat ᵀbread: and they lifted up their eyes and looked, and, behold, a company of Ish'-me-el-ites came from Gil'-e-ad with their camels bearing spicery and ᴿbalm and myrrh, going to carry *it* down to Egypt.   Pr 30:20 • Je 8:22 • *a meal*

26 And Judah said unto his brethren, What profit *is it* if we slay our brother, and ᴿconceal his blood?   Ge 37:20

27 Come, and let us sell him to the Ish'-me-el-ites, and ᴿlet not our hand be upon him; for he *is* our brother *and* our flesh. And his brethren were content.   1 Sa 18:17

28 Then there passed by Mid'-i-an-ites merchantmen; and they drew and lifted up Joseph out of the pit, and sold Joseph to the Ish'-me-el-ites for twenty *pieces* of silver: and they brought Joseph into Egypt.

29 And Reuben returned unto the pit; and, behold, Joseph *was* not in the pit; and he ᴿrentᵀ his clothes.   Job 1:20 • *tore his clothes* in grief

30 And he returned unto his brethren,

37:10 *he told it.* Whether Joseph's two dreams were from God or a product of his own pride is a question. They were only fulfilled in part—his father and deceased mother never bowed down to him. In any event, it was unwise and rather arrogant of him to tell them to his family. It was specifically because of these dreams that his brothers decided to slay him (37:19-20). Nevertheless, God worked all this together for good (Ro 8:28). Joseph's pride, as well as the anger and carnality of his brothers, all needed to be changed before God would deem them ready to found his chosen nation.

37:28 *Midianites.* These traders are called both Midianites (here and in 37:36) and Ishmaelites (here and in 37:25). These two tribes were both descended from Abraham (he was father of both Ishmael through Hagar and Midian through Keturah), both lived in the same region, and undoubtedly both were associated closely in many ways. The result was the interchangeable use of their names.

37:28 *twenty pieces of silver.* Twenty pieces of silver was the going price of a slave. In the time of Zechariah (and of Christ) it was 30 pieces of silver (Ze 11:12-13; Ma 26:14-15).

and said, The [T]child [R]is not; and I, whither shall I go?   Ge 42:13,36 • *lad*

31 And they took [R]Joseph's [T]coat, and killed a kid of the goats, and dipped the coat in the blood;   Ge 37:3,23 • *tunic*

32 And they sent the [T]coat of *many* colours, and they brought *it* to their father; and said, This have we found: know now whether it *be* thy son's coat or no.   *tunic*

33 And he [T]knew it, and said, *It is* my son's [T]coat; an [R]evil[T] beast hath devoured him; Joseph is without doubt [T]rent in pieces.   Ge 37:20 • *recognized* • *tunic* • *wild* • *torn*

34 And Jacob [R]rent[T] his clothes, and put sackcloth upon his loins, and [R]mourned for his son many days.   2 Sa 3:31 • Ge 50:10 • *tore*

35 And all his sons and all his daughters [R]rose up to comfort him; but he refused to be comforted; and he said, For I will go down into the grave unto my son mourning. Thus his father wept for him.   2 Sa 12:17

36 And [R]the Mid'-i-an-ites sold him into Egypt unto Pot'-i-phar, an officer of Pharaoh's, *and* captain of the guard.   Ge 39:1

CHAPTER 38

Joseph's Brethren Sin with the Canaanites

And it came to pass at that time, that Judah went down from his brethren, and [R]turned in to a certain A-dul'-lam-ite, whose name *was* Hi'-rah.   2 Ki 4:8

2 And Judah saw there a daughter of a certain Ca'-naan-ite, whose name *was* Shu'-ah; and he took her, and went in unto her.

3 And she conceived, and bare a son; and he called his name [R]Er.   Ge 46:12

4 And she conceived again, and bare a son; and she called his name O'-nan.

5 And she yet again conceived, and bare a son; and called his name [R]She'-lah: and he was at Che'-zib, when she bare him.   Nu 26:20

6 And Judah [R]took a wife for Er his firstborn, whose name *was* Ta'-mar.   Ge 21:21

7 And [R]Er, Judah's firstborn, was wicked in the sight of the LORD; [R]and the LORD [T]slew him.   Ge 46:12 • 1 Ch 2:3 • *killed*

8 And Judah said unto O'-nan, Go in unto [R]thy brother's wife, and marry her, and raise up seed to thy brother.   De 25:5,6

9 And O'-nan knew that the seed should not be [R]his; and it came to pass, when he went in unto his brother's wife, that he spilled *it* on the ground, lest that he should give seed to his brother.   De 25:6

10 And the thing which he did [T]displeased the LORD: wherefore he slew [R]him also.   Ge 46:12 • Lit. *was evil in the eyes of*

11 Then said Judah to Ta'-mar his daughter in law, [R]Remain a widow at thy father's house, till She'-lah my son be grown: for he said, Lest peradventure he die also, as his brethren *did*. And Ta'-mar went and dwelt [R]in her father's house.   Ru 1:12,13 • Le 22:13

12 And in process of time the daughter of Shu'-ah Judah's wife died; and Judah [R]was comforted, and went up unto his sheepshearers to Tim'-nath, he and his friend Hi'-rah the A-dul'-lam-ite.   2 Sa 13:39

13 And it was told Ta'-mar, saying, Behold thy father in law goeth up [R]to Tim'-nath to shear his sheep.   Jos 15:10,57

14 And she put her widow's garments off from her, and covered her with a vail, and wrapped herself, and [R]sat in an open place,

---

37:35 the grave. The word translated "grave" is actually the Hebrew *sheol*, the great pit in the center of the earth where the spirits of the dead are confined after death, awaiting future resurrection and judgment. This is its first occurrence, and it is significant that righteous Jacob would go there, along with other spirits of the righteous dead, until Christ would take them with Him to paradise after His resurrection. See notes on Luke 16:22-23. The spirits of the lost will remain there until the time of final judgment (Re 20:11-15).

37:36 Potiphar. Archaeological research shows that *Potiphar*, like *Pharaoh*, was a title in Egypt rather than a personal name.

38:6 Tamar. Tamar had a son by Judah through a rather involved and unsavory intrigue, and is the first of four women (the others being Rahab, Ruth and Bathsheba) listed in the kingly genealogy of Jesus Christ (see Ma 1:3). This, among other factors, is surely a testimony of God's grace. Tamar had twin sons, the youngest of which, Phares, was the one in the royal line.

38:8 raise up seed to thy brother. This so-called Levirate marriage relationship (De 25:5-10) was practiced also in other nations at the time, according to the Nuzi tablets.

which *is* by the way to Tim'-nath; for she saw ᴿthat She'-lah was grown, and she was not given unto him to wife. Pr 7:12 • Ge 38:11,26

15 When Judah saw her, he thought her *to be* an harlot; because she had covered her face.

16 And he turned unto her by the way, and said, Go to, I pray thee, let me come in unto thee; (for he knew not that she *was* his daughter in law.) And she said, What wilt thou give me, that thou mayest come in unto me?

17 And he said, ᴿI will send *thee* a kid from the flock. And she said, ᴿWilt thou give *me* a pledge, till thou send *it*? Eze 16:33 • Ge 38:20

18 And he said, What pledge shall I give thee? And she said, ᴿThy signet, and thy bracelets, and thy staff that *is* in thine hand. And he gave *it* her, and came in unto her, and she conceived by him. Ge 38:25; 41:42

19 And she arose, and went away, and ᴿlaid by her vail from her, and put on the garments of her widowhood. Ge 38:14

20 And Judah sent the kid by the hand of his friend the A-dul'-lam-ite, to receive *his* pledge from the woman's hand: but he found her not.

21 Then he asked the men of that place, saying, Where *is* the harlot, that *was* ᵀopenly by the way side? And they said, There was no harlot in this *place*. in full view

22 And he returned to Judah, and said, I cannot find her; and also the men of the place said, *that* there was no harlot in this *place*.

23 And Judah said, Let her take *it* to her, lest we be shamed: behold, I sent this kid, and thou hast not found her.

24 And it came to pass about three months after, that it was told Judah, saying, Ta'-mar thy daughter in law hath ᴿplayed the harlot; and also, behold, she *is* with child by whoredom. And Judah said, Bring her forth, and let her be burnt. Ju 19:2

25 When she *was* brought forth, she sent to her father in law, saying, By the man, whose these *are, am* I with child: and she said, Discern, I pray thee, whose *are* these, the signet, and ᵀbracelets, and staff. cord

26 And Judah acknowledged *them*, and said, She hath been more righteous than I; because that I gave her not to She'-lah my son. And he knew her again no more.

27 And it came to pass in the time of her travail, that, behold, twins *were* in her womb.

28 And it came to pass, when she travailed, that *the one* put out *his* hand: and the midwife took and bound upon his hand a scarlet thread, saying, This came out first.

29 And it came to pass, as he drew back his hand, that, behold, his brother came out: and she said, How hast thou broken forth? *this* breach *be* upon thee: therefore his name was called ᴿPha'-rez. Ge 46:12

30 And afterward came out his brother, that had the scarlet thread upon his hand: and his name was called ᴿZar'-ah. 1 Ch 2:4

CHAPTER 39

Joseph Is Tempted by Potiphar's Wife

And Joseph was brought down to Egypt; and Pot'-i-phar, an officer of Pharaoh, captain of the guard, an Egyptian, bought him of the hands of the Ish'-me-el-ites, which had brought him down thither.

2 And ᴿthe LORD was with Joseph, and he was a prosperous man; and he was in the house of his master the Egyptian. Ac 7:9

3 And his master saw that the LORD *was* with him, and that the LORD ᴿmade all that he did to prosper in his hand. Ps 1:3

38:18 *What pledge.* The Hebrew word for "pledge" is essentially the same as that for "surety" in Genesis 44:32, where Judah was offering himself to Joseph as a substitute to receive Benjamin's punishment, instead of Benjamin. Similarly, Judah's pledge was given to Tamar in substitution for the payment due to Tamar. Both, in effect, can be considered as types of Christ offering His own shed blood in substitution for the death we have deserved.

38:18 *signet.* A signet is a seal used as a signature to confirm a contract.

39:1 *officer of Pharaoh.* The word here used for "officer" actually means "eunuch." The same word later was used for Pharaoh's butler and baker (40:2). Evidently, any man who accepted a high position in Pharaoh's bureaucracy was required to become a eunuch. This situation may have contributed to the adulterous desires of Potiphar's wife.

4 And Joseph [R]found grace in his sight, and he served him: and he made him overseer over his house, and all *that* he had he put into his hand.　　Ge 18:3; 19:19; 39:21

5 And it came to pass from the time *that* he had made him overseer in his house, and over all that he had, that the Lord blessed the Egyptian's house for Joseph's sake; and the blessing of the Lord was upon all that he had in the house, and in the field.

6 And he left all that he had in Joseph's [T]hand; and he knew not [T]ought he had, [T]save the bread which he did eat. And Joseph [R]was *a* goodly *person*, and well favoured.　　1 Sa 16:12 • *care • anything • except*

7 And it came to pass after these things, that his master's wife cast her eyes upon Joseph; and she said, [R]Lie with me.　2 Sa 13:11

8 But he refused, and said unto his master's wife, Behold, my master [T]wotteth not what *is* with me in the house, and he hath committed all that he hath to my hand;　*knows*

9 *There is* none greater in this house than I; neither hath he kept back any thing from me but thee, because thou *art* his wife: [R]how then can I do this great wickedness, and [R]sin against God?　　Pr 6:29,32 • Ps 51:4

10 And it came to pass, as she spake to Joseph day by day, that he hearkened not unto her, to lie by her, *or* to be with her.

11 And it came to pass about this time, that *Joseph* went into the house to do his [T]business; and *there was* none of the men of the house there within.　　*work*

12 And she [R]caught him by his garment, saying, Lie with me: and he left his garment in her hand, and fled, and got him out. Pr 7:13

13 And it came to pass, when she saw that he had left his garment in her hand, and was fled [T]forth,　　*outside*

14 That she called unto the men of her house, and spake unto them, saying, See, he hath brought in an [R]Hebrew unto us to mock

us; he came in unto me to lie with me, and I cried with a loud voice:　　Ge 14:13; 41:12

15 And it came to pass, when he heard that I lifted up my voice and cried, that he left his garment with me, and fled, and got him out.

16 And she laid up his garment by her, until his lord came home.

17 And she [R]spake unto him according to these words, saying, The Hebrew servant, which thou hast brought unto us, came in unto me to mock me:　　Ex 23:1

18 And it came to pass, as I lifted up my voice and cried, that he left his garment with me, and fled out.

19 And it came to pass, when his master heard the words of his wife, which she spake unto him, saying, After this manner did thy servant to me; that [T]his [R]wrath was kindled.　　Pr 6:34,35 • *his anger was aroused*

20 And Joseph's master took him, and [R]put him into the [R]prison, a place where the king's prisoners *were* bound: and he was there in the prison.　　Ps 105:18 • Ge 40:3,15; 41:14

21 But the Lord was with Joseph, and shewed him mercy, and gave him favour in the sight of the keeper of the prison.

22 And the keeper of the prison [R]committed to Joseph's hand all the prisoners that *were* in the prison; and whatsoever they did there, he was the doer *of it*.　Ge 39:4; 40:3,4

23 The keeper of the prison looked not to any thing *that was* under his hand; because the Lord was with him, and *that* which he did, the Lord made *it* to prosper.

CHAPTER 40

Joseph Interprets Dreams in Prison

And it came to pass after these things, *that* the [R]butler of the king of Egypt and *his* baker had offended their lord the king of Egypt.　　Ne 1:11

39:20 *in the prison*. More detailed information about the sufferings of Joseph in the prison are given in Psalm 105:17-18.

40:1 *butler...baker*. These two officials were responsible not only for preparing Pharaoh's drink and food, but also for assuring its safety. It is possible that a cache of some kind of poison had been discovered, with the implication that it would be used in an assassination attempt. Pharaoh's investigative police were trying to determine whether it was intended for his wine or for his bread, and both officials were placed in prison awaiting that determination.

2 And Pharaoh was wroth against two *of* his officers, against the chief of the butlers, and against the chief of the bakers.

3 And he put them in ward in the house of the captain of the guard, into the prison, the place where Joseph *was* bound.

4 And the captain of the guard charged Joseph with them, and he served them: and they continued a season in ward.

5 And they ᴿdreamed a dream both of them, each man his dream in one night, each man according to the interpretation of his dream, the butler and the baker of the king of Egypt, which *were* bound in the prison.   Ge 37:5; 41:1

6 And Joseph came in unto them in the morning, and looked upon them, and, behold, they *were* ᵀsad.   *dejected*

7 And he asked Pharaoh's officers that *were* with him in the ward of his lord's house, saying, ᴿWherefore look ye *so* sadly to day?   Ne 2:2

8 And they said unto him, ᴿWe have dreamed a dream, and *there is* no interpreter of it. And Joseph said unto them, ᴿDo not interpretations *belong* to God? tell me *them,* I pray you.   Ge 41:15 • [Da 2:11,20-22,27,28,47]

9 And the chief butler told his dream to Joseph, and said to him, In my dream, behold, a vine *was* before me;

10 And in the vine *were* three branches: and it *was* as though it budded, *and* her blossoms shot forth; and the clusters thereof brought forth ripe grapes:

11 And Pharaoh's cup *was* in my hand: and I took the grapes, and pressed them into Pharaoh's cup, and I gave the cup into Pharaoh's hand.

12 And Joseph said unto him, ᴿThis *is* the interpretation of it: The three branches ᴿ*are* three days: Da 2:36; 4:18,19 • Ge 40:18; 42:17

13 Yet within three days shall Pharaoh ᴿlift up thine head, and restore thee unto thy ᵀplace: and thou shalt deliver Pharaoh's cup into his hand, after the former manner when thou wast his butler.   2 Ki 25:27 • *position*

14 But ᴿthink on me when it shall be well with thee, and ᴿshew kindness, I pray thee, unto me, and make mention of me unto Pharaoh, and bring me out of this house: Lk 23:42 • Jos 2:12

15 For indeed I was ᴿstolen away out of the land of the Hebrews: ᴿand here also have I done nothing that they should put me into the dungeon.   Ge 37:26-28 • Ge 39:20

16 When the chief baker saw that the interpretation was good, he said unto Joseph, I also *was* in my dream, and, behold, *I had* three white baskets on my head:

17 And in the uppermost basket *there was* of all manner of ᵀbakemeats for Pharaoh; and the birds did eat them out of the basket upon my head.   *baked goods*

18 And Joseph answered and said, ᴿThis *is* the interpretation thereof: The three baskets *are* three days: Ge 40:12

19 ᴿYet within three days shall Pharaoh lift up thy head from off thee, and shall ᴿhang thee on a tree; and the birds shall eat thy flesh from off thee.   Ge 40:13 • De 21:22

20 And it came to pass the third day, *which was* Pharaoh's ᴿbirthday, that he made a feast unto all his servants: and he lifted up the head of the chief butler and of the chief baker among his servants.   Ma 14:6-10

21 And he ᴿrestored the chief butler unto his butlership again; and ᴿhe gave the cup into Pharaoh's hand: Ge 40:13 • Ne 2:1

22 But he ᴿhanged the chief baker: as Joseph had interpreted to them.   Ge 40:19

23 Yet did not the chief butler remember Joseph, but ᴿforgat him.   Ec 9:15,16

40:8 interpretations belong to God. Joseph's own dreams, the meaning of which God had revealed to him (37:5-10), had prepared him for his crucial ministry in Egypt. First he interpreted the dreams of the butler and baker, then eventually of Pharaoh himself. In all these, Joseph realized that God had given both the dream and the interpretation, all in order to accomplish His own purposes.

40:20 lifted up the head. Evidently the butler (or "cupbearer") had been found innocent of the suspected crime against Pharaoh, so Pharaoh "lifted up his head" in the sense of restoring him to his previous high position in the court. The chief baker had been found guilty, so his head was "lifted up" on a gallows.

CHAPTER 41

Pharaoh Calls Joseph from Prison

And it came to pass at the end of two full years, that ᴿPharaoh dreamed: and, behold, he stood by the river.   Ge 40:5

2 And, behold, there came up out of the river seven well favoured kine and fatfleshed; and they fed in a meadow.

3 And, behold, seven other ᵀkine came up after them out of the river, ᵀill favoured and leanfleshed; and stood by the *other* kine upon the brink of the river.   *cows • ugly and gaunt*

4 And the ᵀill favoured and leanfleshed kine did eat up the seven well favoured and fat kine. So Pharaoh awoke.   *ugly and gaunt cows*

5 And he slept and dreamed the second time: and, behold, seven ears of corn came up upon one stalk, ᵀrank and good.   *plump*

6 And, behold, seven thin ᵀears and ᵀblasted with the ᴿeast wind sprung up after them.   Ex 10:13 • *heads* of grain • *blighted*

7 And the seven thin ᵀears devoured the seven rank and full ears. And Pharaoh awoke, and, behold, *it was* a dream.   *heads*

8 And it came to pass in the morning that his spirit was troubled; and he sent and called for all the magicians of Egypt, and all the wise men thereof: and Pharaoh told them his dream; but *there was* none that could interpret them unto Pharaoh.

9 Then spake the ᴿchief butler unto Pharaoh, saying, I do remember my faults this day: Ge 40:1,14,23

10 Pharaoh was ᴿwrothᵀ with his servants, ᴿand put me in ᵀward in the captain of the guard's house, *both* me and the chief baker: Ge 40:2,3 • Ge 39:20 • *angry • custody*

11 And we dreamed a dream in one night, I and he; we dreamed each man according to the interpretation of his dream.

12 And *there was* there with us a young man, an Hebrew, ᴿservant to the captain of the guard; and we told him, and he interpreted to us our dreams; to each man according to his dream he did interpret. Ge 37:36

13 And it came to pass, ᴿas he interpreted to us, so it was; me he restored unto mine office, and him he hanged.   Ge 40:21,22

14 ᴿThen Pharaoh sent and called Joseph, and they ᴿbrought him hastily ᴿout of the dungeon: and he shaved *himself*, and ᴿchanged his raiment, and came in unto Pharaoh.   Ps 105:20 • Da 2:25 • [1 Sa 2:8] • 2 Ki 25:27-29

15 And Pharaoh said unto Joseph, I have dreamed a dream, and *there is* none that can interpret it: ᴿand I have heard say of thee, *that* thou canst understand a dream to interpret it.   Da 5:16

16 And Joseph answered Pharaoh, saying, ᴿ*It is* not in me: God shall give Pharaoh an answer of peace.   Da 2:30

17 And Pharaoh said unto Joseph, ᴿIn my dream, behold, I stood upon the bank of the river: Ge 41:1

18 And, behold, there came up out of the river seven ᵀkine, fatfleshed and well favoured; and they fed in a meadow: *cows*

19 And, behold, seven other ᵀkine came up after them, poor and very ill favoured and leanfleshed, such as I never saw in all the land of Egypt for ᵀbadness: *cows • ugliness*

20 And the lean and the ill favoured ᵀkine did eat up the first seven fat kine: *cows*

21 And when they had eaten them up, it could not be known that they had eaten them; but they *were* still ᵀill favoured, as at the beginning. So I awoke.   *ugly*

22 And I saw in my dream, and, behold, seven ᵀears came up in one stalk, full and good: *heads* of grain

23 And, behold, seven ᵀears, withered, thin, *and* ᵀblasted with the east wind, sprung up after them: *heads • blighted*

24 And the thin ᵀears devoured the seven good ears: and ᴿI told *this* unto the magicians; but *there was* none that could declare *it* to me.   Is 8:19 • *heads*

25 And Joseph said unto Pharaoh, The dream of Pharaoh *is* one: ᴿGod hath shewed Pharaoh what he *is* about to do.   Da 2:28,29,45

26 The seven good ᵀkine *are* seven years; and the seven good ᵀears *are* seven years: the dream *is* one.   *cows • heads* of grain

27 And the seven thin and ᵀill favoured kine that came up after them *are* seven

---

41:1 *by the river*. The river in Pharaoh's dream was undoubtedly the Nile River, which was the primary source of Egypt's great prosperity.

41:5 *rank*. That is, "robust."

41:14 *shaved himself*. The Egyptians were customarily clean-shaven.

years; and the seven empty ᵀears ᵀblasted with the east wind shall be ᴿseven years of famine. 2 Ki 8:1 • *ugly cows* • *heads* • *blighted*

28 ᴿThis *is* the thing which I have spoken unto Pharaoh: What God *is* about to do he sheweth unto Pharaoh. [Ge 41:25,32]

29 Behold, there come ᴿseven years of great plenty throughout all the land of Egypt: Ge 41:47

30 And there shall ᴿarise after them seven years of famine; and all the plenty shall be forgotten in the land of Egypt; and the famine shall consume the land; Ge 41:54,56

31 And the plenty shall not be known in the land by reason of that famine following; for it *shall be* very grievous.

32 And for that the dream was ᵀdoubled unto Pharaoh twice; *it is* because the ᴿthing *is* established by God, and God will shortly bring it to pass. Nu 23:19 • *repeated*

33 Now therefore let Pharaoh look out a man ᵀdiscreet and wise, and set him over the land of Egypt. *discerning*

34 Let Pharaoh do *this*, and let him appoint ᵀofficers over the land, and ᴿtake up the fifth part of the land of Egypt in the seven plenteous years. [Pr 6:6-8] • *overseers*

35 And ᴿlet them gather all the food of those good years that come, and lay up ᵀcorn under the hand of Pharaoh, and let them keep food in the cities. Ge 41:48 • *grain*

36 And that food shall be for store to the land against the seven years of famine, which shall be in the land of Egypt; that the land perish not through the famine.

Joseph Is Exalted over Egypt

37 And ᴿthe thing was good in the eyes of Pharaoh, and in the eyes of all his servants. Ac 7:10

38 And Pharaoh said unto his servants, Can we find *such a one* as this *is*, a man ᴿin whom the Spirit of God *is*? Nu 27:18

39 And Pharaoh said unto Joseph, Forasmuch as God hath shewed thee all this, *there is* none so discreet and wise as thou *art*:

40 ᴿThou shalt be ᵀover my house, and according unto thy word shall all my people be ruled: only in the throne will I be greater than thou. Ps 105:21 • *in charge of*

41 And Pharaoh said unto Joseph, See, I have set thee over all the land of Egypt.

42 And Pharaoh ᴿtook off his ring from his hand, and put it upon Joseph's hand, and arrayed him in vestures of fine linen, and put a gold chain about his neck; Es 3:10

43 And he made him to ride in the second ᴿchariot which he had; and they cried before him, Bow the knee: and he made him *ruler* over all the land of Egypt. Ge 46:29

44 And Pharaoh said unto Joseph, I *am* Pharaoh, and ᵀwithout thee shall no man lift up his hand or foot in all the land of Egypt. *without your consent*

45 And Pharaoh called Joseph's name Zaph'-nath–pa-a-ne'-ah; and he gave him to

---

41:38 *such a one.* In a pagan, idolatrous court, where many nature-gods were worshipped, Joseph was not embarrassed or hesitant to speak again and again about the true God of creation (41:16,25,28,32). As a result, Pharaoh acknowledged God (41:39), and recognized that the Spirit of God was in Joseph.

41:44 *I am Pharaoh.* The identity of this particular Pharaoh has long been a matter of dispute among Bible scholars, as is the entire subject of Egyptian chronology. The generally favorable treatment accorded Joseph and his brethren during this period has been considered by some as support for the view that this Pharaoh was among the Hyksos kings who ruled Egypt for almost 200 years, since their Semitic background possibly would make them more amenable to association with Israelites than would be the case with the native Egyptians, who were Hamitic in background. On the other hand, the Hyksos were notoriously cruel and pagan Baal-worshipers, according to the evidence from ancient historians such as Manetho and Josephus. The question of Egyptian chronology and the identity of the various Pharaohs mentioned in the Bible is still unsettled, but that fact should not undermine our confidence in the biblical records, which are much superior to the highly self-serving and uncertain testimony of the ancient historians and the archaeological inscriptions.

41:45 *Zaphnath-paaneah.* The Egyptian name given to Joseph probably meant something like "God speaks, giving life to the world," but this is uncertain. The name of his wife, Asenath, probably meant "dedicated to the sun." Her father was priest of a temple dedicated to

wife [R]As'-e-nath the daughter of Pot-i-phe'-rah priest of On. And Joseph went out over *all* the land of Egypt. Ge 46:20

46 And Joseph *was* thirty years old when he [R]stood before Pharaoh king of Egypt. And Joseph went out from the presence of Pharaoh, and went throughout all the land of Egypt. 1 Sa 16:21

47 And in the seven plenteous years the earth brought forth [T]by handfuls. Abundantly

48 And he gathered up all the food of the seven years, which were in the land of Egypt, and laid up the food in the cities: the food of the field, which *was* round about every city, laid he up in the same.

49 And Joseph gathered corn as the sand of the sea, very much, until he left numbering; for *it was* without number.

50 [R]And unto Joseph were born two sons before the years of famine came, which As'-e-nath the daughter of Pot-i-phe'-rah priest of On bare unto him. Ge 46:20; 48:5

51 And Joseph called the name of the firstborn [T]Ma-nas'-seh: For God, *said he*, hath made me forget all my toil, and all my [R]father's house. Ps 45:10 • Lit. *Making Forgetful*

52 And the name of the second called he E'-phra-im: For God hath caused me to be fruitful in the land of my affliction.

53 And the seven years of plenteousness, that was in the land of Egypt, were ended.

54 [R]And the seven years of dearth began to come, [R]according as Joseph had said: and the dearth was in all lands; but in all the land of Egypt there was bread. Ac 7:11 • Ge 41:30

55 And when all the land of Egypt was famished, the people cried to Pharaoh for bread: and Pharaoh said unto all the Egyptians, Go unto Joseph; [R]what he saith to you, do. Jo 2:5

56 And the famine was over all the face of the earth: And Joseph opened [T]all the storehouses, and [R]sold unto the Egyptians; and the famine [T]waxed sore in the land of Egypt. Ge 42:6 • Lit. *all that was in them* • *became severe*

57 [R]And all countries came into Egypt to Joseph for to buy *corn*; because that the famine was *so* sore in all lands. Eze 29:12

CHAPTER 42

Joseph's Brethren Travel to Egypt

Now when [R]Jacob saw that there was corn in Egypt, Jacob said unto his sons, Why do ye look one upon another? Ac 7:12

2 And he said, Behold, I have heard that there is [T]corn in Egypt: get you down thither, and buy for us from thence; that we may [R]live, and not die. Ge 43:8 • *grain*

3 And Joseph's ten brethren went down to buy [T]corn in Egypt. *grain*

4 But Benjamin, Joseph's brother, Jacob sent not with his brethren; for he said, [R]Lest peradventure mischief befall him. Ge 42:38

5 And the sons of Israel came to buy [T]corn among those that came: for the famine was [R]in the land of Canaan. Ac 7:11 • Grain

6 And Joseph *was* the governor [R]over the land, *and he it was* that sold to all the peo-

---

the Egyptian sun god. We can probably assume that Joseph led her to worship the true God, since Pharaoh himself apparently recognized His power (note 41:16,25,32,39).

41:51 *Manasseh.* The name of Joseph's first son meant "causing to forget." The name of his second son, Ephraim (41:52), meant "fruitful."

41:54 *the dearth was in all lands.* An ancient tablet was discovered in Yemen in the 19th century, indicating that in that land there had been seven years of abundance followed by a number of years of severe famine. The age of the tablet was uncertain but it is possible that it correlates with the Egyptian years of abundance and famine at the time of Joseph.

42:1 *look one upon another.* Jacob's sons probably realized that they might eventually have to get grain in Egypt, but they also knew that was where they had dispatched Joseph. Their furtive glances at this time suggest that they had already discussed this situation among themselves.

42:6 *bowed down themselves.* When his brothers bowed before Joseph, they were fulfilling the prophecy of his first dream, as he had reported it to them some 21 or more years earlier (37:5-10).

42:7 *saw his brethren.* It seems very likely that Joseph knew that his brothers would eventually have to come to him to buy grain, and had planned how he would handle

ple of the land: and Joseph's brethren came, and bowed down themselves before him *with* their faces to the earth. Ge 41:41,55

7 And Joseph saw his brethren, and he knew them, but ᵀmade himself ᴿstrange unto them, and spake ᵀroughly unto them; and he said unto them, Whence come ye? And they said, From the land of Canaan to buy food. Ge 45:1,2 • *acted as a stranger to them* • *harshly*

8 And Joseph knew his brethren, but they knew not him.

9 And Joseph ᴿremembered the dreams which he dreamed of them, and said unto them, Ye *are* spies; to see the ᵀnakedness of the land ye are come. Ge 37:5-9 • *exposed parts*

10 And they said unto him, Nay, my lord, but to buy food are thy servants come.

11 We *are* all one man's sons; we *are* ᵀtrue *men*, thy servants are no spies. *honest*

12 And he said unto them, Nay, but to see the nakedness of the land ye are come.

13 And they said, Thy servants *are* twelve brethren, the sons of one man in the land of Canaan; and, behold, the youngest *is* this day with our father, and one *is* not.

14 And Joseph said unto them, That *is it* that I spake unto you, saying, Ye *are* spies:

15 Hereby ye shall be proved: By the life of Pharaoh ye shall not go forth hence, except your youngest brother come hither.

16 Send one of you, and let him fetch your brother, and ye shall be kept in prison, that your words may be ᵀproved, whether *there be any* truth in you: or else by the life of Pharaoh surely ye *are* spies. *tested*

17 And he put them all together into ᵀward ᴿthree days. Ge 40:4,7,12 • *prison*

18 And Joseph said unto them the third day, This do, and live; ᴿfor I fear God: Le 25:43

19 If ye *be* true *men*, let one of your brethren be bound in the house of your prison: go ye, carry ᵀcorn for the famine of your houses: *grain*

20 But bring your youngest brother unto me; so shall your words be verified, and ye shall not die. And they did so.

21 And they said one to another, We *are* verily guilty concerning our brother, in that we saw the anguish of his soul, when he besought us, and we would not hear; therefore is this distress come upon us.

22 And Reuben answered them, saying, ᴿSpake I not unto you, saying, Do not sin against the ᵀchild; and ye would not hear? therefore, behold, also his blood is ᴿrequired. Ge 37:21,22,29 • Ge 9:5,6 • *boy*

23 And they knew not that Joseph understood *them*; for he spake unto them by an interpreter.

24 And he turned himself ᵀabout from them, and ᴿwept; and returned to them again, and ᵀcommuned with them, and took from them Simeon, and bound him before their eyes. Ge 43:30; 45:14,15 • *away* • *talked*

---

the situation when they would finally appear—no doubt after much thought and prayer. He was most concerned that God's promises to Abraham, Isaac and Jacob be fulfilled in the descendants of Israel, but this would first require full reconciliation of all the family members to each other. He was not seeking revenge but restoration, and this would necessarily require recognition of their sin by his brothers, followed by forgiveness by himself. Accordingly, the several stages of his plan to bring this about were set in motion at this time.

42:16 *fetch your brother*. It was important for Joseph to learn whether the ten older brothers resented Benjamin, as they had him, since he and Benjamin were the only sons of Jacob's beloved Rachel.

42:21 *verily guilty*. For the first time, Joseph knew that his brothers had recognized, and were confessing their sin. This was what he wanted to hear.

42:23 *an interpreter*. Since Babel, it had been necessary to develop a profession of linguists, who could translate one language into another. This explains the frequent accounts of Abraham and others being able to communicate with people of other nations.

42:24 *Simeon*. Joseph longed to be reconciled to his family, but first had to learn their attitude to him, to their father and to his younger brother Benjamin. Therefore, he subjected them to a number of tests. After hearing them express regret for what they had done to him (42:21-22), Joseph took Simeon hostage while he sent the older brothers back for Benjamin, since Simeon had taken the lead part in their action against Joseph. This was calculated to further stir their consciences.

25 Then Joseph ᴿcommanded to fill their sacks with ᵀcorn, and to ᴿrestore every man's money into his sack, and to give them provision for the way: and ᴿthus did he unto them. Ge 44:1 • Ge 43:12 • [Ro 12:17,20,21] • *grain*

26 And they ᵀladed their ᵀasses with the ᵀcorn, and departed thence. *loaded • donkeys • grain*

27 And as ᴿone of them opened his sack to give his ᵀass ᵀprovender in the inn, he ᵀespied his money; for, behold, it *was* in his sack's mouth. Ge 43:21,22 • *donkey • feed • saw*

28 And he said unto his brethren, My money is restored; and, lo, *it is* even in my sack: and ᵀtheir heart failed *them*, and they were afraid, saying one to another, What *is* this *that* God hath done unto us? *their hearts sank*

29 And they came unto Jacob their father unto the land of Canaan, and told him all that befell unto them; saying,

30 The man, *who is* the lord of the land, ᴿspake ᵀroughly to us, and took us for spies of the country. Ge 42:7 • *harshly*

31 And we said unto him, We *are* ᵀtrue *men*; we are no spies: *honest*

32 We *be* twelve brethren, sons of our father; one *is* not, and the youngest *is* this day with our father in the land of Canaan.

33 And the man, the lord of the country, said unto us, ᴿHereby shall I know that ye *are* true *men*; leave one of your brethren *here* with me, and take *food for* the famine of your households, and be gone: Ge 42:15,19,20

34 And bring your ᴿyoungest brother unto me: then shall I know that ye *are* no spies, but *that* ye *are* true *men:* so will I deliver you your brother, and ye shall ᴿtraffickᵀ in the land. Ge 42:20; 43:3,5 • Ge 34:10 • *trade*

35 And it came to pass as they emptied their sacks, that, behold, ᴿevery man's bundle of money *was* in his sack: and when *both* they and their father saw the bundles of money, they were afraid. Ge 43:12,15,21

36 And Jacob their father said unto them, Me have ye ᴿbereaved *of my children:* Joseph *is* not, and Simeon *is* not, and ye will take ᴿBenjamin *away:* all these things are against me. Ge 43:14 • [Ro 8:28,31]

37 And Reuben spake unto his father, saying, Slay my two sons, if I bring him not to thee: deliver him into my hand, and I will bring him to thee again.

38 And he said, My son shall not go down with you; for ᴿhis brother is dead, and he is left alone: ᴿif mischief befall him by the way in the which ye go, then shall ye bring down my gray hairs with sorrow to the grave. Ge 37:22; 42:13; 44:20,28 • Ge 42:4; 44:29

CHAPTER 43

Joseph's Brethren Return to Egypt

And the famine *was* sore in the land. 2 And it came to pass, when they had eaten up the corn which they had brought out of Egypt, their father said unto them, Go ᴿagain, buy us a little food. Ge 42:2; 44:25

3 And Judah spake unto him, saying, The man did solemnly ᵀprotest unto us, saying, Ye shall not see my face, except your ᴿbrother *be* with you. Ge 42:20; 43:5; 44:23 • Lit. *warn*

4 If thou wilt send our brother with us, we will go down and buy thee food:

5 But if thou wilt not send *him*, we will not go down: for the man said unto us, Ye shall not see my face, except your brother *be* with you.

6 And Israel said, Wherefore dealt ye *so* ᵀill with me, *as* to tell the man whether ye had yet a brother? *wickedly*

7 And they said, The man asked us ᵀstraitly of our state, and of our kindred, saying, *Is* your father yet alive? have ye *another* brother? and we told him according to ᵀthe tenor of these words: could we certainly know that he would say, Bring your brother down? *pointedly about ourselves • Lit. these words*

8 And Judah said unto Israel his father, Send the lad with me, and we will arise and go; that we may ᴿlive, and not die, both we, and thou, *and* also our little ones. Ge 42:2; 47:19

42:27 *provender.* An old word for "animal fodder."

42:37 *Slay my two sons.* Poor Reuben, out of favor with Jacob because of his incest with Bilhah, desperately sought his father's favor by this absurd offer. What possible satisfaction did he think Jacob would derive from the death of two of his grandsons?

43:9 *surety for him.* Judah was only the fourth of Jacob's sons, but at this crisis, he begins to assume the family leadership. His offer to be "surety" for Benjamin, if necessary,

9 I will be surety for him; of my hand shalt thou require him: ᴿif I bring him not unto thee, and set him before thee, then let me bear the blame for ever: Ge 42:37; 44:32

10 For except we had lingered, surely now we had returned this second time.

11 And their father Israel said unto them, If *it must be* so now, do this; take ᵀof the best fruits in the land in your vessels, and ᴿcarry down the man a present, a little ᴿbalm, and a little honey, spices, and myrrh, nuts, and almonds: Ge 32:20; 33:10; 43:25,26 • Je 8:22 • *some of*

12 And take double money in your hand; and the money that was brought again in the mouth of your sacks, carry *it* again in your hand; peradventure it *was* an oversight:

13 Take also your brother, and arise, go again unto the man:

14 And God Almighty give you mercy before the man, that he may send away your other brother, and Benjamin. ᴿIf I be bereaved *of my children*, I am bereaved. Es 4:16

15 And the men took that present, and they took double money in their hand, and Benjamin; and rose up, and went ᴿdown to Egypt, and stood before Joseph. Ge 39:1; 46:3,6

16 And when Joseph saw Benjamin with them, he said to the ᴿruler of his house, Bring *these* men home, and ᵀslay, and make ready; for *these* men shall ᵀdine with me at noon. Ge 24:2; 39:4; 44:1 • *slaughter an animal* • Lit. *eat*

17 And the man did as Joseph ᵀbade; and the man brought the men into Joseph's house. *ordered*

18 And the men were ᴿafraid, because they were brought into Joseph's house; and they said, Because of the money that was returned in our sacks at the first time are we brought in; that he may seek occasion against us, and fall upon us, and take us for bondmen, and our asses. Ge 42:28

19 And they came near to the steward of Joseph's house, and they communed with him at the door of the house,

20 And said, O sir, ᴿwe came indeed down at the first time to buy food: Ge 42:3,10

21 And ᴿit came to pass, when we came to the ᵀinn, that we opened our sacks, and, behold, *every* man's money *was* in the mouth of his sack, our money in full weight: and we have brought it again in our hand. Ge 42:27,35 • *encampment*

22 And other money have we brought down in our hands to buy food: we cannot tell who put our money in our sacks.

23 And he said, Peace *be* to you, fear not: your God, and the God of your father, hath given you treasure in your sacks: I had your money. And he brought ᴿSimeon out unto them. Ge 42:24

24 And the man brought the men into Joseph's house, and ᴿgave *them* water, and they washed their feet; and he gave their ᵀasses ᵀprovender. Ge 18:4; 19:2; 24:32 • *donkeys* • *feed*

25 And they made ready the present against Joseph came at noon: for they heard that they should eat bread there.

26 And when Joseph came home, they brought him the present which *was* in their hand into the house, and ᴿbowed themselves to him to the earth. Ge 37:7,10; 42:6; 44:14

27 And he asked them of *their* ᵀwelfare, and said, *Is* your father well, the old man of whom ye spake? *Is* he yet alive? *well-being*

28 And they answered, Thy servant our father *is* in good health, he *is* yet alive. ᴿAnd they bowed down their heads, and ᵀmade obeisance. Ge 37:7,10 • *prostrated themselves*

29 And he lifted up his eyes, and saw his brother Benjamin, ᴿhis mother's son, and said, *Is* this your younger brother, ᴿof whom ye spake unto me? And he said, God be gracious unto thee, my son. Ge 35:17,18 • Ge 42:13

30 And Joseph made haste; for ᴿhis bowels did yearn upon his brother: and he sought *where* to weep; and he entered into *his* chamber, and wept there. 1 Ki 3:26

31 And he washed his face, and went out, and ᵀrefrained himself, and said, ᵀSet on ᴿbread. Ge 43:25 • *restrained* • *Serve the bread*

32 And they set on for him by himself, and for them by themselves, and for the Egyptians, which did eat with him, by themselves: because the Egyptians might not eat

---

substituting his life for Benjamin's life (44:32-33), reveals a sacrificial character that is Christlike.

43:26 bowed themselves. There were at least five times when Joseph's brothers fulfilled the prophecy in his long-ago dream (37:7) by bowing down to him (42:6; 43:26,28; 44:14; 50:18).

bread with the ᴿHebrews; for that *is* an abomination unto the Egyptians. Ge 41:12

33 And they sat before him, the firstborn according to his ᴿbirthright, and the youngest according to his youth: and the men marvelled one at another. Ge 27:36; 42:7

34 And he took *and sent* ᵀmesses unto them from before him: but Benjamin's ᵀmess was ᴿfive times so much as any of theirs. And they drank, and were merry with him. Ge 35:24; 45:22 • *servings* • *serving*

CHAPTER 44

And he commanded the steward of his house, saying, Fill the men's sacks *with* food, as much as they can carry, and put every man's money in his sack's mouth.

2 And put my cup, the silver cup, in the sack's mouth of the youngest, and his ᵀcorn money. And he did according to the word that Joseph had spoken. *grain*

3 As soon as the morning was light, the men were sent away, they and their ᵀasses.

4 *And* when they were gone out of the city, *and* not *yet* far off, Joseph said unto his steward, Up, follow after the men; and when thou dost overtake them, say unto them, Wherefore have ye ᴿrewardedᵀ evil for good? 1 Sa 25:21 • *repaid*

5 *Is* not this *it* in which my lord drinketh, and whereby indeed he ᵀdivineth? ye have done evil in so doing. *practises divination*

6 And he overtook them, and he spake unto them these same words.

7 And they said unto him, Wherefore saith my lord these words? ᵀGod forbid that thy servants should do according to this thing: *Far be it from us that*

8 Behold, ᴿthe money, which we found in our sacks' mouths, we brought again

unto thee out of the land of Canaan: how then should we steal out of thy lord's house silver or gold? Ge 43:21

9 With whomsoever of thy servants it be found, ᴿboth let him die, and we also will be my lord's ᵀbondmen. Ge 31:32 • *slaves*

10 And he said, Now also *let it be* according unto your words: he with whom it is found shall be my ᵀservant; and ye shall be blameless. *slave*

11 Then they speedily took down every man his sack to the ground, and opened every man his sack.

12 And he searched, *and* began at the eldest, and ᵀleft at the youngest: and the cup was found in Benjamin's sack. *finished with*

13 Then they ᴿrentᵀ their clothes, and laded every man his ᵀass, and returned to the city. 2 Sa 1:11 • *tore* • *donkey*

14 And Judah and his brethren came to Joseph's house; for he *was* yet there: and they ᴿfell before him on the ground. Ge 37:7,10

15 And Joseph said unto them, What deed *is* this that ye have done? wot ye not that such a man as I can certainly divine?

16 And Judah said, What shall we say unto my lord? what shall we speak? or how shall we clear ourselves? God hath ᴿfound out the iniquity of thy servants: behold, ᴿwe *are* my lord's servants, both we, and *he* also with whom the cup is found. [Nu 32:23] • Ge 44:9

17 And he said, ᴿGodᵀ forbid that I should do so: *but* the man in whose hand the cup is found, he shall be my servant; and as for you, get you up in peace unto your father. Pr 17:15 • *Far be it from me that*

18 Then Judah came near unto him, and said, Oh my lord, let thy servant, I pray thee, speak a word in my lord's ears, and ᴿlet not thine anger burn against thy servant: for thou *art* even as Pharaoh. Ex 32:22

43:33 *the men marvelled.* No wonder they marveled! The probability that 11 men could be "accidentally" arranged in order of age is only one chance out of 39,917,000 (calculated by multiplying the numbers one through eleven together). Putting it another way, there are almost 40 million different ways in which eleven men could be seated.

44:5 *he divineth.* It is very unlikely that godly Joseph would ever have used such an occult device as a divining cup. It was, however, a costly silver cup and, if the brothers thought it was really a divining cup, they would be terrified of imminent retribution if the superstitious Egyptians thought they had stolen it. Probably the penalty for such a crime would be death (44:9); Joseph wanted to put them to the final test, to see if they would take advantage of this opportunity to rid themselves of Benjamin, as they had

19 My lord asked his servants, saying, Have ye a father, or a brother?

20 And we said unto my lord, We have a father, an old man, and [R]a child of his old age, a little one; and his brother is [R]dead, and he alone is left of his mother, and his father loveth him.   Ge 37:3; 43:8; 44:30 • Ge 42:38

21 And thou saidst unto thy servants, [R]Bring him down unto me, that I may set mine eyes upon him.   Ge 42:15,20

22 And we said unto my lord, The lad cannot leave his father: for *if* he should leave his father, *his father* would die.

23 And thou saidst unto thy servants, Except your youngest brother come down with you, ye shall see my face no more.

24 And it came to pass when we came up unto thy servant my father, we told him the words of my lord.

25 And [R]our father said, Go again, *and* buy us a little food.   Ge 43:2

26 And we said, We cannot go down: if our youngest brother be with us, then will we go down: for we may not see the man's face, except our youngest brother *be* with us.

27 And thy servant my father said unto us, Ye know that my wife bare me two *sons:*

28 And the one went out from me, and I said, [R]Surely he is torn in pieces; and I saw him not since: Ge 37:31-35

29 And if ye take this also from me, and mischief befall him, ye shall bring down my gray hairs with sorrow to the grave.

30 Now therefore when I come to thy servant my father, and the lad *be* not with us; seeing that [R]his life is bound up in the lad's life;   [1 Sa 18:1; 25:29]

31 It shall come to pass, when he seeth that the lad *is* not *with us,* that he will die: and thy servants shall bring down the gray hairs of thy servant our father with sorrow to the grave.

32 For thy servant became surety for the lad unto my father, saying, [R]If I bring him not unto thee, then I shall bear the blame to my father for ever.   Ge 43:9

33 Now therefore, I pray thee, [R]let thy servant [T]abide instead of the lad [T]a bondman to my lord; and let the lad go up with his brethren.   Ex 32:32 • *remain* • *as a slave*

34 For how shall I go up to my father, and the lad *be* not with me? lest peradventure I see the evil that shall come on my father.

CHAPTER 45

Then Joseph could not [T]refrain himself before all them that stood by him; and he cried, Cause every man to go out from me. And there stood no man with him, [R]while Joseph made himself known unto his brethren.   Ac 7:13 • *restrain*

2 And he [R]wept aloud: and the Egyptians and the house of Pharaoh heard. Ge 43:30; 46:29

3 And Joseph said unto his brethren, [R]I *am* Joseph; doth my father yet live? And his brethren could not answer him; for they were [T]troubled at his presence. Ac 7:13 • *dismayed*

---

once thought to do with Joseph. As it turned out, they passed this test with flying colors.

45:1 *could not refrain himself.* This scene is surely the most dramatic confrontation and reunion in all literature, but it is far more than literature. This was the event which established the miracle nation of Israel. This was the founding of that unique people through whom would be given to the world the Scriptures and of whom one day the Savior would come. Had this scene not occurred, the children of Israel would soon have scattered and merged with the other peoples of the Middle East. It had been a long time in preparation, but God had a long-range goal.

45:1 *known unto his brethren.* There is a great similarity here to another dramatic confrontation that will come at the end of this age, when the Lord Jesus Christ returns to meet His brethren of the house of Israel, those who rejected Him and even urged His crucifixion, and who have continued to deny Him through all the centuries since. "And I will pour upon the house of David, and upon the inhabitants of Jerusalem, the spirit of grace and of supplications: and they shall look upon me whom they have pierced, and they shall mourn for him, as one mourneth for his only son, and shall be

4 And Joseph said unto his brethren, Come near to me, I pray you. And they came near. And he said, I *am* Joseph your brother, whom ye sold into Egypt.

5 Now therefore be not grieved, nor angry with yourselves, that ye sold me hither: ^Rfor God did send me before you to preserve life.   Ge 45:7,8; 50:20

6 For these two years *hath* the ^Rfamine *been* in the land: and yet *there are* five years, in the which *there shall* neither *be* ^Tearing nor harvest.   Ge 43:1; 47:4,13 • *plowing*

7 And God sent me before you to preserve you a ^Tposterity in the earth, and to save your lives by a great deliverance. *a remnant*

8 So now *it was* not you *that* sent me hither, but ^RGod: and he hath made me ^Ra father to Pharaoh, and lord of all his house, and a ^Rruler throughout all the land of Egypt.   [Ro 8:28] • Is 22:21 • Ge 41:43; 42:6

9 Haste ye, and go up to my father, and say unto him, Thus saith thy son Joseph, God hath made me lord of all Egypt: come down unto me, ^Ttarry not: *do not delay*

10 And ^Rthou shalt dwell in the land of Go'-shen, and thou shalt be near unto me, thou, and thy children, and thy children's children, and thy flocks, and thy herds, and all that thou hast: Ge 46:28,34; 47:1,6

11 And there will I ^Rnourish^T thee; for yet *there are* five years of famine; lest thou, and thy household, and all that thou hast, come to poverty.   Ge 47:12 • *provide for*

12 And, behold, your eyes see, and the eyes of my brother Benjamin, that *it is* ^Rmy mouth that speaketh unto you.   Ge 42:23

13 And ye shall tell my father of all my glory in Egypt, and of all that ye have seen; and ye shall haste and ^Rbring down my father hither.   Ac 7:14

14 And he fell upon his brother Benjamin's neck, and wept; and Benjamin wept upon his neck.

15 Moreover he ^Rkissed all his brethren, and wept upon them: and after that his brethren talked with him.   Ge 48:10

16 And the ^Tfame thereof was heard in Pharaoh's house, saying, Joseph's brethren are come: and it pleased Pharaoh well, and his servants.   *report*

17 And Pharaoh said unto Joseph, Say unto thy brethren, This do ye; ^Tlade your beasts, and go, get you unto the land of Canaan;   *load*

18 And take your father and your households, and come unto me: and I will give you the good of the land of Egypt, and ye shall eat ^Rthe fat of the land.   Ge 27:28; 47:6

19 Now thou art commanded, this do ye; take you wagons out of the land of Egypt for your little ones, and for your wives, and bring your father, and come.

20 Also regard not your stuff; for the good of all the land of Egypt *is* yours.

21 And the children of Israel did so: and Joseph gave them ^Rwagons,^T according to the commandment of Pharaoh, and gave them provision for the way.   Ge 45:19; 46:5 • *carts*

22 To all of them he gave each man ^Rchanges of ^Traiment; but to Benjamin he gave three hundred *pieces* of silver, and ^Rfive changes of raiment.   2 Ki 5:5 • Ge 43:34 • *clothing*

23 And to his father he sent after this *manner*; ten ^Tasses ^Tladen with the good things of Egypt, and ten she asses laden with ^Tcorn and bread and ^Tmeat for his father ^Tby the way.   *donkeys • loaded • grain • food • for*

24 So he sent his brethren away, and they departed: and he said unto them, See that ye ^Tfall not out by the way.   *be not troubled*

25 And they went up out of Egypt, and came into the land of Canaan unto Jacob their father,

26 And told him, saying, Joseph *is* yet alive, and he *is* governor over all the land of

---

in bitterness for him, as one that is in bitterness for his firstborn" (Ze 12:10). It is largely because of this striking parallel that many have taken Joseph to be a type of Christ, even though the New Testament writers nowhere speak explicitly of Him in such a comparison.

45:8 *but God.* This event is not only a stirring testimonial to the forgiving grace of Joseph, who was far more concerned with reconciliation than vengeance, but also of the truth of Romans 8:28, "all things work together for good to them that love God." For He "worketh all things after the counsel of his own will" (Ep 1:11).

45:10 *land of Goshen.* This land was at the northeast corner of Egypt, and was sparsely

Egypt. RAnd Jacob's heart fainted, for he believed them not.   Job 29:24

27 And they told him all the words of Joseph, which he had said unto them: and when he saw the wagons which Joseph had sent to carry him, the spirit Rof Jacob their father revived: Ju 15:19

28 And Israel said, *It is* enough; Joseph my son *is* yet alive: I will go and see him before I die.

CHAPTER 46

Joseph's Family Dwells in Egypt

And Israel took his journey with all that he had, and came to RBe'-er–she'-ba, and offered sacrifices unto the God of his father Isaac.   Ge 21:31,33; 26:32,33; 28:10

2 And God spake unto Israel Rin the visions of the night, and said, Jacob, Jacob. And he said, Here *am* I.   Ge 15:1; 22:11; 31:11

3 And he said, I *am* God, the God of thy father: fear not to go down into Egypt; for I will there make of thee a great nation:

4 I will go down with thee into Egypt; and I will also surely bring thee up *again:* and Joseph shall put his hand upon thine eyes.

5 And RJacob rose up from Be'-er–she'-ba: and the sons of Israel carried Jacob their father, and their little ones, and their wives, in the wagons Rwhich Pharaoh had sent to carry him.   Ac 7:15 • Ge 45:19-21

6 And they took their Tcattle, and their goods, which they had gotten in the land of Canaan, and came into Egypt, RJacob, and all his seed with him: De 26:5 • livestock

7 His sons, and his sons' sons with him, his daughters, and his sons' daughters, and all his seed brought he with him into Egypt.

8 And these *are* the names of the children of Israel, which came into Egypt, Jacob and his sons: Reuben, Jacob's firstborn.

9 And the sons of Reuben; Ha'-noch, and Phal'-lu, and Hez'-ron, and Car'-mi.

10 And Rthe sons of Simeon; TJem'-u-el, and Ja'-min, and O'-had, and Ja'-chin, and Zo'-har, and Sha'-ul the son of a Ca'-naan-i-tish woman.   Ex 6:15 • Nemuel, 1 Ch 4:24

11 And the sons of RLevi; Ger'-shon, Ko'-hath, and Me-ra'-ri.   1 Ch 6:1,16

12 And the sons of RJudah; Er, and O'-nan, and She'-lah, and TPha'-rez, and Za'-rah: but REr and O'-nan died in the land of Canaan. And Rthe sons of Pha'-rez were Hez'-ron and Ha'-mul.   1 Ch 2:3; 4:21 • Ge 38:3,7,10 • Ge 38:29 • Or Perez

13 And the sons of Is'-sa-char; To'-la, and Phu'-vah, and Job, and Shim'-ron.

14 And the Rsons of Zeb'-u-lun; Se'-red, and E'-lon, and Jah'-le-el.   Nu 26:26

15 These *be* the sons of Leah, which she bare unto Jacob in Pa'-dan–a'-ram, with his daughter Dinah: all the souls of his sons and his daughters *were* thirty and three.

16 And the sons of Gad; TZiph'-i-on, and Hag'-gi, Shu'-ni, and Ez'-bon, E'-ri, and Ar'-o-di, and A-re'-li.   Sam., LXX Zephon, and Nu 26:15

17 RAnd the sons of Asher; Jim'-nah, and Ish'-u-ah, and Is'-u-i, and Be-ri'-ah, and Se'-rah their sister: and the sons of Be-ri'-ah; He'-ber, and Mal'-chi-el.   1 Ch 7:30

18 RThese *are* the sons of Zil'-pah, Rwhom Laban gave to Leah his daughter, and these she bare unto Jacob, *even* sixteen Tsouls.   Ge 30:10; 37:2 • Ge 29:24 • persons

19 The Rsons of Ra'-chel RJacob's wife; Joseph, and Benjamin.   Ge 35:24 • Ge 44:27

20 RAnd unto Joseph in the land of Egypt were born Ma-nas'-seh and E'-phra-im, which As'-e-nath the daughter of Pot-i-phe'-rah priest of On bare unto him.   Ge 41:45,50-52; 48:1

21 RAnd the sons of Benjamin *were* Be'-lah, and Be'-cher, and Ash'-bel, Ge'-ra, and Na'-a-man, RE'-hi, and Rosh, Mup'-pim, and Hup'-pim, and Ard.   1 Ch 7:6; 8:1 • Nu 26:38

occupied at this early period of history. It was in the fertile Nile delta and was an ideal region for Jacob's family to settle and grow into a new nation. It was well suited also for the grazing of their cattle.

46:4 upon thine eyes. That is, Jacob would be with his beloved Joseph at his death, and Joseph then would lovingly close his father's eyes as he died.

46:5 from Beersheba. This was the southern boundary of Jacob's homeland, so he passed by to sacrifice and pray there before his permanent departure for Egypt. God appeared to him one last time, assuring him that this move was in the will of God.

46:15 and his daughters. Jacob apparently had three or more daughters in addition to his

22 These *are* the sons of Ra'-chel, which were born to Jacob: all the souls *were* fourteen.

23 And the sons of Dan; Hu'-shim.

24 And the sons of Naph'-ta-li; Jah'-ze-el, and Gu'-ni, and Je'-zer, and Shil'-lem.

25 ᴿThese *are* the sons of Bil'-hah, ᴿwhich Laban gave unto Ra'-chel his daughter, and she bare these unto Jacob: all the souls *were* seven.   Ge 30:5,7 • Ge 29:29

26 ᴿAll the ᵀsouls that came with Jacob into Egypt, which came out of his loins, ᴿbesides Jacob's sons' wives, all the souls *were* threescore and six;   Ex 1:5 • Ge 35:11 • *persons who went*

27 And the sons of Joseph, which were born him in Egypt, *were* two souls: ᴿall the souls of the house of Jacob, which came into Egypt, *were* threescore and ten.   De 10:22

28 And he sent Judah before him unto Joseph, to direct his face unto Go'-shen; and they came into the land of Go'-shen.

29 And Joseph made ready his ᴿchariot, and went up to meet Israel his father, to Go'-shen, and presented himself unto him; and he ᴿfell on his neck, and wept on his neck a good while.   Ge 41:43 • Ge 45:14,15

30 And Israel said unto Joseph, ᴿNow let me die, since I have seen thy face, because thou *art* yet alive.   Lk 2:29,30

31 And Joseph said unto his brethren, and unto his father's house, I will go up, and shew Pharaoh, and say unto him, My brethren, and my father's house, which *were* in the land of Canaan, are come unto me;

32 And the men *are* ᴿshepherds, for their ᵀtrade hath been to feed ᵀcattle; and they have brought their flocks, and their herds, and all that they have. Ge 47:3 • *occupation* • *livestock*

33 And it shall come to pass, when Pharaoh shall call you, and shall say, ᴿWhat *is* your occupation?   Ge 47:2,3

34 That ye shall say, Thy servants' ᴿtrade hath been about cattle ᴿfrom our youth even until now, both we, *and* also our fathers: that ye may dwell in the land of Go'-shen; for every shepherd *is* an abomination unto the Egyptians.   Ge 47:3 • Ge 30:35; 34:5; 37:17

CHAPTER 47

Then Joseph ᴿcame and told Pharaoh, and said, My father and my brethren, and their flocks, and their herds, and all that they have, are come out of the land of Canaan; and, behold, they *are* in ᴿthe land of Go'-shen.   Ge 46:31 • Ge 45:10; 46:28; 50:8

2 And he took some of his ᵀbrethren, *even* five men, and ᴿpresented them unto Pharaoh.   Ac 7:13 • *brothers*

3 And Pharaoh said unto his brethren, ᴿWhat *is* your occupation? And they said unto Pharaoh, Thy servants *are* shepherds, both we, *and* also our fathers.   Ge 46:33

4 They said moreover unto Pharaoh, ᴿFor to sojourn in the land are we come; for thy servants have no pasture for their flocks; for the famine *is* sore in the land of Canaan: now therefore, we pray thee, let thy servants dwell in the land of Go'-shen.   De 26:5

5 And Pharaoh spake unto Joseph, saying, Thy father and thy brethren are come unto thee:

6 The land of Egypt *is* before thee; in the best of the land make thy father and brethren to dwell; ᴿin the land of Go'-shen let them dwell: and if thou knowest *any* men of activity among them, then make them rulers over my cattle.   Ge 47:4

7 And Joseph brought in Jacob his father, and set him before Pharaoh: and Jacob ᴿblessed Pharaoh.   Ge 47:10; 48:15,20

8 And Pharaoh said unto Jacob, How old *art* thou?

9 And Jacob said unto Pharaoh, ᴿThe days of the years of my pilgrimage *are* an

---

twelve sons, even though only Dinah is specifically mentioned. Dinah seems never to have married.

46:27 threescore and ten. "The souls that came with Jacob into Egypt, which came out of his loins" (46:26) are said to total 66, whereas the totals as given for his four wives (46:15,18,22,25) add to 70. These, however, include Joseph and his two sons (46:19-20), accounting for 69. Since Jacob himself is included in the 70 of this verse, there was probably an unnamed daughter of Leah (46:15 mentions "daughters," but only Dinah is named) who died on the trek into Egypt, or soon after. Thus the total stands at 70, as indicated in Genesis 46:27.

47:9 *an hundred and thirty years.* Jacob died at 147 (47:28), whereas Isaac had lived to 180, Abraham to 175, and Terah to 205. Their distant ancestor Shem lived to age 600. Life

Rhundred and thirty years: Rfew and evil have the days of the years of my life been, and have not attained unto the days of the years of the life of my fathers in the days of their pilgrimage. [He 11:9,13] • Ge 47:28 • [Job 14:1]

10 And Jacob Rblessed Pharaoh, and went out from before Pharaoh. Ge 47:7

11 And Joseph placed his father and his brethren, and gave them a possession in the land of Egypt, in the best of the land, in the land of RRam'-e-ses, Ras Pharaoh had commanded. Ex 1:11; 12:37 • Ge 47:6,27

12 And Joseph nourished his father, and his brethren, and all his father's household, with bread, according to *their* families.

13 And *there was* no bread in all the land; for the famine *was* very Tsore, Rso that the land of Egypt and *all* the land of Canaan fainted by reason of the famine. Ge 41:30 • *severe*

14 RAnd Joseph gathered up all the money that was found in the land of Egypt, and in the land of Canaan, for the corn which they bought: and Joseph brought the money into Pharaoh's house. Ge 41:56; 42:6

15 And when money failed in the land of Egypt, and in the land of Canaan, all the Egyptians came unto Joseph, and said, Give us bread: for Rwhy should we die in thy presence? for the money faileth. Ge 47:19

16 And Joseph said, Give your Tcattle; and I will Tgive you for your cattle, if money fail. *livestock • give you* bread

17 And they brought their Tcattle unto Joseph: and Joseph gave them bread *in exchange* for horses, and for the flocks, and for the cattle of the herds, and for the Tasses: and he fed them with bread for all their cattle for that year. *livestock • donkeys*

18 When that year was ended, they came unto him the second year, and said unto him, We will not hide *it* from my lord, how that our money is spent; my lord also hath our herds of Tcattle; there is Tnot ought left in the sight of my lord, but our bodies, and our lands: *livestock • nothing*

19 Wherefore shall we die before thine eyes, both we and our land? buy us and our land for bread, and we and our land will be servants unto Pharaoh: and give *us* seed, that we may Rlive, and not die, that the land be not desolate. Ge 43:8

20 And Joseph Rbought all the land of Egypt for Pharaoh; for the Egyptians sold every man his field, because the famine Tprevailed over them: so the land became Pharaoh's. Je 32:43 • *was severe upon them*

21 And as for the people, he Tremoved them to cities from *one* end of the borders of Egypt even to the *other* end thereof. *moved*

22 ROnly the land of the Rpriests bought he not; for the priests had a portion *assigned them* of Pharaoh, and did eat their portion which Pharaoh gave them: wherefore they sold not their lands. Ez 7:24 • Ge 41:45

23 Then Joseph said unto the people, Behold, I have bought you this day and your land for Pharaoh: lo, *here is* seed for you, and ye shall sow the land.

24 And it shall come to pass in the increase, that ye shall give the fifth *part* unto Pharaoh, and four parts shall be your own, for seed of the field, and for your food, and for them of your households, and for food for your little ones.

25 And they said, Thou hast saved our lives: let us find grace in the sight of my lord, and we will be Pharaoh's servants.

26 And Joseph made it a law over the land of Egypt unto this day, *that* Pharaoh should have the fifth *part*; Rexcept the land

---

spans were still declining after the traumatic changes of the great flood and would continue to do so until about the time of Moses.

47:9 *days of their pilgrimage.* Jacob considered his life on earth to be merely a "pilgrimage," like that of his fathers. Though not much is said about it, they evidently recognized that their eternal home would be with God. "These all died in faith, not having received the promises, but having seen them afar off, and were persuaded of them, and embraced them, and confessed that they were strangers and pilgrims on the earth" (He 11:13).

47:10 *Jacob blessed Pharaoh.* It is significant that "Jacob blessed Pharaoh," not the other way around. Even though Pharaoh was probably the greatest king on earth at the time, "without all contradiction the less is blessed of the better" (He 7:7), and in God's sight, Jacob was the greatest man of his generation.

47:26 *the fifth part.* In effect, the people became Pharaoh's "servants" merely in the sense

of the priests only, *which* became not Pharaoh's.   Ge 47:22

Jacob Blesses His Children

27 And Israel ᴿdwelt in the land of Egypt, in the country of Go'-shen; and they had possessions therein, and ᴿgrew, and multiplied exceedingly.   Ge 47:11 • Ge 17:6; 26:4; 35:11; 46:3

28 And Jacob lived in the land of Egypt seventeen years: so the whole age of Jacob was an hundred forty and seven years.

29 And the time drew nigh that Israel must die: and he called his son Joseph, and said unto him, If now I have found grace in thy sight, put, I pray thee, thy hand under my thigh, and deal kindly and truly with me; bury me not, I pray thee, in Egypt:

30 But ᴿI will lie with my fathers, and thou shalt carry me out of Egypt, and ᴿbury me in their buryingplace. And he said, I will do as thou hast said.   2 Sa 19:37 • Ge 49:29; 50:5-13

31 And he said, Swear unto me. And he sware unto him. And ᴿIsrael bowed himself upon the bed's head.   1 Ki 1:47

CHAPTER 48

And it came to pass after these things, that *one* told Joseph, Behold, thy father *is* sick: and he took with him his two sons, Ma-nas'-seh and E'-phra-im.

2 And *one* told Jacob, and said, Behold, thy son Joseph cometh unto thee: and Israel ᵀstrengthened himself, and sat upon the bed.   *collected his strength*

3 And Jacob said unto Joseph, God ᴿAlmighty appeared unto me at Luz in the land of Canaan, and blessed me,   Ge 43:14; 49:25

4 And said unto me, Behold, I will ᴿmake thee fruitful, and multiply thee, and I will make of thee a multitude of people; and will ᴿgive this land to thy seed after thee *for* an everlasting possession.   Ge 46:3 • Ex 6:8

5 And now thy ᴿtwo sons, E'-phra-im and Ma-nas'-seh, which were born unto thee in the land of Egypt before I came unto thee into Egypt, *are* mine; as Reuben and Simeon, they shall be mine.   Jos 13:7; 14:4

6 And thy ᵀissue, which ᵀthou begettest after them, shall be thine, *and* shall be called after the name of their brethren in their inheritance.   *offspring • are born to you*

7 And as for me, when I came from Pa'-dan, ᴿRa'-chel died ᵀby me in the land of Canaan in the way, when yet *there was* but a little way to come unto Eph'-rath: and I buried her there in the way of Eph'-rath; the same *is* Beth'-le-hem.   Ge 35:9,16,19,20 • *beside*

8 And Israel beheld Joseph's sons, and said, Who *are* these?

9 And Joseph said unto his father, They *are* my sons, whom God hath given me in this *place*. And he said, Bring them, I pray thee, unto me, and ᴿI will bless them.   Ge 27:4

10 Now ᴿthe eyes of Israel were dim for age, *so that* he could not see. And he brought them near unto him; and he ᴿkissed them, and embraced them.   Ge 27:1 • Ge 27:27; 45:15; 50:1

11 And Israel said unto Joseph, ᴿI had not thought to see thy face: and, lo, God hath shewed me also thy ᵀseed.   Ge 45:26 • *offspring*

12 And Joseph brought them out from ᵀbetween his knees, and he bowed himself with his face to the earth.   *beside*

13 And Joseph took them both, E'-phra-im in his right hand toward Israel's left hand, and Ma-nas'-seh in his left hand toward Israel's right hand, and brought *them* near unto him.

14 And Israel stretched out his right hand, and ᴿlaid *it* upon E'-phra-im's head, who *was* the younger, and his left hand upon Ma-nas'-seh's head, ᴿguiding his hands ᵀwittingly; for Ma-nas'-seh *was* the ᴿfirstborn.   Ma 19:15 • Ge 48:19 • Jos 17:1 • *knowingly*

15 And ᴿhe blessed Joseph, and said, God, before whom my fathers Abraham and Isaac did walk, the God which fed me all my life long unto this day,   [He 11:21]

---

that Joseph established a "flat tax" of 20 percent of their income that would go to the government. Otherwise, they still had full control over their individual property. The government provided seed for their use, and presumably all the standard government services. Furthermore, these governmental regulations as established by Joseph had literally "saved their [our] lives" (47:25). Their enforced savings during the seven years of prosperity had not only enabled them to survive the seven years of famine but also to help other nations as well. "Saving for a rainy day" has always been good policy, for individuals and for nations.

48:15 *all my life long.* Jacob had seen many troubles and afflictions during his 147 years,

126

16 The Angel ᴿwhich redeemed me from all evil, bless the lads; and let ᴿmy name be named on them, and the name of my fathers Abraham and Isaac; and let them grow into a multitude in the midst of the earth. Ge 22:11,15-18; 28:13-15; 31:11 • Am 9:12

17 And when Joseph saw that his father laid his right hand upon the head of E′-phra-im, it displeased him: and he held up his father's hand, to remove it from E′-phra-im's head unto Ma-nas′-seh's head.

18 And Joseph said unto his father, Not so, my father: for this *is* the firstborn; put thy right hand upon his head.

19 And his father refused, and said, ᴿI know *it*, my son, I know *it*: he also shall become a people, and he also shall be great: but truly ᴿhis younger brother shall be greater than he, and his seed shall become a multitude of nations. Ge 48:14 • Nu 1:33,35

20 And he blessed them that day, saying, In thee shall Israel bless, saying, God make thee as E′-phra-im and as Ma-nas′-seh: and he set E′-phra-im before Ma-nas′-seh.

21 And Israel said unto Joseph, Behold, I die: but God shall be with you, and bring you again unto the land of your fathers.

22 Moreover ᴿI have given to thee one portion above thy brethren, which I took out of the hand ᴿof the Am′-or-ite with my sword and with my bow. Jos 24:32 • Ge 34:28

CHAPTER 49

And Jacob called unto his sons, and said, Gather yourselves together, that I may ᴿtell you *that* which shall befall you ᴿin the last days. De 33:1,6-25 • Is 2:2; 39:6

2 Gather yourselves together, and hear, ye sons of Jacob; and hearken unto Israel your father.

3 Reuben, thou *art* ᴿmy firstborn, my might, and the beginning of my strength, the excellency of dignity, and the excellency of power: Ge 29:32

4 Unstable as water, thou shalt not excel; because thou ᴿwentest up to thy father's bed; then defiledst thou *it*: he went up to my couch. Ge 35:22

5 Simeon and Levi *are* brethren; instruments of cruelty *are in* their habitations.

6 O my soul, ᴿcome not thou into their

---

but God had never forsaken him, just as He had promised (28:15). When Jacob testified that God had "fed me," the concept was that of a shepherd feeding his sheep. This in effect is the first biblical reference to the Lord as our Shepherd.

48:16 *The Angel which redeemed me*. This verse contains the first mention of the important biblical word "redeem." Significantly it attributes the work of redemption to God, not man, and not a sacrificial animal. The "Angel of the Lᴏʀᴅ" is none other than the pre-incarnate Christ (see note on 16:7). It must always be stressed, when evaluating other religions, that only biblical Christianity offers the gospel that can save, for only the Creator Himself is sufficient to accomplish the work of redemption.

48:19 *multitude of nations*. The tribe of Ephraim eventually became larger and more important than any of the other tribes except Judah. Its name was even made synonymous with all 10 tribes in the Northern Kingdom when they rebelled against Rehoboam and became a separate nation.

48:22 *one portion above thy brethren*. Although this may refer only to a specific tract of land in Canaan, the principle is here established that Joseph, rather than Reuben, will be granted the birthright (see 1 Ch 5:1-2) with its double inheritance, so that Ephraim and Manasseh, Joseph's sons, are established as each equal with the other eleven sons of Israel.

48:22 *Amorite*. This incident is not referred to elsewhere in the account of Jacob's life, but that doesn't mean that it did not happen. A reasonable explanation might be that an Amorite neighbor of Jacob's had attacked him, but that Jacob defeated and slew his attacker, thereby acquiring possession of his land. This particular portion he wanted to reserve for Joseph's inheritance in addition to the ultimate twelve-fold division of the land. It is likely that this is "the parcel of ground" referred to in John 4:5.

49:3 *Reuben*. No prophet, judge, king, or other notable leader ever came from Reuben's tribe. He lost his birthright because of incest with his father's concubine.

secret; Runto their assembly, mine honour, be not thou united: Rfor in their anger they slew a man, and in their selfwill they digged down a wall.   Pr 1:15,16 • Ps 26:9 • Ge 34:26

7 Cursed *be* their anger, for *it was* fierce; and their wrath, for it was cruel: RI will divide them in Jacob, and scatter them in Israel.   Jos 19:1,9; 21:1-42

8 RJudah, thou *art he* whom thy brethren shall praise: Rthy hand *shall be* in the neck of thine enemies; thy father's children shall bow down before thee.   De 33:7 • Ps 18:40

9 Judah *is* Ra lion's whelp: from the prey, my son, thou art gone up: he stooped down, he couched as a lion, and as an old lion; who shall rouse him up?   [Re 5:5]

10 RThe sceptre shall not depart from Judah, nor Ra lawgiver from between his feet, until Shi'-loh come; and unto him *shall* the gathering of the people *be*.   Nu 24:17 • Ps 60:7

11 Binding his Tfoal unto the vine, and his Tass's colt unto the choice vine; he washed his garments in wine, and his clothes in the blood of grapes: *donkey • donkey's*

12 His eyes *shall be* Tred with wine, and his teeth Twhite with milk.   *darker than • whiter than*

13 Zeb'-u-lun shall dwell at the haven of the sea; and he *shall be* for an haven of ships; and his border *shall be* unto RZi'-don.

14 RIs'-sa-char *is* a strong Tass couching down between two burdens: 1 Ch 12:32 • *donkey*

15 And he saw that rest *was* good, and the land that *it was* pleasant; and bowed Rhis shoulder to Tbear, and became a servant unto tribute.   1 Sa 10:9 • *bear a burden*

16 RDan shall judge his people, as one of the tribes of Israel.   De 33:22

17 Dan shall be a serpent by the way, an adder in the path, that biteth the horse heels, so that his rider shall fall backward.

18 RI have waited for thy salvation, O LORD.   Is 25:9

49:7 *divide them...and scatter.* The tribe of Simeon had an inheritance surrounded by that of Judah except at the south, which opened on the Negev Desert. The tribe of Levi was scattered through all the tribes, having been designated as the priestly tribe because of their opposition to the golden calf (Ex 32:26).

49:9 *couched.* That is, "crouched down" or "laid down."

49:10 *not depart from Judah.* This important prophecy has been strikingly fulfilled. Judah was not Jacob's firstborn son nor his favorite son nor the son who would produce the priestly tribe, yet he was the son through whom God would fulfill His promises to Israel and to the world. The leadership, according to Jacob, was to go to Judah, but this did not happen for over 600 years. Moses came from Levi, Joshua from Ephraim, Gideon from Manasseh, Samson from Dan, Samuel from Ephraim, and Saul from Benjamin. But when David finally became king, Judah held the sceptre and did not relinquish it until after Shiloh came. Shiloh, of course, is a name for the Messiah, probably related to the Hebrew word for "peace" (*shalom*) and meaning in effect "the one who brings peace."

49:13 *at the haven.* The word "at" is only inferred from the context, but could just as well be "toward." That is Zebulun's interests would lie toward the sea and trade from the sea, whether or not any of her borders would actually lie on the sea coast. The same applies to her northern border, not actually adjacent to Zidon, but with trade from Zidon. She did border in part on the Sea of Galilee, and encompassed the future cities of Cana and Nazareth in Galilee.

49:14 *Issachar.* The tribe of Issachar, like their father, was strong physically, but lethargic and led by others.

49:18 *thy salvation.* This is the first mention of the word "salvation" in the Bible. The Hebrew word, *yeshua*, is actually the same as the name "Jesus." In the context, Jacob, in giving his prophetic comments concerning Dan, called the tribe "a serpent by the way, an adder in the path, that biteth the horse heels, so that his rider shall fall backward" (49:17). The prophecy probably had reference to the fact that it would be the Danites who first introduced the satanic practice of idolatry into Israel on a regular official basis (Ju 18:30-31). As he uttered the prophecy, Jacob surely would have recalled the primeval promise of the coming Seed of the woman, whose heel would be bitten by the serpent (Satan), but who would

19 ᴿGad, a troop shall overcome him: but he shall overcome at the last.   De 33:20

20 ᴿOut of Asher his bread *shall be* fat, and he shall yield royal dainties.   De 33:24

21 ᴿNaph'-ta-li *is* a ᵀhind let loose: he giveth ᵀgoodly words.   De 33:23 • *deer* • Lit. *beautiful*

22 Joseph *is* a fruitful bough, *even* a fruitful bough by a well; *whose* branches run over the wall:

23 The archers have ᴿsorely grieved him, and shot *at him*, and hated him: Ge 37:4,24

24 But his ᴿbow abode in strength, and the arms of his hands were made strong by the hands of ᴿthe mighty *God* of Jacob; (ᴿfrom thence *is* the shepherd, the stone of Israel:)   Job 29:20 • Ps 132:2,5 • Ge 45:11; 47:12

25 ᴿ*Even* by the God of thy father, who shall help thee; ᴿand by the Almighty, who shall bless thee with blessings of heaven above, blessings of the deep that lieth under, blessings of the breasts, and of the womb: Ge 28:13; 32:9; 35:3; 43:23; 50:17 • Ge 17:1; 35:11

26 The blessings of thy father have prevailed above the blessings of my progenitors unto the utmost bound of the everlasting hills: they shall be on the head of Joseph, and on the crown of the head of him that was separate from his brethren.

27 Benjamin shall ᴿravin *as* a wolf: in the morning he shall devour the prey, and at night he shall divide the spoil.   Ju 20:21,25

28 All these *are* the twelve tribes of Israel: and this *is it* that their father spake unto them, and blessed them; every one according to his blessing he blessed them.

29 And he charged them, and said unto them, I am to be gathered unto my people: ᴿbury me with my fathers in the cave that *is* in the field of E'-phron the Hit'-tite,   Ge 47:30

30 In the cave that *is* in the field of Machpe'-lah, which *is* before Mam'-re, in the land of Canaan, ᴿwhich Abraham bought with the field of E'-phron the Hit'-tite for a possession of a buryingplace.   Ge 23:3-20

31 There they buried Abraham and Sarah his wife; there they buried Isaac and Rebekah his wife; and there I buried Leah.

32 The purchase of the field and of the cave that *is* therein *was* from the children of Heth.

The Death of Jacob

33 And when Jacob had made an end of commanding his sons, he ᵀgathered up his

---

in turn finally crush the serpent's head and bring eternal salvation (3:15). It was in reference to this messianic promise that he had just spoken to Judah. It is natural, therefore, that right at this point, he would cry out: "I have waited for thy salvation, O LORD!" It might not be out of line to suggest that he was even personifying God's coming salvation and saying: I have waited for Jesus, O LORD!"

49:19 *Gad*. Gad's territory was on the east of the Jordan, often attacked by the warlike descendants of Ishmael, Esau and others. However, they were valiant fighters and usually prevailed.

49:20 *Asher*. Asher's western border was the northern sea coast and the northern border near Sidon of the Phoenicians. These circumstances tended to produce both material prosperity and spiritual degeneracy.

49:21 *Naphtali*. Barak was probably the greatest leader from the tribe of Naphtali (Ju 4:6), but the tribe as a whole was characterized by both courage and eloquence. Note the song of Deborah and Barak (Ju 5).

49:26 *everlasting hills*. No hills could be everlasting, of course. The Hebrew word is *olam*, and is better translated "ancient." The hills of Canaan presumably dated back some 700 hundred years or more to the time of the great flood.

49:26 *head of Joseph*. It is a significant fulfillment of prophecy that the two sons on whom Jacob pronounced the longest and fullest blessings later became the two dominant tribes in Israel, Judah and Ephraim.

49:27 *Benjamin*. The future Benjamites would be like a ravenous and successful wolf. In terms of success, such men as King Saul and the apostle Paul were from Benjamin's tribe. In terms of uncaring rapacity the deplorable actions described in Judges 19 and 20 almost resulted in the destruction of the whole tribe.

49:27 *ravin*. To ravin is to "devour," like a raven.

feet into the bed, and yielded up the ghost, and was gathered unto his people.   *drew up*

CHAPTER 50

And Joseph fell upon his father's face, and wept upon him, and kissed him.

2 And Joseph commanded his servants the physicians to ᴿembalm his father: and the physicians embalmed Israel.   Ge 50:26

3 And forty days were fulfilled for him; for so are fulfilled the days of those which are embalmed: and the Egyptians ᴿmournedᵀ for him threescore and ten days.   De 34:8 • Lit. *wept*

4 And when the days of his mourning were past, Joseph spake unto ᴿthe house of Pharaoh, saying, If now I have found ᵀgrace in your eyes, speak, I pray you, in the ears of Pharaoh, saying,   Es 4:2 • *favour*

5 ᴿMy father made me swear, saying, Lo, I ᵀdie: in my grave ᴿwhich I have digged for me in the land of Canaan, there shalt thou bury me. Now therefore let me go up, I pray thee, and bury my father, and I will come again.   Ge 47:29-31 • Is 22:16 • *am dying*

6 And Pharaoh said, Go up, and bury thy father, according as he made thee swear.

7 And Joseph went up to bury his father: and with him went up all the servants of Pharaoh, the elders of his house, and all the elders of the land of Egypt,

8 And all the house of Joseph, and his brethren, and his father's house: only their little ones, and their flocks, and their herds, they left in the land of Go'-shen.

9 And there went up with him both chariots and horsemen: and it was a very great company.

10 And they came to the threshingfloor of A'-tad, which *is* beyond Jordan, and there they ᴿmourned with a great and very ᵀsore lamentation: ᴿand he made a mourning for his father seven days.   Ac 8:2 • 1 Sa 31:13 • *solemn*

11 And when the inhabitants of the land, the Ca'-naan-ites, saw the mourning in the floor of A'-tad, they said, This *is* a grievous mourning to the Egyptians: wherefore the name of it was called ᵀA'-bel–miz'-ra-im, which *is* beyond Jordan.   Lit. *Mourning of Egypt*

12 And his sons did unto him according as he commanded them:

13 For ᴿhis sons carried him into the land of Canaan, and buried him in the cave of the field of Mach-pe'-lah, which Abraham ᴿbought with the field for a possession of a buryingplace of E'-phron the Hit'-tite, before Mam'-re.   Ac 7:16 • Ge 23:16-20

14 And Joseph returned into Egypt, he, and his brethren, and all that went up with him to bury his father, after he had buried his father.

The Death of Joseph

15 And when Joseph's brethren saw that their father was dead, they said, Joseph will peradventure hate us, and will certainly requite us all the evil which we did unto him.

16 And they sent a messenger unto Joseph, saying, Thy father did command before he died, saying,

17 So shall ye say unto Joseph, Forgive, I pray thee now, the trespass of thy brethren, and their sin; ᴿfor they did unto thee evil: and now, we pray thee, forgive the trespass of the servants of ᴿthe God of thy father. And Joseph wept when they spake unto him.   [Pr 28:13] • Ge 49:25

18 And his brethren also went and ᴿfell down before his face; and they said, Behold, we *be* thy servants.   Ge 37:7-10; 41:43; 44:14

19 And Joseph said unto them, ᴿFear not: ᴿfor *am* I in the place of God?   Ge 45:5 • 2 Ki 5:7

20 ᴿBut as for you, ye ᵀthought evil against me; but ᴿGod meant it unto good, to bring to pass, as *it is* this day, to save much people alive.   Ps 56:5 • [Ac 3:13-15] • *intended*

21 Now therefore fear ye not: ᴿI will ᵀnourish you, and your little ones. And he comforted them, and spake kindly ᵀunto them.   [Ma 5:44] • *provide for* • Lit. *to their hearts*

22 And Joseph dwelt in Egypt, he, and his father's house: and Joseph lived an hundred and ten years.

23 And Joseph saw E'-phra-im's children ᴿof the third *generation*: the children also of Ma'-chir the son of Ma-nas'-seh were brought up upon Joseph's knees.   Job 42:16

24 And Joseph said unto his brethren, ᵀI die: and ᴿGod will surely visit you, and

---

50:2 *embalm his father.* Both Jacob and later Joseph (50:26) were embalmed in the manner of the Egyptians, and the remains of both were ultimately carried back for permanent burial in the promised land.

bring you out of this land unto the land Rwhich he sware to Abraham, to Isaac, and to Jacob.   Ex 3:16,17 • Ge 26:3; 35:12; 46:4 • *I am dying*

25 And RJoseph took an oath of the children of Israel, saying, God will surely Tvisit you, and Rye shall carry up my Rbones from hence.   Ex 13:19 • De 1:8; 30:1-8 • Ex 13:19 • *visit* to help

26 So Joseph died, *being* an hundred and ten years old: and they embalmed him, and he was put in a coffin in Egypt.

50:26 *an hundred and ten years old.* Joseph lived some 54 years after Jacob died, but his life span was considerably shorter than Jacob's 147 years. Longevity was still declining as a result of the traumatic changes in the earth's climatology and biology during the flood. Although Joseph was buried in Egypt, the Israelites under Moses eventually reburied him in Canaan as he had requested (Ex 13:19; Jos 24:32).

50:26 *coffin in Egypt.* Note the dramatic significance of this ending. The Book of Genesis begins with the magnificent words: "In the beginning God created." But sin and the curse intervened, and it ends with the sad testimony of God's people away from the land of promise, and their leader "in a coffin in Egypt."

PLEASE NOTE: *The Henry Morris Study Bible* contains 22 appendices within its text. The following is a selection of these that are most relevant to the important foundational context of many of Dr. Morris's notes on the Book of Genesis.

Authenticity of Biblical Text

Although none of the original manuscripts written by Moses or Paul or the other biblical writers have been preserved (no doubt providentially; otherwise they might have become objects of worship), we can have full confidence in the integrity and canonicity of the text as transmitted to us. Some of the considerations supporting this confidence are summarized below.

Authenticity of the New Testament Text

Logical Basis of Confidence in the Text

- Over 20,000 hand-copied manuscripts of the Greek text are in existence, far more than for any other documents of comparable antiquity.

- Some papyrus fragments, especially of John, are preserved from the middle of the second century.

- Although there are some differences in the preserved manuscripts, there is no doubt that at least 95 percent of the text is intact from the apostolic period.

- The complete text of all New Testament books was available to those who had lived at the time of the apostles, and they were satisfied with it.

- In particular, the portrait of Christ as given in the New Testament was accepted as authentic by the earliest Christians.

- The conclusion is that the New Testament as we now have it (in any version) is substantially identical with the original writings.

Secondary Attestations of Authenticity

- Hundreds of quotations are included in the writings of the early church fathers, probably adequate to construct the entire New Testament, if necessary.

- Accuracy of most New Testament historical and geographical references has been confirmed by archaeological and historical research, and no such reference has been found to be in error.

- Large numbers of undesigned correlations within the New Testament books have been found, with no proven inconsistencies.

- The New Testament books were originally written in *Koine* Greek, the common language of the New Testament era, rather than classical Greek.

- Consistency of church ordinances (baptism, Lord's Supper) can only be explained if the documents were authentic as practiced by the early church prior to the circulation and collection of the New Testament books since early church practices were consistent with Scripture.

Authenticity of the Old Testament Text

New Testament Attestation

- Traditional authorship accepted by Christ (Lk 24:27; Jo 5:46-47; Ma 24:15-21).
- At least 320 direct quotations from the Old Testament, plus hundreds of allusions.
- Confirmation in the New Testament of supernatural events recorded in the Old Testament (Ma 12:39-40, 19:4-5; Lk 17:26; Jo 6:32).

Preservation of the Hebrew Text

- Over 1,000 hand-copied manuscripts of the Masoretic Text are available.
- Meticulous study and compilation of all earlier texts by the Masoretes in A.D. 500.
- Extremely careful copying and cross-checking of Old Testament text by the Hebrew scribes.
- Completion of writing and editing about the time of Ezra, with probably the first Old Testament canon developed at that time.
- Careful preservation and transmission from still earlier times.

Indirect Confirmation of Old Testament Text

- Other ancient versions (Septuagint, Vulgate, Syriac, Samaritan, etc.).
- Dead Sea Scrolls (containing most of the Old Testament).
- Acceptance by Jews and early Christians.
- Old Testament quotations in pre-Christian writings.

Fallacious Documentary (JEPD) Hypothesis

- Supposed basis (especially in relation to Pentateuch).
    Different styles and vocabularies.
    Inability of Moses and other patriarchs to write.
    Assumed low stage of cultural evolution.
    Alleged derivation from Babylonian myths.
    Impossibility of miracles and fulfilled prophecies.
- Refutation.
    Archaeological confirmations.
        High culture, writing skills in evidence long before Abraham.
        Geographical and historical accuracy.
        Superiority of biblical records to ethnic myths.
    Witness of Passover to Mosaic authorship.
    Claims of writers; universal acceptance by Jews.

Conclusion

The biblical text as we have it is authentic, confirmed wherever it can be tested. Entirely apart from the question of divine inspiration, the text has been accurately transmitted from the original writings. Furthermore, the most difficult part to believe in the Old Testament (the creation and the flood) is supported by all true science, and the most difficult to believe in the New Testament (the bodily resurrection of Christ) is confirmed by all sound history.

CREATION VERSUS EVOLUTION AS WORLDVIEWS

The origins controversy is not fundamentally a scientific issue, but rather a life-and-death struggle between two basic worldviews, each embracing the origin, destiny, and meaning of the cosmos and all things in the cosmos—material, biological, and spiritual.

Comparison of the Two Worldviews

Creation	Evolution
1. Self-existing eternal Creator	1. Self-originating or self-existing cosmos
2. Cosmos created by divine fiat	2. Cosmos organized by itself
3. Basic systems completed in the past by supernatural processes	3. All systems developed by still-continuing natural processes
4. Net changes in created systems "downward" toward disorganization	4. Net changes in evolving systems "upward" toward higher organization

Each model of origins entails a comprehensive worldview, embracing the whole of reality, and each is basically philosophical or, better, religious. It is a common misconception that evolution is science and creation is religion. Since it is impossible for scientists actually to *observe* or *repeat* unique events of the past. Evolution is based on the premise of naturalism, not science. In fact, evolution is the underlying premise (either atheism or pantheism, both of which preclude true creation) of more religions than creation. Note the tabulation below.

Religions Based on the Two Worldviews

Creation	Evolution
Biblical Christianity Orthodox Judaism Orthodox Islam	Non-Biblical Christianity (liberalism, esoteric cults, etc.) Non-Orthodox Judaism (Reform Judaism, Nationalistic Zionism) Non-Orthodox Islam Ancient Pagan Religions (Babylon, Greece, Rome, Egypt, etc.) New-Age Mysticism (Witchcraft, Goddess Worship, Satanism, etc.) Hinduism (incl. Sikhism, Jainism, etc.) Confucianism Buddhism Taoism Shintoism Animism Humanism Atheism

Of the three creationist religions, only biblical Christianity acknowledges that the Creator must also become the Redeemer and Savior. Thus Islam and Judaism become humanistic in effect, relying on human works in addition to faith in the Creator. All others are basically evolutionary religions, assuming an eternal space-time cosmos, the intrinsic processes of which (often personified as various gods and goddesses) have developed the cosmos into its present form.

Fruits of the Two Worldviews

The Lord Jesus Christ said, "A good tree cannot bring forth evil fruit, neither can a corrupt tree bring forth good fruit" (Ma 7:18). By this test, the evolution "tree" is certainly corrupt, for its "fruit" has been uniformly evil. Note the following list of harmful philosophies and evil practices. The leading advocates of these philosophies have in every case based their pseudo-scientific rationale on evolutionism.

Evolutionist Fruits

Harmful Philosophies		Evil Practices	
Communism	Nazism	Abortion	Drug Culture
Racism	Imperialism	Promiscuity	Slavery
Atheism	Humanism	Pornography	Genocide
Materialism	Amoralism	Chauvinism	New-Agism
Scientism	Pantheism	Euthanasia	Pollution
Monopolism	Anarchism	Bestiality	Satanism
Occultism	Social Darwinism	Homosexuality	Criminality
Behaviorism	Freudianism	Cannibalism	Witchcraft

The above list could be extended. On the other hand, true biblical creationism has produced good fruits. Consider the following:

Creationist Fruits

Wholesome Human Social Relationships

- Monogamous marriage was established by God with the first human couple (Ge 2:21-25; Ma 19:4-6).
- Dominion mandate established human stewardship of man under God over the physical and animal creation, viewing every honorable occupation as a service to God (Ge 1:26-28; Col 3:23).
- Human government ordained to maintain order in society (Ge 9:1-7; Ro 13:1-7) as service to the Creator.

True Science

- Founding fathers of modern science (Newton, Kepler, Boyle) were creationists, "thinking God's thoughts after Him."
- Scientific method based on premise of orderly creation, capable of being understood and described rationally, because it was designed by an intelligent Creator.

True Education

- Transmitting truth learned by obedience to dominion mandate from one generation to another, thereby "subduing" the earth.
- Centered and controlled in the home and family, stressing obedience to God and His Word (Ge 18:18-19; Ep 6:4).
- Transmission of truth through God's people (Ma 28:19-20; 2 Ti 3:16).

True Americanism

- Founding fathers of American system—though not all Bible-believing Christians—were all creationists.
- Declaration of Independence assumes that American freedom is ensured by obedience to the Creator (e.g., "all men created equal").
- Background of the U.S. Constitution based on English common law, which was derived mainly from Scripture, and efforts of many Bible-believing founding fathers.

True Christianity—every major doctrine and practice based on creationist foundation

- Christology—Christ as Creator (Jo 1:3; Col 1:16).
- Gospel—founded "everlastingly" on God first as Creator (Re 14:6-7), then as incarnate saving Word.
- Saving faith—centered on God's work as Creator (He 10:38–11:3).
- Sound evangelism—note John's example, along with his purpose in writing his Gospel (Jo 20:30-31; 1:1-12).
- Sound missionary effort—see Paul's example (Ac 14:1,15-17; 17:2-4,23-34).
- Fellowship (Ep 3:8-12).
- Christian life (Col 3:10; 2 Co 5:17).
- Christian home and family (Ma 19:3-6).
- Biblical revelation and inerrancy (Ps 119:89-90; He 1:1-2).
- Redemption (1 Pe 1:18-21; 2 Ti 1:9; Tit 1:2).

Conclusion

The true worldview is not evolutionary humanism, as taught in the majority of the world's educational institutions, but biblical creationism, centered in the Lord Jesus Christ as Creator, Redeeming Savior, and coming King and Lord of all.

THE LOGIC OF BIBLICAL CREATION

The biblical account of creation is ridiculed by atheists, patronized by liberals, and often allegorized even by conservatives. The fact is, however, that it is God's own account of creation, corroborated by Jesus Christ (Mk 10:6-8) who was there.

We are well advised to take it seriously and literally, for God is able to say what He means, and will someday hold us accountable for believing what He says. Furthermore, the account is reasonable and logical, fully in accord with all true science and history. The following chain of logic, while not compelling belief on the part of those who refuse to believe, at least demonstrates the reasonableness of biblical creation.

There are only two possible basic models of origins—that is, of the origin of the universe, of the earth, of animate life, of human life, and of all the basic systems of the cosmos. These are, in simplest terms, evolution or creation. Either the origin of things can be understood in terms of continuing natural processes, or they cannot—one or the other. If they cannot, then we must resort to completed supernatural processes to explain the origin of at least the basic systems of the cosmos. Evolution and creation thus exhaust the possibilities, as far as origins are concerned.

This necessarily means that if we can demonstrate to be false either model of origins, then the other must be true. There is no other option. By definition, evolution should still be occurring now, since it is to be explained by present processes.

Present Processes

If there is anything certain in this world, however, it is that there is no evidence whatever that evolution is occurring today—that is, true vertical evolution, from some simpler kind to some more complex kind. No one has ever observed a star evolve from hydrogen, life evolve from chemicals, a higher species evolve from a lower species, a man from an ape, or anything else of this sort. Not only has no one ever observed true evolution in action, no one knows how evolution works, or even how it might work. No one has ever seen it happen (despite thousands of experiments that have tried to produce it), and no one yet has come up with a workable mechanism to explain it, so it would seem that it has been falsified, at least as far as the present world is concerned. This does not prove that it did not happen in the past, of course, but the evolutionist should recognize that this means it is not science, since it is not observable. Evolution must be accepted on faith.

What about the Past?

Actually, there is no evidence at all that evolution ever took place in the past, either. In all recorded history, extending back nearly 5,000 years, no one has ever recorded the natural evolution of any kind of creature (living or non-living) into a more complex kind. Furthermore, all known vertical changes seem to go in the wrong direction. An average of at least one species has become extinct every day since records have been kept, but no new species has evolved during that time. Stars explode, comets and meteorites disintegrate, the biosphere deteriorates, and everything eventually dies, so far as all historical observations go, but nothing has ever evolved into higher complexity.

But how about prehistoric changes? The only real records we have of this period are presumably to be found in the sedimentary rocks of the earth's crust, where billions of fossil remains of former living creatures have been preserved for our observation. Again, however, the story is one of extinction, not evolution. Numerous kinds of extinct animals are found (e.g., dinosaurs), but never, in all of these billions of fossils, is a truly incipient or transitional form found. No fossil has ever been found with half scales and half feathers, half legs and half wings, half-developed heart, half-developed eye, or any other such thing.

If evolution were true, there should be millions of transitional types among these multiplied billions of fossils—in fact, *everything* should show transitional features. But they do not! If one were to rely strictly on the observed evidence, he would have to agree that past evolution has also been falsified.

The Necessity of Creation

If evolution did not occur in the past, and does not occur at present, then it is entirely imaginary—not a part of the real world at all. This leaves creation as the necessary explanation of origins.

This fact is confirmed by the best-proved laws of science—the law of conservation in quantity and the law of decay in complexity, or the famous First and Second Laws of Thermodynamics.

The First Law notes that, in all real processes, the total quantity of matter and energy stays constant, even though it frequently changes form. A parallel principle in biology notes that "like begets like"—dogs are always dogs, for example, though they occur in many varieties. The Second Law notes that the quality of any system always tends to decrease—that is, its usefulness, its complexity, its information value. In living organisms, true vertical changes go down, not up—mutations cause deterioration, individuals die, species become extinct. In fact, everything in the universe seems to be headed downhill toward ultimate cosmic death.

Furthermore, the First Law states in effect that *nothing* is being either "created" or "evolved" by present processes. The Second Law notes that there is, instead, a universal *tendency* for everything to disintegrate, to run down, and finally, to "die." The whole universe is growing old, wearing out, headed toward ultimate stillness and death. This universal "increase in entropy" leads directly to the conclusion that there must have been a creation of things in the past; otherwise, everything would now be dead (since they are universally dying in the present).

Again, we are driven to the logical necessity of a primal creation—a creation that was accomplished not by present natural processes, but by past supernatural processes. This means, however, that we cannot deduce anything about that creation except just the *fact* of creation. The processes of creation, the duration of the period of creation, the order of events—all are hidden from us by virtue of the fact that our present observed processes do not create, they only conserve in quantity and deteriorate in quality.

Nevertheless, there must have been a creation, and, therefore, a Creator. The Creator of the infinitely complex, highly energized cosmos must be omniscient and omnipotent. Having created life, as well as human personalities, He must also be a living Person. No effect can be greater than its cause.

Therefore, He is fully capable of revealing to us knowledge about His creation—knowledge which could never be learned through studying present processes. It almost seems that He *must* do this, in fact, since He surely is not capricious. He would not create men and women who long to know the meaning of their lives, yet neglect or refuse to tell them anything about it.

Assuming, then, that He *has* revealed this information to His creatures, just where is His revelation to be found? There are numerous books of religion, ancient and modern, but they do *not* contain any account at all of the *creation* of the universe.

The answer, therefore, has to be in His record of creation in the Book of Genesis, for there is no alternative. There are only three creationist "religions" in the world—Christianity, Islam, and Judaism—and all three base their belief in creation on the record of Genesis. Without exception, all the other religions and philosophies of the world have based their beliefs concerning origins on some form of evolutionism. That is, they all begin with the universe (space, time, matter) already in existence, then speculate how the forces of nature (often personified as various gods and goddesses) may have generated all the systems and living creatures of the world out of some primordial watery chaos. Only Genesis even *attempts* to tell how the universe itself came to be.

Whether most people believe it or not, therefore, the creation account in Genesis is God's record of His creation. Jesus Christ also taught this truth, so surely any true Christian should believe it. This account does not allow even the possibility of evolution, since everything was created "after his kind" (Ge 1:24), and since God "rested from all His work" (Ge 2:3) after six days of creating and making things, and so is no longer using processes which "create" things, as theistic evolutionists believe. Instead, He now is "upholding all things" (He 1:3) through His law of conservation—the "First Law of Thermodynamics."

The entrance of sin into the world brought a disordering principle into the Creator's perfect creation, in the form of God's "curse" on the "whole creation"—the principle of decay and death—the "Second Law." Thus, the natural laws now governing the processes of the universe are not laws of origin and development, as evolution requires, but of conservation and decay, in accordance with the truth of primeval special creation.

If we now wish to know how *long* it took for God to make all things, we can learn this from His Genesis record—and *only* there—since we cannot legitimately project present processes back into the creation period. That account says He did it in just six days of work followed by a day of rest, thus providing the pattern by which men and women were to order their daily lives throughout history. Ever since that first week, people have actually done this—even those who reject His account of creation.

"But how long were those days?" someone may still ask. Only God can answer that question, and He does define His terms. "God called the light Day," says the account, in the very first use of the word "day" in the Bible (Ge 1:5). The "day" thus is the light-period in the diurnal light and darkness cycle, which began on "the first day," and has continued every day since.

"But what about the evidences for the earth's great age?" others will ask. The answer is that there are no such *evidences*. All calculations that purport to give this kind of evidence are based on present natural processes, and, as we have seen, it is not legitimate to project these into the creation period. Furthermore, all such processes invariably involve the principle of decay, and these can never be assumed to have operated uniformly in the past. Thermodynamics specifies that all processes must be decay processes, but the *rate* of decay depends on the science of kinetics—not thermodynamics. Every process functions at its own rate, which may vary widely with time, depending on the many "variables." Making allowance for tremendous acceleration of most processes at the time of the global hydraulic cataclysm described in Genesis will lead us to conclude that these processes, instead of pointing to the earth's great age, really point to the earth's great flood.

One may escape from this chain of logic if he wishes, but the fact remains that the chain *is* logical and reasonable. When mixed with faith, there is peace and joy in believing God's straightforward, rational, simple, satisfying, and truly scientific account of creation in Genesis.

This appendix was originally published as an "Impact" article in the Institute for Creation Research newsletter, *Acts and Facts* (July 1990).

OUTLINE OF EARTH HISTORY AS REVEALED IN THE BOOK OF GENESIS

I. Introduction

The Book of Genesis is the most important book ever written, in the sense that it is the foundational book of the 66 books of the Bible, the written Word of God. It is the true record of primeval history and lays the foundation for every key doctrine of the Bible and the Christian faith.

An understanding of Genesis is prerequisite to any real understanding of the New Testament. The books of the New Testament contain over 200 quotations from or clear allusions to, the Genesis record (see appendix on page 156).

Jesus Christ Himself frequently quoted from Genesis (Mk 10:6) or alluded to its histories (Jo 3:14). He began in Genesis in His biblical exposition of all the "things concerning Himself" while walking on the road to Emmaus after His resurrection (see Lk 24:25-27). This constitutes an excellent example for us. We should, as He did, begin with Genesis.

II. Authorship of Genesis

Moses is the traditional author of Genesis, as well as the other books of the Pentateuch. However, he was not living during the times recorded in Genesis, as he was during the times of Exodus, Leviticus, Numbers, and Deuteronomy. Therefore, he probably incorporated previous records as did the authors of other historical books in the Bible (e.g., Kings).

That is, the various sections of Genesis were actually recorded by eyewitnesses of the events described—by Adam, Noah, Shem, Terah, Isaac, Jacob, and others. Their respective tablets were then later compiled and edited by Moses into the present format of Genesis, with the various sections demarked by the recurring phrase, "These are the generations of . . ."

See the "Introduction to Genesis" for further discussion of this important subject. Supervising and guiding the entire operation, of course, was the inspiration of the Holy Spirit (2 Ti 3:16; 2 Pe 1:21).

III. The Only True Account of Origins

The false philosophy of evolution has led modern scientific and educational establishments to develop elaborate naturalistic development scenarios for the universe and its many components, including human beings. The only true account of origins, however, is given in Genesis. The sequence of origins events as revealed in Genesis is as follows:

- Creation of Space/Mass/Time Universe (Ge 1:1).
- Formation of Solid Earth and Biosphere (Ge 1:9-10).
- Origin of Stars and Solar System (Ge 1:14-19).
- Formation of Marine and Atmospheric Life (Ge 1:20).
- Creation of Conscious Animal Life (Ge 1:21-25).

- Creation of Man in the Image of God (Ge 1:26,27).
- Origin of Marriage and Home (Ge 1:28; 2:23-24).
- Origin of Decay and Death (Ge 3:17-19).
- Origin of Agriculture and Animal Husbandry (Ge 4:2).
- Origin of Urbanization (Ge 4:17).
- Origin of Technology (Ge 4:20-22).
- Origin of the Nations (Ge 10).
- Origin of Different Languages (Ge 11:1-9).
- Origin of the Chosen Nation of Israel (Ge 12).

IV. The Chronological Framework of Earth History

The major events in the history of the world and life are interpreted by evolutionists in terms of their system of naturalistic cosmology and geologic ages on earth. The biblical creationist framework of history is vastly different. These two chronologies are summarized below.

Evolutionary Framework

- Matter and energy are either infinitely old or else originated in a quantum fluctuation from "nothing."
- The present universe originated in a "Big Bang" as an infinitesimal particle of space and time about 10 to 20 billion years ago.
- The solar system condensed either out of a cloud of cosmic dust or by an accumulation of colliding planetoids about 4.6 billion years ago.
- Life evolved from complex non-living chemicals in a primeval soup 3.5 to 4.0 billion years ago.
- Multi-cellular life evolved in the ocean about one billion years ago.
- Human life evolved from non-human animal life three to four million years ago.
- Culture and civilization evolved about 9,000 years ago.
- Man and civilization will continue to evolve in the unknown future.

Biblical Framework

- The universe was created by God's command about 6,000 years ago (possibly up to 10,000 years ago).
- The perfect creation was completed in six 24-hour days (Ge 1:1–2:3; Ex 20:8-11).
- Man's sin brought God's curse on the whole creation, with suffering and death (Ge 3:14-18).
- A cataclysmic deluge, destroyed the primeval world-system and earth structure in the days of Noah (Ge 7:14-19).
- Languages were confused and the nations were dispersed at Babel (Ge 11:1-9).
- Creation was redeemed at Calvary (Jo 19-20; Col 1:16-20).
- In the future, perfect creation will be restored and eternal order will be established (Re 21–22).

V. Attempts to Reconcile Biblical and Evolutionary Frameworks

Because of the peer pressure of leaders in science, education, and society in general, many Christians have tried to accommodate the evolutionary framework within the biblical framework, or vice versa. Such attempts, however, are futile, and there is no valid reason for Christians not to accept the biblical record at face value. The various compromise theories, attempting to harmonize the astronomic and geological ages with the creation week of Genesis, are as follows:

Literary Framework Theory

- Evolutionary ages taken as literally true, but creation week merely an allegory or some other literary device.
- Interpretive system: "Theistic Evolution" (Evolution taken as God's method of creation).

Day-Age Theory

- Evolutionary ages assumed to be same as creation week (Geological "ages" = creation "days").
- Interpretive system: "Progressive Creation" (Intermittent acts of creation interspersed between long ages of either slow evolution or no evolution).

Gap Theory

- Evolutionary ages taken as completed before the creation week, with the ages terminated by a global catastrophe followed by reconstruction.
- Interpretive system: Dispensationalism (Geological ages relegated to a former dispensation not relevant to present human dispensation).

All three compromise theories have a number of variants, but all make the basic error of accepting the evolutionary ages of astronomy and geology as real history, and then trying to find a place for the Genesis record of six-day creation. This can only be done, however, by gross distortion of the plain sense of the Genesis record.

VI. Fallacies in Accepting Evolutionary Ages as Real History

Biblical Fallacies

- Permanence of created "kinds" (Ge 1:25, etc., 1 Co 15:35-44) does not accommodate theistic evolution.
- Completion of creation (Ge 2:1-3; He 4:3-4,10) does not allow use of present natural processes to "create" or "make" complex systems.
- New Testament accepts historicity of Genesis creation and flood accounts.
- "Day" defined as literal day at first mention (Ge 1:5).
- Exodus 20:8-11 and 31:15-18 require literal days.
- Contextual use of "day" in Genesis precludes figurative meaning (i.e., "day" defined by numerical sequence and bounded by "evening and morning"—always literal in Old Testament usage).
- No contextual basis for "gap" between Genesis 1:1 and 1:2 (note Hebrew conjunction "and," beginning each verse in Genesis, indicating continuity for sequence of events).
- No clear reference in Bible to pre-Adamic race or pre-Adamic cataclysm.

Theological Fallacies

- Evolutionary ages are the most wasteful and cruel process conceivable by which to produce man.
- Geological ages are identified specifically by their fossils (billions of fossils known in these "ages") indicating global suffering, decay, and death prior to entrance of sin and Satan into the world.
- Evolutionary ages imply no purpose in creation. (Why dinosaurs, for example?)
- Evolution and eternal pre-worlds characterize all pagan religions and philosophies.

Scientific Fallacies

- There is no legitimate scientific evidence of any kind for any form of evolution.
- There are many more natural processes indicating a young earth than an old earth (see appendix on page 146).
- There are at least 25 discrepancies between the evolutionary order of events and the creation order (e.g., plant life before the sun, earth originally covered by water, birds before land animals, fruit trees before fishes, earth before the stars, etc.).
- Geological ages assumed to be continuous with present, leaving no room for a pre-Adamic cataclysm.
- The global cataclysm required by the gap theory would destroy all geological evidences for the "ages."

VII. The Flood Theory of Geology

If the geological ages did not actually take place, as the biblical record clearly stipulates, then the vast geological systems must be explained some other way—especially the billions of fossils in the rocks of the earth's crust. The obvious explanation is the Genesis record of the flood. If the flood did occur as the global cataclysm so clearly described in the Bible, it would have destroyed any previous geological deposits. Thus the "geological column" is really telling of the destruction of life in one age instead of telling of the evolution of life over many ages.

See appendix on page 150 for a listing of both biblical and scientific evidences of the world-wide flood. Those who accept the evolutionary ages must reject these evidences, for such a flood would have destroyed all the evidences for any geological ages before the flood.

Two theories have been proposed by Christians who wish to retain the evolutionary ages in their interpretations of Scripture: the local flood theory and the tranquil flood theory. Neither will suffice.

Fallacies in the Local Flood Theory

- Requires breaking the Noahic covenant promising no more such flood.
- Ignores the many references in both Old and New Testaments to the global flood.
- Requires a 17,000 foot-high local flood to cover Mount Ararat, where the ark landed when the flood waters abated.
- Makes the construction of a vast ark to hold all land animals redundant, if not ridiculous.

Fallacies in the Tranquil Flood Theory

- Local floods are not tranquil, so how could a global flood be tranquil?
- If all geological strata have been formed by local flood action, how could a global flood not accomplish even greater geological work?

VIII. The Creative and Formative Works of God

The creation chapter (Ge 1) describes two basic types of God's work in creating and making all things. His work of "creating" (Hebrew *bara*) involved calling into existence out of nothing (except His own power) basic entities out of which all things would be made. His work of "making" (Hebrew *asah*) and "forming" (Hebrew *yatsar*) involved building up complex systems out of those basic entities. Only God can "create;" whenever creation is mentioned in the Bible, God is the one doing it. Man, with enough effort and ingenuity, can make and form complex systems, but God did it instantaneously during creation week.

Creative Works of God

- Creation of the physical elements of the universe—space, mass, energy, time (Ge 1:1).
- Creation of conscious life (Hebrew *nephesh*), including both soul and spirit (in the sense of "breath"). Animals possess components of both the created physical elements and conscious life (Ge 1:21).
- Creation of human beings in the image of God. Men and women are tri-unities of body, soul and spirit (in the sense of the divine image). The human body is much more complex than that of the highest animal, as is the human soul/breath complex. Only men and women possess, in addition, the image of God (Ge 1:27).

Formative Works of God

- **Day One:** Energizing the cosmos, as centered in light energy (Ge 1:2-5).
- **Day Two:** Formation of the atmosphere ("firmament") and hydrosphere, both of which are necessary for life and are unique to earth among the planets (Ge 1:6-8).
- **Day Three:** Formation of the lithosphere (the solid earth) and biosphere (earth's cover of vegetation), a necessity for animal life (Ge 1:9-13).
- **Day Four:** Formation of astrosphere in a different "firmament" (Hebrew *raqia*, referring to an "expanse" of stretched-out place), including all the stars, galaxies and planets (Ge 1:14-19).
- **Day Five:** Formation of different kinds of animals for the atmosphere (birds) and hydrosphere (fishes), each to reproduce only "after its kind" (Ge 1:20-23).
- **Day Six:** Formation of different kinds of land animals for the lithosphere and biosphere, as well as one male body and one female body (Adam and Eve) to serve as progenitors of all later human beings (Ge 1:24-31).
- **Day Seven:** Completion and sanctification of "all the work which God created and made" (Ge 1:31–2:3).

IX. Outline of World History According to Peter

The World that Then Was (2 Pe 3:6)

- Global greenhouse provided by the "waters above the firmament" (probably a thermal blanket of invisible water vapor, which would also prevent strong winds and rains, and filter out harmful radiation from space).
- Extensive habitable lands, with abundant plant and animal life everywhere (no deserts, ice caps).
- Man's dominion and stewardship.
- Committed to man's care (Ge 1:28-30; 2:15,20).
- Cursed for man's sake (Ge 3:17-19).
- Corrupted by man's sin (Ge 4:11; 6:11-12).
- Destroyed by the Genesis Flood (Ge 6–8).
- Precipitation of vapor canopy.
- Eruption of primeval crust.
- Formation of present fossil-bearing crust.
- Initiation of atmospheric circulation.
- Initiation of Ice Age (pluvial age in lower latitudes).
- Residual catastrophes (ongoing intermittent local floods, volcanic eruptions, earthquakes, etc.).

The World that Is Now (2 Pe 3:7)

- Held together ("sustained") by its Creator (Col 1:17).
- Subjected to ongoing decay (Ro 8:20).
- Naturalistic uniformity of processes (Ge 8:22; Ec 1:4-10).
- Ultimate disintegration by fiery cataclysm (not annihilation but conversion of mass to other forms of energy) (2 Pe 3:10).

The World that Shall Be (2 Pe 3:13)

- Suffering and death removed forever (Re 21:4).
- Everything made new again (Ac 3:21; Re 21:5).
- Eternal (Da 12:3; Is 66:22).
- No more sin (2 Pe 3:13; 1 Jo 3:1-3).

GLOBAL PROCESSES INDICATING RECENT CREATION

It is widely taught today that the earth is 4.6 billion years old and the age of the universe anywhere from 8 billion years to eternal. The Bible, on the other hand, indicates the universe to be only a few thousand years old, and all known human history (as recorded in the historical annals of Egypt, Sumeria, and other ancient nations) also is limited to a few thousand years.

The great ages needed to make evolutionism appear feasible are based mainly on a handful of very slow radioactive decay processes (e.g., uranium to lead, potassium to argon, etc.). These must each be based on at least three unprovable assumptions:

- Known initial boundary conditions (e.g., assumption of no initial radiogenic lead in the uranium/lead mineral).

- Isolated system (i.e., no ingress or egress of components of the system during the time it is functioning).

- Constant rate of process (i.e., no effect of environmental radiations or any other force on the decay rate).

None of these assumptions are capable of either proof or disproof, since conditions are unknown prior to recorded history. All are known to be wrong in almost all natural processes.

On the other hand, there are scores of worldwide natural processes which will indicate ages far too brief for evolution to be feasible, even with the above "uniformitarian" assumptions. Some of these are listed in the accompanying tabulation, with references for each.

These may all be wrong, of course, because they are all based on the same unreasonable assumptions as for the very few processes that yield old ages.

However, there are many more of them, and the assumptions are more likely to be valid for short time periods than for long periods. Therefore, the weight of scientific evidence is that the universe is young, entirely apart from the definitive and conclusive evidence of biblical revelation.

This tabulation is modified from the tabulation originally published as an ICR "Impact" article in *Acts and Facts*, then also *What is Creation Science?* by Henry M. Morris and Gary Parker (San Diego, Master Books, 1987), pp. 288-293.

Uniformitarian Estimates—Age of the Earth

Process	Estimated Age of Earth in Years	Reference
1. Decay of earth's magnetic field	10,000	1
2. Influx of radiocarbon to the earth system	10,000	2
3. Continuous rapid deposition of geologic column	too small to calculate	3
4. Influx of juvenile water to oceans	340,000,000	3
5. Influx of magma from mantle to form crust	500,000,000	3
6. Growth of oldest living part of biosphere	5,000	3
7. Origin of human civilizations	5,000	3
8. Efflux of Helium-4 into the atmosphere	1,750—175,000	4
9. Development of total human population	4,000	5
10. Influx of sediment to the ocean via rivers	30,000,000	6
11. Erosion of sediment from continents	14,000,000	6
12. Leaching of sodium from continents	1,000,000	7
13. Leaching of chlorine from continents	1,000,000	7
14. Leaching of calcium from continents	12,000,000	7
15. Influx of carbonate to the ocean	100,000	7
16. Influx of sulphate to the ocean	10,000,000	7
17. Influx of chlorine to the ocean	164,000,000	7
18. Influx of calcium to the ocean	1,000,000	7
19. Influx of uranium to the ocean	1,260,000	8
20. Efflux of oil from traps by fluid pressure	10,000—100,000	9
21. Formation of radiogenic lead by neutron capture	too small to measure	9
22. Formation of radiogenic strontium by neutron capture	too small to measure	9
23. Decay of natural remanent paleomagnetism	100,000	9
24. Parentless polonium halos	too small to measure	10
25. Decay of uranium with initial "radiogenic" lead	too small to measure	11
26. Decay of potassium with entrapped argon	too small to measure	11
27. Formation of river deltas	5,000	12
28. Submarine oil seepage into oceans	50,000,000	13
29. Decay of natural plutonium	80,000,000	14
30. Decay of lines of galaxies	10,000,000	15
31. Expanding interstellar gas	60,000,000	16
32. Decay of short-period comets	10,000	17
33. Decay of long-period comets	1,000,000	18
34. Influx of small particles to the sun	83,000	18
35. Maximum life of meteor showers	5,000,000	18
36. Instability of rings of Saturn	1,000,000	18
37. Escape of methane from Titan	20,000,000	18
38. Accumulation of dust on the moon	uncertain	19
39. Deceleration of earth by tidal friction	500,000,000	20
40. Cooling of the earth by heat efflux	24,000,000	20

Process	Estimated Age of Earth in Years	Reference
41. Accumulation of calcareous ooze on sea floor	5,000,000	21
42. Influx of sodium to the ocean via rivers	62,000,000	22
43. Influx of nickel to the ocean via rivers	9,000	23
44. Influx of magnesium to the ocean via rivers	45,000,000	23
45. Influx of silicon to the ocean via rivers	8,000	23
46. Influx of potassium to the ocean via rivers	11,000,000	23
47. Influx of copper to the ocean via rivers	50,000	23
48. Influx of gold to the ocean via rivers	560,000	23
49. Influx of silver to the ocean via rivers	2,100,000	23
50. Influx of mercury to the ocean via rivers	42,000	23
51. Influx of lead to the ocean via rivers	2,000	23
52. Influx of tin to the ocean via rivers	100,000	23
53. Influx of aluminum to the ocean via rivers	100	23
54. Influx of lithium into ocean via rivers	20,000,000	23
55. Influx of titanium into ocean via rivers	160	23
56. Influx of chromium into ocean via rivers	350	23
57. Influx of manganese into ocean via rivers	1,400	23
58. Influx of iron into ocean via rivers	140	23
59. Influx of cobalt into ocean via rivers	18,000	23
60. Influx of zinc into ocean via rivers	180,000	23
61. Influx of rubidium into ocean via rivers	270,000	23
62. Influx of strontium into ocean via rivers	19,000,000	23
63. Influx of bismuth into ocean via rivers	45,000	23
64. Influx of thorium into ocean via rivers	350	23
65. Influx of antimony into ocean via rivers	350,000	23
66. Influx of tungsten into ocean via rivers	1,000	23
67. Influx of barium into ocean via rivers	84,000	23
68. Influx of molybdenum into ocean via rivers	500,000	23

Reference Documentation for Age Estimates

1. Thomas G. Barnes, *Origin and Destiny of the Earth's Magnetic Field* (San Diego: Institute for Creation Research, 1983), 132 pp.
2. Melvin A. Cook, "Do Radiological Clocks Need Repair?" *Creation Research Society Quarterly* 5 (Oct. 1968): 70. Also see, *Radiocarbon and the Age of the Earth*, by Gerald Aardsma (San Diego: Institute for Creation Research, 1991).
3. Henry M. Morris, ed., *Scientific Creationism* (San Diego: Master Books, 1985).
4. Melvin A. Cook, "Where is the Earth's Radiogenic Helium?" *Nature* 179 (Jan. 26, 1957): 213. See also *The Age of the Earth's Atmosphere*, by Larry Vardiman (San Diego: Institute for Creation Research, 1990).
5. Henry M. Morris, "*Evolution and the Population Problem*," ICR Impact Series, *Acts and Facts*, no. 21 (Nov. 1974).
6. Stuart E. Nevins, "*Evolution: The Ocean Says No*," ICR Impact Series, *Acts and Facts* 2, no. 8 (Oct. 1973).
7. Dudley J. Whitney, *The Face of the Deep* (New York: Vantage, 1955).
8. Salman Bloch, "Some Factors Controlling the Concentration of Uranium in the World Ocean," *Geochimica et Cosmochimica Acta* 44 (1980): 373-77. See also *What is Creation Science?* by Henry M. Morris and Gary Parker (San Diego: Master Books, 1987), pp. 283-284.
9. Melvin A. Cook, *Prehistory and Earth Models* (London: Max Parrish, 1966).
10. Robert Gentry, *Creation's Tiny Mystery* (Knoxville: Earth Science Associates, 1988).
11. Harold S. Slusher, *Critique of Radiometric Dating* (San Diego: Institute for Creation Research, 1980), 58 pp.
12. Benjamin F. Allen, "The Geologic Age of the Mississippi River," *Creation Research Society Quarterly* 9 (Sept. 1972): 96-114.

13. R. D. Wilson, *et al.*, "Natural Marine Oil Seepage," *Science* 184 (May 24, 1974): 857-65.
14. "Natural Plutonium," *Chemical and Engineering News* 49 (Sept. 20, 1971): 29.
15. Halton Arp, "Observational Paradoxes in Extragalactic Astronomy," *Science* 174 (Dec. 17, 1971): 1189-1200.
16. V. A. Hughes and D. Routledge, "An Expanding Ring of Interstellar Gas with Center Close to the Sun," *Astronomical Journal* 77, no. 3 (1972): 210-14.
17. Harold S. Slusher, "Some Astronomical Evidences for a Youthful Solar System," *Creation Research Society Quarterly* 8 (June 1971): 55-57.
18. Harold S. Slusher, *Age of the Cosmos* (San Diego: Institute for Creation Research, 1980), 76 pp.
19. John D. Morris, *The Young Earth* (Colorado Springs, Master Books, 1994), pp. 87, 88.
20. Thomas G. Barnes, "Physics, a Challenge to Geologic Time," ICR Impact Series, *Acts and Facts* 16 (July 1974).
21. Maurice Ewing, J. I. Ewing, and M. Talwan, "Sediment Distribution in the Oceans—Mid-Atlantic Ridge," *Bulletin of the Geophysical Society of America* 75 (Jan. 1967): 17-36.
22. Steven A. Austin and Russell D. Humphries, "The Sea's Missing Salt: A Dilemma for Evolutionists," *Proceedings of the Second International Conference on Creationism* 2 (1991): 17-33.
23. J. P. Riley and G. Skirrow, eds., *Chemical Oceanography* 1 (London: Academic Press, 1965): 164. See also Harold Camping, "Let the Oceans Speak," *Creation Research Society Quarterly* 11 (June 1974): 39-45. Uniformitarian geologists, making the unwarranted assumption that ocean chemicals are all in a steady state, have noted that the same method of calculation would give the so-called "residence time" of each element in the ocean, if the influx and efflux of the elements are assumed to be equal. This assumption is wrong, however, as shown in References 8 and 22, for uranium and sodium in particular.

THE UNIVERSAL FLOOD

Central to the question of the historicity of the early chapters of Genesis is the question of whether the Noahic flood was global or only regional. A worldwide flood would have cataclysmically changed the entire surface of the globe, including any fossil-bearing sedimentary rocks that may have been formed prior to that time. Consequently, the earth's present fossil sediments must date largely from the time of their being deposited by the waters of the great flood.

On the other hand, the modern evolutionary system of earth history denies any such global cataclysm and is based on the assumption of uniformitarianism. The sedimentary rocks and their fossil contents have been interpreted as evidence of a vast series of evolutionary ages extending over billions of years of time, deposited slowly and generally uniformly over the earth as living organisms gradually evolved into higher and higher forms during those ages.

The "day-age theory" is the attempt by Bible expositors to accommodate these evolutionary ages *within* the framework of the six days of creation. The "gap theory" is the attempt by other expositors to accommodate them *outside* the framework of the six days of creation. Both such theories, if consistent, are associated with the "local flood theory," since a universal flood would have destroyed the sedimentary framework of the geological ages. That is, a universal flood precludes the historicity of the geological ages, and vice versa.

If the Genesis flood actually was worldwide, then the strained exegesis associated with the day-age and gap theories becomes unnecessary and harmful. In the tabulation below, therefore, are listed one hundred reasons why the flood should be accepted as a true global cataclysm.

From References in Genesis

Genesis Reference	Argument
1. 1:7	Water above the atmosphere must have been global in extent
2. 2:5	No rain on the earth must have been worldwide condition
3. 2:6	Earth mist watered the whole face of the ground
4. 2:10-14	Edenic geography no longer in existence
5. 4:22	High civilization at dawn of history not continuous with present world
6. 5:5	Longevity of antediluvian patriarchs indicates distinctive biosphere
7. 6:1	Man had multiplied on the face of the earth
8. 6:2	Demonic-human unions co-extensive with mankind
9. 6:5	Universal evil inexplicable in post-diluvian society
10. 6:6-7	Repentance of God extended to the whole animal creation
11. 6:11	Earth was filled with violence and corruption before God
12. 6:12	All flesh was corrupted (possibly including animals)
13. 6:13	God decided to destroy both man and the earth
14. 6:15	Ark too large for regional fauna
15. 6:17	Everything with the breath of life to die
16. 6:19	Purpose of ark was to keep two of every sort alive
17. 6:20	Animals of all kinds migrated to the ark
18. 6:21	All kinds of edible food taken on the ark
19. 7:4	Every living substance on the ground to be destroyed
20. 7:10	"The flood" (Hebrew *mabbul*) applies solely to Noah's flood.
21. 7:11	All the fountains of the great deep cleaved open in one day.

Genesis Reference		Argument
22.	7:11	The "sluiceways from the floodgates" of heaven were opened
23.	7:12	Rain poured continuously for forty days and forty nights
24.	7:18	The waters prevailed and increased greatly
25.	7:19	High hills under the whole heaven were covered
26.	7:20	Waters fifteen cubits above highest mountains
27.	7:21	Every man died on the earth
28.	7:22	All flesh with the breath of life in the dry land died
29.	7:23	Every living substance destroyed off the face of the ground
30.	7:24	Waters at maximum height for five months
31.	8:2	Windows of heaven open for five months
33.	8:4	Ark floated over 17,000-ft. mountains for five months
34.	8:5	Water receded 2½ months before mountain tops seen
35.	8:9	Dove found no suitable ground even after four months of receding waters
36.	8:11	Plants began budding nine months after the flood
37.	8:14	Occupants were in the ark for over a year
38.	8:19	All present nonmarine animals came from the ark
39.	8:21	God smote all living things only once
40.	8:22	Present uniformity of nature dates from the end of the flood
41.	9:1	Earth was to be filled with descendants of Noah
42.	9:2	Changed relation between man and animals followed the flood
43.	9:3	Man permitted animal food after flood
44.	9:6	Institution of human government dates from flood
45.	9:10	God's covenant made with every living creature
46.	9:11	God promised the flood would never come again on the earth
47.	9:13	Rainbow placed in sky after the flood
48.	9:19	Whole earth overspread by the sons of Noah
49.	11:1	Whole earth spoke one language after the flood
50.	11:9	All men lived in one place after the flood

From Other Biblical Writers

Reference		Argument
51.	Job 12:15	The waters overturned the earth
52.	Ps 29:10	The flood testified God as eternal king
53.	Ps 104:8	Flood terminated by crustal tectonics
54.	Is 54:9	Waters of Noah went over the earth
55.	Ma 24:37	The days of Noah like those when Christ comes
56.	Ma 24:39	The flood took them all away
57.	Lk 17:27	The flood destroyed them all
58.	He 11:7	Noah warned of things never seen before
59.	He 11:7	Noah condemned the world by his faith
60.	1 Pe 3:20	Only eight souls saved on the ark through the flood
61.	2 Pe 2:5	God spared not the old world (Greek *kosmos*)
62.	2 Pe 2:5	God brought the flood on the world of the ungodly
63.	2 Pe 2:5	The "flood" (Greek *kataklusmos*) applied solely to Noah's flood
64.	2 Pe 3:6	The world that then was, perished by the watery cataclysm

From Nonbiblical Evidence

Argument
65. Worldwide distribution of flood traditions
66. Origin of civilization near Ararat-Babylon region in post-flood time
67. Convergence of population growth statistics on date of flood
68. Dating of oldest living things at post-flood time
69. Worldwide occurrence of water-laid sediments and sedimentary rocks
70. Recent uplift of major mountain ranges
71. Marine fossils on crests of mountains
72. Evidence of former worldwide warm climate
73. Necessity of catastrophic burial and rapid lithification of fossil deposits
74. Recent origin of many datable geological processes
75. Worldwide distribution of all types of fossils
76. Uniform physical appearance of rocks from different "ages"
77. Frequent mixing of fossils from different "ages"
78. Near-random deposition of formational sequences
79. Equivalence of total organic material in present world and fossil world
80. Wide distribution of recent volcanic rocks
81. Evidence of recent drastic rise in sea level
82. Worldwide occurrence of raised shore lines and river terraces
83. Evidence of recent drastic rise in sea level
84. Universal occurrence of rivers in valleys too large for the present stream
85. Sudden extinction of dinosaurs and other prehistoric animals
86. Rapid onset of glacial period
87. Existence of polystrate fossils
88. Preservation of tracks and other ephemeral markings throughout geologic column
89. Worldwide occurrence of sedimentary fossil "graveyards" in rocks of all "ages"
90. Absence of any physical evidence of chronologic boundary between rocks of successive "ages"
91. Occurrence of all rock types (shale, limestone, granite, etc.) in all "ages"
92. Parallel of supposed evolutionary sequence through different "ages" with modern ecological zonation in the one present age
93. Lack of correlation of most radiometric "ages" with assumed paleontologic "ages"
94. Absence of meteorites in geological column
95. Absence of hail imprints in geological column, despite abundance of fossil ripple-marks and raindrop imprints
96. Evidence of man's existence during earliest of geologic "ages" (e.g., human footprints in Cambrian, Carboniferous, and Cretaceous formations)
97. Similar structural features (rifts, faults, folds, thrusts, etc.) in rocks of all "ages"
98. Absence of evidence of drainage systems in sediments of any "ages" except the most recent
99. Hydraulic evidence of rapid deposition of each stratum and of continuous formation of every sequence of strata, with no worldwide time gap between any formation and another above it
100. Numerous modern sightings of probable remains of Noah's ark at about 15,000 feet elevation in ice cap on Mount Ararat

From *The Genesis Record* by Henry M. Morris (Grand Rapids: Baker Book House, 1976), pp. 683-686.

BIBLE-BELIEVING SCIENTISTS
OF THE PAST

Many scientists today insist that no true scientist can believe in special creation or in the inspiration of the Bible. They are wrong, however, for there are thousands of living scientists who believe in special, recent creation, who believe in Christ and have accepted Him as personal Savior, and who believe in the inerrancy and full authority of the Bible. Over a thousand such men have belonged to one particular organization, the Creation Research Society, and there are numerous similar organizations around the world.

Furthermore, many—probably most—of the greatest scientists of all time, the founding fathers of science in fact, believed in a personal Creator God, the inspiration of the Bible and special creation, and they professed faith in Christ and the gospel. Whether all were truly "born-again," as we would understand that term in a Bible-believing church today, we cannot know. Some were unorthodox in their specific doctrinal beliefs, but all were creationists.

A tabulation follows of some of these great scientists of the past, with the disciplines they founded or the particular discoveries or inventions they made. It is surely wrong for anyone to allege that one cannot be a true scientist and still believe in special creation.

Scientific Disciplines Established by Bible-believing Scientists

	Discipline	Scientist
1.	Antiseptic Surgery	Joseph Lister (1827 – 1912)
2.	Bacteriology	Louis Pasteur (1822 – 1895)
3.	Calculus	Isaac Newton (1642 – 1727)
4.	Celestial Mechanics	Johann Kepler (1571 – 1630)
5.	Chemistry	Robert Boyle (1626 – 1691)
6.	Comparative Anatomy	Georges Cuvier (1769 – 1832)
7.	Computer Science	Charles Babbage (1792 – 1871)
8.	Dimensional Analysis	Lord Rayleigh (1842 – 1919)
9.	Dynamics	Isaac Newton (1642 – 1727)
10.	Electrodynamics	James Clerk Maxwell (1831 – 1879)
11.	Electromagnetics	Michael Faraday (1791 – 1867)
12.	Electronics	Ambrose Fleming (1849 – 1945)
13.	Energetics	Lord Kelvin (1824 – 1907)
14.	Entomology of Living Insects	Henri Fabre (1823 – 1915)
15.	Field Theory	Michael Faraday (1791 – 1867)
16.	Fluid Mechanics	George Stokes (1819 – 1903)
17.	Galactic Astronomy	William Herschel (1738 – 1822)
18.	Gas Dynamics	Robert Boyle (1627 – 1691)
19.	Genetics	Gregor Mendel (1822 – 1884)
20.	Glacial Geology	Louis Agassiz (1807 – 1873)
21.	Gynecology	James Simpson (1811 – 1870)
22.	Hydraulics	Leonardo da Vinci (1452 – 1519)
23.	Hydrography	Matthew Maury (1806 – 1873)

Discipline	Scientist
24. Hydrostatics	Blaise Pascal (1623 – 1662)
25. Ichthyology	Louis Agassiz (1807 – 1873)
26. Isotopic Chemistry	William Ramsay (1852 – 1916)
27. Model Analysis	Lord Rayleigh (1842 – 1919)
28. Natural History	John Ray (1627 – 1705)
29. Non-Euclidean Geometry	Bernhard Riemann (1826 – 1866)
30. Oceanography	Matthew Maury (1806 – 1873)
31. Optical Mineralogy	David Brewster (1781 – 1868)
32. Paleontology	John Woodward (1665 – 1728)
33. Pathology	Rudolph Virchow (1821 – 1902)
34. Physical Astronomy	Johann Kepler (1571 – 1630)
35. Reversible Thermodynamics	James Joule (1818 – 1889)
36. Statistical Thermodynamics	James Clerk Maxwell (1831 – 1879)
37. Stratigraphy	Nicholas Steno (1631 – 1686)
38. Systematic Biology	Carolus Linnaeus (1707 – 1778)
39. Thermodynamics	Lord Kelvin (1824 – 1907)
40. Thermokinetics	Humphrey Davy (1778 – 1829)
41. Vertebrate Paleontology	Georges Cuvier (1769 – 1832)

Notable Inventions, Discoveries, or Developments by Bible-Believing Scientists

Contribution	Scientists
1. Absolute Temperature Scale	Lord Kelvin (1824 – 1907)
2. Actuarial Tables	Charles Babbage (1792 – 1871)
3. Barometer	Blaise Pascal (1623 – 1662)
4. Biogenesis Law	Louis Pasteur (1822 – 1895)
5. Calculating Machine	Charles Babbage (1792 – 1871)
6. Chloroform	James Simpson (1811 – 1870)
7. Classification System	Carolus Linnaeus (1707 – 1778)
8. Double Stars	William Herschel (1738 – 1822)
9. Electric Generator	Michael Faraday (1791 – 1867)
10. Electric Motor	Joseph Henry (1797 – 1878)
11. Ephemeris Tables	Johann Kepler (1571 – 1630)
12. Fermentation Control	Louis Pasteur (1822 – 1895)
13. Galvanometer	Joseph Henry (1797 – 1878)
14. Global Star Catalog	John Herschel (1792 – 1871)
15. Inert Gases	William Ramsay (1852 – 1916)
16. Kaleidoscope	David Brewster (1781 – 1868)
17. Law of Gravity	Isaac Newton (1642 – 1727)
18. Mine Safety Lamp	Humphrey Davy (1778 – 1829)
19. Pasteurization	Louis Pasteur (1822 – 1895)
20. Reflecting Telescope	Isaac Newton (1642 – 1727)
21. Scientific Method	Francis Bacon (1561 – 1626)
22. Self-induction	Joseph Henry (1797 – 1878)
23. Telegraph	Samuel F. B. Morse (1791 – 1872)

Contribution	Scientists
24. Thermionic Valve	Ambrose Fleming (1849 – 1945)
25. Transatlantic Cable	Lord Kelvin (1824-1907)
26. Vaccination and Immunization	Louis Pasteur (1822 – 1895)

This tabulation, showing that many of the founding fathers of modern science were men who believed in God, the Bible and creation, was first published as an ICR "Impact Article" in *Acts and Facts*, (Jan. 1982), then in *Men of Science, Men of God*, by Henry M. Morris (San Diego: Master Books, 1982, 1988), 107 pp.

QUOTATIONS FROM OR ALLUSIONS TO GENESIS IN THE NEW TESTAMENT

One measure of the foundational importance of the Book of Genesis is the fact that allusions and quotations referring to Genesis occur so frequently in the New Testament, as much as or more than any other book of the Old Testament. These are listed in the following table. Note especially the "observations" at the end of the table.

	Genesis Reference	Topic	New Testament Reference
1.	1:1	God in the beginning	Jo 1:1
2.	1:1	Beginning of the world	2 Ti 1:9
3.	1:1	Beginning of the world	Tit 1:2
4.	1:1	Creation of universe	He 11:3
5.	1:1	Earth and heaven in the beginning	He 1:10
6.	1:3-5	Light out of darkness	2 Co 4:6
7.	1:5-7	Earth out of water and in water	2 Pe 3:4-5
8.	1:11	Every seed his own body	1 Co 15:38-39
9.	1:11-12	Earth bringing forth herbs	He 6:7
10.	1:26-27	Made male and female	Mk 10:6-7
11.	1:26-27	Made in image of God	Col 3:10
12.	1:27	In the image of God	1 Co 11:7
13.	1:29-31	All creatures good	1 Ti 4:4
14.	1:31	All things made by God	Ac 17:24
15.	2:1	All that in them is	Ac 14:15
16.	2:1	All things created in heaven and earth	Re 10:6
17.	2:1	First heaven and first earth	Re 21:1
18.	2:1–3	All things created	Col 1:16
19.	2:1	Works finished	He 4:3
20.	2:2	Rest on the seventh day	He 4:4
21.	2:3	Ceased from His works	He 4:10
22.	2:3	Created all things	Ep 3:9
23.	2:3	World made by Him	Jo 1:10
24.	2:3	Created all things	Re 4:11
25.	2:4	Creation which God created	Mk 13:19
26.	2:4	He that made heaven and earth	Re 14:7
27.	2:4–6	Things that were made	Ro 1:20
28.	2:7	Adam a living soul	1 Co 15:45
29.	2:7	Man formed	1 Ti 2:13
30.	2:9	Tree of life in paradise	Re 2:7
31.	2:9	Fruit of tree of life	Re 22:14
32.	2:17	Death by sin	Ro 5:12
33.	2:18	Woman for the man	1 Co 11:9
34.	2:22	Woman of the man	1 Co 11:8
35.	2:23	Bone of his bone	Ep 5:30

Genesis Reference	Topic	New Testament Reference
36. 2:24	Leave father and mother	Ep 5:31
37. 2:24	One flesh	1 Co 6:16
38. 2:24	Cleave to his wife	Ma 19:5
39. 2:24	One flesh	Mk 10:8
40. 3:1	That old serpent	Re 20:2
41. 3:1	Subtlety of serpent	2 Co 11:3
42. 3:4	Father of lies	Jo 8:44
43. 3:6	Woman deceived	1 Ti 2:14
44. 3:13	Serpent beguiled Eve	2 Co 11:3
45. 3:14	Devil sinneth from the beginning	I Jo 3:8
46. 3:15	Made of a woman	Ga 4:4
47. 3:15	Satan bruised under foot	Ro 16:20
48. 3:15	Enmity with the woman	Re 12:13-17
49. 3:15	That old serpent	Re 12:9
50. 3:15	Treading on serpents	Lk 10:19
51. 3:16	Saved in child-bearing	I Ti 2:15
52. 3:16	Woman under obedience	1 Co 14:34
53. 3:16	Sorrow in travail	Jo 16:20
54. 3:16	Man the head of the woman	1 Co 11:3
55. 3:17	No more curse	Re 22:3
56. 3:18	Thorns and briers	He 6:8
57. 3:18-19	Bondage of corruption	Ro 8:21-22
58. 3:18-19	No more death, sorrow, pain	Re 21:4
59. 3:19	Work for your own bread	2 Th 3:12
60. 3:19	By man came death	1 Co 15:21
61. 3:20	Mother of us all	Ga 4:26
62. 3:22	Fruit of tree of life	Re 22:2
63. 3:23	Man from the earth	1 Co 15:47
64. 4:3-5	Abel a more excellent sacrifice	He 11:4
65. 4:4	Righteous Abel	Ma 23:35
66. 4:8	Cain slew his brother	1 Jo 3:12
67. 4:10	Blood of Abel	He 12:24
68. 4:11	Blood of Abel	Lk 11:51
69. 4:16	The way of Cain	Jude 11
70. 4:26	Prophets since the world began	Lk 1:70
71. 5:1	Book of the generations	Ma 1:1
72. 5:1	Similitude of God	Jam 3:9
73. 5:2	Created male and female	Ma 19:4
74. 5:2	Beginning of the creation of God	Re 3:14
75. 5:4	Death reigned from Adam	Ro 5:14-19
76. 5:5	In Adam all die	1 Co 15:22
77. 5:3-6	Adam to Enos	Lk 3:38
78. 5:12-21	Cainan to Methuselah	Lk 3:37
79. 5:18	Enoch, seventh from Adam	Jude 14
80. 5:24	Enoch translated	He 11:5
81. 5:28-32	Lamech to Shem	Lk 3:36
82. 5:29	Subjected to curse in hope	Ro 8:20

Genesis Reference	Topic	New Testament Reference
83. 6:2	Angels that sinned	2 Pe 2:4
84. 6:3	Spirit striving with flesh	Ga 5:17
85. 6:4	Angels left their habitation	Jude 6
86. 6:4	Marrying wives	Lk 17:27
87. 6:5	Days of Noah	Ma 24:37
88. 6:12-13	The days of Noah	Lk 17:26
89. 6:13	God spared not old world	2 Pe 2:5
90. 6:14-16	Ark preparing	1 Pe 3:20
91. 7:1	Saving of his house	He 11:7
92. 7:13-16	Noah entered the ark	Ma 24:38
93. 7:17-18	The flood came	Ma 24:39
94. 7:19-20	Overflowed with water	2 Pe 3:6
95. 8:21	Sweet savour	Ph 4:18
96. 8:22	Fruitful seasons	Ac 14:17
97. 9:2	All things subjected to man	He 2:7-8
98. 9:3	Everything meat for you	1 Ti 4:3
99. 9:4	Blood not to be eaten	Ac 15:20
100. 9:6	Life for life	Ma 26:52
101. 10:8-11	Babylon, the mother of abominations	Re 17:5
102. 10:32	All nations on face of earth	Ac 17:26
103. 11:4-5	That great city	Re 17:18
104. 11:10-13	Shem to Cainan	Lk 3:36
105. 11:14-20	Salah to Serug	Lk 3:35
106. 11:22-26	Nahor to Abraham	Lk 3:34
107. 11:31	Abraham dwelt in Haran	Ac 7:4
108. 12:1	Abraham to leave his kindred	Ac 7:3
109. 12:3	All families of earth to be blessed	Ac 3:25
110. 12:3	All nations blessed	Ga 3:8
111. 12:4	Abraham went out	He 11:8
112. 12:5	From Haran to Canaan	Ac 7:4
113. 12:7	Unborn seed given the land	Ac 7:5
114. 13:15	Promise to the seed	Ga 3:16
115. 14:18	Melchizedek met Abraham	He 7:1
116. 14:19	Abraham blessed of Melchizedek	He 7:6-7
117. 14:20	Tithes to Melchizedek	He 7:4-5
118. 15:5	So shall thy seed be	Ro 4:18
119. 15:5	Seed as the stars	He 11:12
120. 15:6	Faith counted for righteousness	Ro 4:3,5,9,22
121. 15:6	Abraham believed God	Ga 3:6
122. 15:6	Imputed righteousness	Jam 2:23
123. 15:13	Afflicted 400 years	Ac 7:6
124. 15:14	Nation to be judged	Ac 7:7
125. 15:16	Iniquity to be filled up	1 Th 2:16
126. 16:1	No children	Ac 7:5
127. 16:15	A son by Hagar	Ga 4:22
128. 17:5	Father of many nations	Ro 4:17
129. 17:7	With Abram's seed forever	Lk 1:55

Genesis Reference	Topic	New Testament Reference
130. 17:8	Oath sworn to Abraham	Lk 1:73
131. 17:10	Circumcision of the fathers	Jo 7:22
132. 17:11	Sign of circumcision	Ro 4:11
133. 17:13	Covenant of circumcision	Ac 7:8
134. 17:17	Abraham and Sarah past age	Ro 4:19
135. 18:2	Angels unawares	He 13:2
136. 18:10,14	Sarah to bear at appointed time	Ro 9:9
137. 18:12	Sarah called Abraham "lord"	1 Pe 3:6
138. 18:20	Sin of Sodom and Gomorrah	Ma 10:15
139. 19:1-3	Entertaining angels	He 13:2
140. 19:5	Going after strange flesh	Jude 7
141. 19:9	Lot dwelling among wicked	2 Pe 2:7-8
142. 19:24	Fire and brimstone from heaven	Lk 17:29
143. 19:25	Judgment on Sodom	Lk 10:12
144. 19:26	Lot's wife	Lk 17:32
145. 21:1	Promise fulfilled	Ga 4:23
146. 21:2	Sarah conceived seed	He 11:11
147. 21:3	Abraham begat Isaac	Ma 1:2
148. 21:4	Isaac the son of Abraham	Lk 3:34
149. 21:9	Son of promise persecuted	Ga 4:29
150. 21:10	Bondwoman cast out	Ga 4:30
151. 21:12	Isaac the seed of promise	Ga 4:28
152. 21:13	Seed of Abraham	Ro 9:7
153. 21:13	Isaac the seed called	He 11:18
154. 21:14	Hagar in the wilderness	Ga 4:24-25
155. 22:1-3	Abraham offered up Isaac	He 11:17
156. 22:5	Accounting that God could raise him up	He 11:19
157. 22:9	Isaac on the altar	Jam 2:21
158. 22:16	God swearing by Himself	He 6:13
159. 22:17	Blessing and multiplying	He 6:14
160. 22:17	As the sand and stars	He 11:12
161. 22:18	Heir of all nations of earth	Ro 4:13
162. 23:4	Stranger and sojourner	He 11:9
163. 23:16-20	Sepulcher bought	Ac 7:16
164. 25:21	Rebekah conceived	Ro 9:10
165. 25:23	Elder to serve the younger	Ro 9:12
166. 25:25-26	Jacob and Esau	Ro 9:13
167. 25:33	Birthright despised	He 12:16
168. 26:3	Blessing of Abraham	Ga 3:14
169. 26:4-5	Covenant confirmed	Ga 3:17
170. 27:27-29,39-40	Isaac blessed Jacob and Esau	He 11:20
171. 27:34,38	No place of repentance	He 12:17
172. 28:12	Angels descending	Jo 1:51
173. 28:15	Never leave thee	He 13:5
174. 29:35	Judah, son of Jacob	Lk 3:33
175. 30:13	Called blessed	Lk 1:48
176. 30:23	Reproach taken away	Lk 1:25

Genesis Reference	Topic	New Testament Reference
177. 31:42	God of Abraham, Isaac, and Jacob	Ma 22:32
178. 32:12	Seed as the sand	He 11:12
179. 33:19	Jacob's parcel of ground	Jo 4:5
180. 35:16-17	Rachel weeping	Ma 2:18
181. 37:28	Joseph sold into Egypt	Ac 7:9
182. 38:29	Judah begat Pharez	Ma 1:3
183. 39:2,23	The Lord with Joseph	Ac 7:9
184. 41:41-44	Joseph exalted	Ac 7:10
185. 41:54	Dearth in Egypt	Ac 7:11
186. 42:1-2	Corn in Egypt	Ac 7:12
187. 42:5	Famine in Canaan	Ac 7:11
188. 42:13	Twelve brethren	Ac 7:8
189. 45:1-4	Joseph revealed to his brethren	Ac 7:13
190. 45:9-11	Joseph sending for Jacob	Ac 7:14
191. 46:5-6	Jacob going to Egypt	Ac 7:15
192. 46:26-27	Seventy-five souls	Ac 7:14
193. 47:9	Strangers and pilgrims	He 11:13
194. 47:31	Leaning on top of staff	He 11:21
195. 48:13-20	Jacob blessed sons of Joseph	He 11:21
196. 49:9-10	Lion of tribe of Judah	Re 5:5
197. 49:10	Lord sprang from Judah	He 7:14
198. 49:11	Washed garments in blood	Re 7:14
199. 49:29-30	Jacob buried in Canaan	Ac 7:16
200. 50:24-26	Death of Joseph	He 11:22

Observations

- The references listed above do not include references to "Israel" as a nation, or to "Judah," "Benjamin," and so forth, as tribes, even though such names are first encountered in Genesis.
- The references listed do not include verses in which there is merely a similarity in wording (Jo 2:5 with Ge 41:55) unless there is evidence that the New Testament writer consciously was incorporating the Genesis phraseology into his own writings.
- All books of the New Testament except Philemon, 1 John, and 3 John contain allusions to Genesis.
- Of the 50 chapters in Genesis, only seven (chapters 20, 24, 34, 36, 40, 43, 44) are not quoted or cited in the New Testament.
- More than half of the 200 New Testament allusions to Genesis are from the first 11 chapters of Genesis.
- 63 of the allusions are to the first three chapters of Genesis.
- 14 of the allusions are from the "flood chapters" (6–8).
- 58 references are related to Abraham.
- None of the 200 New Testament references to Genesis are explicitly ascribed to Moses as their author, indicating a probable recognition that he was editor and compiler, rather than author.
- 25 of the references were directly from Christ Himself (from chapters 1–7; 9; 17–19; 28; 31).

Taken from *The Genesis Record* by Henry M. Morris (Grand Rapids: Baker Book House, 1976), pp. 677-682.

"FIRST MENTIONS" OF IMPORTANT BIBLICAL WORDS IN GENESIS

Word	Text	Word	Text	Word	Text
Altar	8:20	Give	1:29	Reward	15:1
Angel	16:7	Glory	31:1	Righteous (just)	6:9
Atonement (pitch)	6:14	Good	1:4	Righteousness	15:6
Believe	15:6	Grace	6:8	Salvation	49:18
Bless	1:22	Hear	3:8	Sanctify	2:3
Blood	4:10	Heart	6:5	Say	1:3
Book	5:1	Holy (sanctified)	2:3	Science (knowledge)	2:17
Choose	6:2	House	7:1	See	1:4
City	4:17	I am	15:1	Seed	1:11
Clothe	3:21	Impute (count)	15:6	Send	3:23
Command	2:16	Just	6:9	Shed (pour out)	9:6
Complete (perfect)	6:9	Kingdom	10:10	Shield	15:1
Conception	3:16	Knowledge	2:17	Sign	1:14
Covenant	6:18	Law	26:5	Sin	4:7
Create	1:1	Life	2:7	Sorrow	3:16
Curse	3:14	Light	1:3	Soul (creature)	1:21
Darkness	1:2	Love	22:2	Sow	26:12
Day	1:5	Make	1:7	Speak (say)	1:3
Die	2:17	Man	1:26	Strength	4:12
Door	4:7	Mercy	19:16	Tempt	22:1
Drunken	9:21	Obey	22:18	Tithe	14:20
Everlasting (forever)	3:22	Peace (Salem)	14:18	Truth	24:27
Evil	2:9	Perfect (complete)	6:9	Vision	15:1
Faith (believed)	15:6	Power (strength)	4:12	Will	24:5
Fear (afraid)	3:10	Praise (commend)	12:15	Wine	9:21
Fear not	15:1	Pray	20:7	Woman	2:22
Fire	19:24	Prophet	20:7	Word	15:1
Forever	3:22	Redeem	48:16	Work	2:2
Fruit	1:11	Rest	2:2	Worship (bow down)	18:2

From *The Genesis Record*, by Henry M. Morris (Grand Rapids: Baker Book House, 1976), p. 687.

THE CREATIONIST FAITH OF
OUR FOUNDING FATHERS

Many of the foundations of our American Christian heritage are being undermined in today's hedonistic society, and this sad fact is surely related to the prior undermining of biblical creationism in our schools and colleges. It is therefore relevant to the emphasis of this study Bible to note that most of the founding fathers of our nation believed in special creation as taught in the Bible. Thus, defending our Christian creationist faith is also a vital component of the true defense of our country and its system of constitutional government "under God."

A favorite patriotic song of yesteryear, "My Country, 'Tis of Thee," is not sung much anymore, especially in our public schools, probably because the last verse is a prayer, directed to "Our fathers' God…Author of liberty…Great God our King." (The Supreme Court decided several years ago that it is unconstitutional to pray in school.)

In fact, it is now considered unconstitutional to acknowledge God in any way at all in the public schools, especially as our "Author" and "King"—that is, as our Creator and Lord. Yet, when our nation was first established on that memorable fourth of July in 1776, the signing of the Declaration was preceded by prayer, at the urging of Ben Franklin, to the Author of liberty. It was no accident that the Declaration of Independence acknowledged God as Creator (that is, as "Nature's God") in its very first sentence. Then, in its second sentence, the Declaration affirmed that "all men are *created* equal…endowed by their *Creator* with certain unalienable rights." In its last sentence, it expressed "firm reliance on the protection of *divine providence*." Our nation's founding document thus expressed faith in God as both Creator and Sustainer of men, and there is bound to be a correlation between our nation's strong foundation and God's blessing on it for these some 225 years since that first fourth of July.

Franklin may not have been an orthodox Bible-believing Christian, but he did believe in God and creation. He wrote, for example, as follows:

> Here is my creed. I believe in one God, the Creator of the universe. That He governs it by His Providence. That He ought to be worshiped.[1]

The same could be said of Thomas Jefferson, reputedly a deist, but nevertheless a believer in God and special creation. Some of his testimonies are actually inscribed on the walls of the Jefferson Memorial, in Washington, D.C. For example:

> Almighty God hath created the mind free. All attempts to influence it by temporal punishments or burthens…are a departure from the plan of the Holy Author of our religion.…

> God who gave us life gave us liberty. Can the liberties of a nation be secure when we have removed a conviction that these liberties are the gift of God?

A modern evolutionary historian has noted Jefferson's keen insight in reference to the growing pre-Darwinian propaganda for uniformitarianism and evolution, as follows:

When Jefferson, in his old age, was confronted with the newly developing science of geology, he rejected the evolutionary concept of the creation of the earth on the grounds that no all-wise and all-powerful Creator would have gone about the job in such a slow and inefficient way.[2]

It was Jefferson, of course, who had the major responsibility for the wording in the Declaration of Independence.

James Madison is often considered the chief architect of the Constitution as well as the Bill of Rights, and he was a profound Bible student studying for the ministry during his college days at Princeton (then known as the College of New Jersey). He eventually became a lawyer and statesman, and his Christian convictions never wavered. It was his influence especially that eventually established religious freedom in our country. He later wrote that "belief in a God All Powerful, wise and good, is…essential to the moral order of the world and to the happiness of man."[3]

Madison's theology had been largely shaped by the teachings of President John Witherspoon of the College of New Jersey (also a signer of the Declaration) whose strong biblical Calvinist faith included the doctrine of natural depravity of man. This truth in turn was behind Madison's unique insistence on a government of checks-and-balances in which the innate sinfulness of men attaining power could be prevented from usurping total power. This doctrine, of course, rests squarely on the biblical record of the creation and fall of man.

His manuscripts also include elaborate notes on the four Gospels and Acts in particular, specifically acknowledging the deity and bodily resurrection of Christ, and praising the example of the Berean Christians in studying the Scriptures.[4]

John Hancock, who was the first to sign the Declaration, had been president of the Provincial Congress of Massachusetts a year before when he issued a proclamation calling for "A Day of Public Humiliation, Fasting, and Prayer," referring to "that God who rules in the Armies of Heaven and without whose Blessing the best human Counsels are but Foolishness—and all created Power Vanity."[5] That same year, the Continental Congress also passed a stirring resolution expressing "humble confidence in the mercies of the Supreme and impartial God and ruler of the universe."[6]

George Washington (often called "the father of our country") was also a strong Bible-believing Christian and literal creationist. Among other things, he once commented:

> A reasoning being would lose his reason, in attempting to account for the great phenomena of nature, had he not a Supreme Being to refer to; and well has it been said, that if there had been no God, mankind would have been obligated to imagine one.[7]

Washington also said:

> It is impossible to account for the creation of the universe, without the agency of a Supreme Being.…It is impossible to govern the universe without the aid of a Supreme Being. It is impossible to reason without arriving at a Supreme Being.[8]

Consider also the testimony of John Jay, the first Chief Justice of the United States Supreme Court. In an address to the American Bible Society (of which he was then president) he said:

> The Bible will also inform them that our gracious Creator has provided for us a Redeemer, in whom all the nations of the earth shall be blessed; that this Redeemer has made atonement for the sins of the whole world, and…has opened a way for our redemption and salvation.[9]

In fact, all the signers of the Declaration and the delegates to the Constitutional Convention, as well as the delegates to the various sessions of the Continental Congress—at least so far as known—

were men who believed in God and the special creation of the world and mankind. Nearly all were members of Christian churches and believed the Bible to be the inspired Word of God.

This had been true of their forebears as well:

> In colonial times, the Bible was the primary tool in the educational process. In fact, according to Columbia University Professor Dr. Lawrence A. Cremin, the Bible was "the single most primary source for the intellectual history of Colonial America." From their knowledge of the Bible, a highly literate, creative people emerged. Their wise system of education was later replaced by a man-centered system that has caused a steady decline in literacy and creativity.[10]

An interesting admission from Fred Edwords, Executive Director of the American Humanist Association and a strong opponent of modern creationism, has noted that the nation's founders

> ...all mentioned God—and not merely the clockwork God of deism, but a God actively involved in history. Their "public religion"...harked back to the Old Testament with its view of America as "the promised land." This was prevalent in many writings of the time.[11]

In many ways the history of the founding of our country as well as our continuing modern history does seem to parallel that of God's chosen nation of Israel in ancient times. One fascinating example of this is found in a very early Independence Day address by Dr. Elias Boudinot, President of the Continental Congress in 1783.

> No sooner had the great Creator of the heavens and the earth finished His almighty work, and pronounced all very good, but He set apart...one day in seven for the commemoration of His inimitable power in producing all things out of nothing....The deliverance of the children of Israel from a state of bondage to an unreasonable tyrant was perpetuated by the Paschal lamb, and enjoining it on their posterity as an annual festival forever....The resurrection of the Savior of mankind is commemorated by keeping the first day of the week....Let us then, my friends and fellow citizens, unite all our endeavors this day to remember, with reverential gratitude to our Supreme Benefactor, all the wonderful things He has done for us, in our miraculous deliverance from a second Egypt—another house of bondage.[12]

Sad to say, ancient Israel gradually forgot their Sabbaths and their Passovers, and even forgot God and served the gods of nature, so that God finally judged them and sent them into captivity.

Similarly, our own nation was greatly blessed of God in its miraculous formation and early history. On that first great Liberty Day, when the Liberty Bell first rang out, the founders sent forth a testimony to all colonies taken from God's Word: "Proclaim liberty throughout all the land unto all the inhabitants thereof" (Le 25:10). Yet now, we also are rapidly forgetting the true God, His Creation, His Word, and His great salvation. Will the time come when America, like Israel, will fall under the chastening hand of our offended Creator and be enslaved by the coming humanistic pagan world government?

Actually, multitudes of our people, including many of our national leaders, have already abandoned their God-given Christian American heritage of liberty through our Creator and Savior, and have thereby become slaves themselves—some to drugs, some to alcohol, some to crime, immorality, greed, pleasure, or various other exacting slavemasters. In a word, they have become slaves to sin, even in this once-sweet land of liberty. As Jesus said, "Whosoever committeth sin is the servant of sin" (Jo 8:34).

The agents of the Enemy entrap many into such slavery by their deceptive promises of freedom from God and His Word, but "while they promise them liberty, they themselves are the servants of corruption; for of whom a man is overcome, of the same is he brought in bondage" (2 Pe 2:19).

True liberty, for both time and eternity, is secured only by faith in the saving work of Christ, and "if the Son therefore shall make you free, ye shall be free indeed" (Jo 8:36). People all over the world and Americans in particular need urgently to come back to the true God and Savior before it is too late.

Notes

[1] *The Writings of Ben Franklin* (New York: Macmillan Co., vol. 10, 1905–1907), p. 84.

[2] Gilman M. Ostrander, *The Evolutionary Outlook*, 1875–1900 (Clio, Michigan: Marston Press, 1971), p. 1.

[3] Princeton University Library Chronicle (Spring 1961, p. 125), cited by Eidsmoe, p. 110.

[4] See volume I in Biography of James Madison, pp. 3,34, as cited in *A Cloud of Witnesses*, ed. by Stephen A. Northrop (Portland, Oregon: American Heritage Ministries, 1987), p. 307.

[5] Cited in William J. Federer, *America's God and Country* (Coppell, Texas: Fame Publishing Co., 1996), p. 275.

[6] Ibid., p. 140.

[7] *Maxims of Washington*, ed. by John F. Schroeder (Mt. Vernon, Virginia: Mt. Vernon Ladies Association, 1942), p. 209.

[8] Quoted in *Maxims of Washington*, ed. by John P. Schroeder (Mt. Vernon, Virginia: Mt. Vernon Ladies Association, 1942), p. 275.

[9] Cited in *A Cloud of Witnesses*, ed. by Stephen A. Northrop (Reprinted by American Heritage Ministries, Portland, Oregon, 1987), p. 251.

[10] Mary-Elaine Swanson, "Teaching Children the Bible," *Mayflower Institute Journal* (vol. 1, July/August 1983), p. 5.

[11] Frederick Edwords, "The Religious Character of American Patriotism," *The Humanist* (vol. 47, Nov./Dec. 1987), p. 20.

[12] Address in New Jersey on July 4, 1783, cited in *Foundation for Christian Self-Government* (July 1982), p. 3.

Addressing Alternate Explanations for Age of the Earth

The evolutionary system has been entrenched for so long that many people who otherwise accept the Bible as infallible have deemed it expedient to compromise on this issue. Thus, evolution has been called, "God's method of creation"; and the Genesis record of the six days of creation has been reinterpreted in terms of the evolutionary ages of historical geology. These geological ages themselves have been accommodated in Genesis either by placing them in an assumed "gap" between Genesis 1:1 and 1:2 or by changing the "days" of creation into the "ages" of evolution.

Theories of this kind raise more problems than they solve, however. It is more productive to take the Bible literally and then to interpret the actual facts of science within its revelatory framework. If the Bible cannot be understood, it is useless as revelation. If it contains scientific fallacies, it could not have been given by inspiration.

The specific purpose of this study is to show that all such theories which seek to accommodate the Bible to evolutionary geology are invalid and, therefore, should be abandoned.

Theistic Evolution

Evolution is believed by its leading advocates to be a basic principle of continual development, of increasing order and complexity, throughout the universe. The complex elements are said to have developed from simpler elements, living organisms to have evolved from non-living chemicals, complex forms of life from simpler organisms, and even man himself to have gradually evolved from some kind of ape-like ancestor. Religions, cultures, and other social institutions are likewise believed to be continually evolving into higher forms.

Thus, evolution is a complete worldview, an explanation of origins and meanings without the necessity of a personal God who created and upholds all things. Since this philosophy is so widely and persuasively taught in our schools, Christians are often tempted to accept the compromise position of "theistic evolution," according to which evolution is viewed as God's method of creation. However, this is basically an inconsistent and contradictory position. A few of its fallacies are as follows:

- It contradicts the Bible record of creation. Ten times in the first chapter of Genesis, it is said that God created plants and animals to reproduce "after their kinds." The biblical "kind" may be broader than our modern "species" concept, but at least it implies definite limits to variation. The New Testament writers accepted the full historicity of the Genesis account of creation. Even Christ Himself quoted from it as historically accurate and authoritative (Matthew 19:4–6).

- It is inconsistent with God's methods. The standard concept of evolution involves the development of innumerable misfits and extinctions, useless and even harmful organisms. If this is God's "method of creation," it is strange that He would use such cruel, haphazard, inefficient, wasteful processes. Furthermore, the idea of the "survival of the fittest," whereby the stronger animals eliminate the weaker in the "struggle for existence" is the essence of Darwin's theory of evolution by natural selection, and this whole scheme is flatly contradicted by the biblical doctrine of love, of unselfish sacrifice, and of Christian charity. The God of the Bible is a God of order and of grace, not a

God of confusion and cruelty.

- The evolutionary philosophy is the intellectual basis of all anti-theistic systems. It served Hitler as the rationale for Nazism and Marx as the supposed, scientific basis for communism. It is the basis of the various modern methods of psychology and sociology that treat man merely as a higher animal and which have led to the misnamed "new morality" and ethical relativism. It has provided the pseudo-scientific rationale for racism and military aggression. Its whole effect on the world and mankind has been harmful and degrading. Jesus said: "A good tree cannot bring forth evil fruit" (Matthew 7:18). The evil fruit of the evolutionary philosophy is evidence enough of its evil roots.

Thus, evolution is biblically unsound, theologically contradictory, and sociologically harmful.

Progressive Creation

Some Christians use the term "progressive creation" instead of "theistic evolution," the difference being the suggestion that God interjected occasional acts of creation at critical points throughout the geological ages. Thus, for example, man's soul was created, though his body evolved from an ape-like ancestor.

This concept is less acceptable than theistic evolution, however. It not only charges God with waste and cruelty (through its commitment to the geologic ages) but also with ignorance and incompetence. God's postulated intermittent creative efforts show either that He didn't know what He wanted when He started the process or else that He couldn't provide it with enough energy to sustain it until it reached its goal. A god who would have to create man by any such cut-and-try discontinuous, injurious method as this can hardly be the omniscient, omnipotent, loving God of the Bible.

The Day-Age Theory

According to the established system of historical geology, the history of the earth is divided into a number of geological ages. The earth is supposed to have evolved into its present form and inhabitants over a vast span of geologic ages, beginning about a billion years ago.

In contrast, the biblical revelation tells us that God created the entire universe in six days only a few thousand years ago. Consequently, many Christian scholars have tried to find some way of reinterpreting Genesis to fit the framework of history prescribed by the geologists.

The most popular of these devices has been the "day-age" theory, by which the "days" of creation were interpreted figuratively as the "ages" of geology. However, there are many serious difficulties with this theory.

The Hebrew word for "day" is yom and the word can occasionally be used to mean an indefinite period of time, if the context warrants. In the overwhelming preponderance of its occurrences in the Old Testament, however, it means a literal day, that is, either an entire solar day or the daylight portion of a solar day. It was, in fact, defined by God Himself the very first time it was used, Genesis 1:5, where we are told that "God called the light, day." It thus means, in the context, the "day" in the succession of "day and night" or "light and darkness."

Furthermore, the word is never used to mean a definite period of time, in a succession of similar periods (that is, "the first day," "the second day," etc.) or with definite terminal points (that is, noted by "evening and morning," etc.) unless the period is a literal solar day. And there are hundreds of instances of this sort in the Bible.

Still further, the plural form of the word (Hebrew yamim) is used over 700 times in the Old Testament and always, without exception, refers to literal "days." A statement in the Ten Commandments written on a tablet of stone directly by God Himself is very significant in this connection, where He uses this word and says plainly: "In six days, the LORD made heaven and earth, the sea, and all that in them is" (Exodus 20:11).

Not only is the day-age theory unacceptable scripturally, but it also is grossly in conflict with the geological position with which it attempts to compromise. There are more than 20 serious contradictions between the biblical order and events of the creative days and the standard geologic history of the earth and its development, even if it were permissible to interpret the "days" as "ages." For example, the Bible teaches that the earth existed before the stars, that it was initially covered by water, that fruit trees appeared before fishes, that plant life preceded the sun, that the first animals created were the whales, that birds were made before insects, that man was created before woman, and many other such things, all of which are contradicted by historical geologists and paleontologists.

But the most serious fallacy in the day-age theory is theological. It charges God with the direct responsibility for five billion years of history of purposeless variation, accidental changes, evolutionary blind alleys, numerous misfits and extinctions, a cruel struggle for existence, with preservation of the strong and extermination of the weak, of natural disasters of all kinds, rampant disease, disorder, and decay, and, above all, with death. The Bible teaches that, at the end of the creation period, God pronounced His whole creation to be "very good," in spite of all this. It also teaches plainly that this present type of world, "groaneth and travaileth in pain" (Romans 8:22) only resulted from man's sin and God's curse thereon. "By one man sin entered into the world, and death by sin" (Romans 5:12). "God is not the author of confusion" (1 Corinthians 14:33).

The Gap Theory

Two theories for harmonizing the first chapter of Genesis with the geologic ages have been advanced, one placing the geologic ages "during" the six days of creation (thus making the "days" into "ages"), and the other placing the geologic ages "before" the six days (thus making them days of "recreation" following a great cataclysm which had destroyed the primeval earth). The "day-age theory" has been shown to be an impossible compromise, both biblically and scientifically.

The "gap theory" likewise involves numerous serious fallacies. The geologic ages cannot be disposed of merely by ignoring the extensive fossil record on which they are based. These supposed ages are inextricably involved in the entire structure of the evolutionary history of the earth and its inhabitants, up to and including man. The fossil record is the best evidence for evolution (in fact, the only such evidence which indicates evolution on more than a trivial scale). Furthermore, the geologic ages are recognized and identified specifically by the fossil contents of the sedimentary rocks in the earth's crust. The very names of the ages show this. Thus, the "Paleozoic Era" is the era of "ancient life," the "Mesozoic Era" of "intermediate life." and the "Cenozoic Era" of "recent life." As a matter of fact, the one primary means for dating these rocks in the first place has always been the supposed "stage-of-evolution" of the contained fossils.

Thus, acceptance or the geologic ages implicitly involves acceptance of the whole evolutionary package. Most of the fossil forms preserved in the sedimentary rocks have obvious relatives in the present world, so that the "re-creation" concept involves the Creator in "re-creating" in six days of the same animals and plants which had been previously developed

slowly over long ages, only to perish violently in a great pre-Adamic cataclysm.

The gap theory, therefore, really does not face the evolution issue at all, but merely pigeon-holes it in an imaginary gap between Genesis 1:1 and 1:2. It leaves unanswered the serious problem as to why God would use the method of slow evolution over long ages in the primeval world, then destroy it, and then use the method of special creation to re-create the same forms He had just destroyed.

Furthermore, there is no geologic evidence of such a worldwide cataclysm in recent geologic history. In fact, the very concept of a worldwide cataclysm precludes the geologic ages, which are based specifically on the assumption that there have been no such worldwide cataclysms. As a device for harmonizing Genesis with geology, the gap theory is self-defeating.

The greatest problem with the theory is that it makes God the direct author of evil. It implies that He used the methods of struggle, violence, decay, and death on a worldwide scale for at least three billion years in order to accomplish His unknown purposes in the primeval world. This is the testimony of the fossils and the geologic ages which the theory tries to place before Genesis 1:2. Then, according to the theory, Satan sinned against God in heaven (Isaiah 14:12–15; Ezekiel 28:11–17), and God cast him out of heaven to the earth, destroying the earth in the process in the supposed pre-Adamic cataclysm. Satan's sin in heaven, however, cannot in any way account for the age-long spectacle of suffering and death in the world during the geologic ages which preceded his sin! Thus, God alone remains responsible for suffering, death, and confusion, and without any reason for it.

The Scripture says, on the other hand, at the end of the six days of creation, "And God saw every thing that he had made [e.g., including not only the entire earth and all its contents, but all the heavens as well — note Genesis 1:16, 2:2, etc.], and, behold, it was very good" (Genesis 1:31). Death did not "enter the world" until man sinned (Romans 5:12; 1 Corinthians 15:21). Evidently even Satan's rebellion in heaven had not yet taken place, because everything was pronounced "very good" there, too.

The real answer to the meaning of the great terrestrial graveyard — the fossil contents of the great beds of hardened sediments all over the world — will be found neither in the slow operation of uniform natural processes over vast ages of time nor in an imaginary cataclysm that took place before the six days of God's perfect creation. Rather, it will be found in a careful study of the very real worldwide cataclysm described in Genesis 6 through 9 and confirmed in many other parts of the Bible and in the early records of nations and tribes all over the world, namely, the great Flood of the days of Noah. Evidences for and results of this worldwide Flood are discussed in detail in Impact Series No. 6.

Conclusion

Only a few of the many difficulties with the various accommodationist theories have been discussed, but even these have shown that it is impossible to devise a legitimate means of harmonizing the Bible with evolution. We must conclude, therefore, that if the Bible is really the Word of God (as its writers allege and as we believe) then evolution and its geological age-system must be completely false. Since the Bible cannot be reinterpreted to correlate with evolution, Christians must diligently proceed to correlate the facts of science with the Bible.

—Henry M. Morris, PhD